AFTER JOYCE

AFTERJOYCE
Studies in Fiction After Ulysses

Robert Martin Adams

NEW YORK

OXFORD UNIVERSITY PRESS

1977

Every new form limits the succeeding innovations in the same series. Every such form is itself one of a finite number of possibilities open in any temporal situation. Hence every innovation reduces the duration of its class.
George Kubler, *The Shape of Time*

CONTENTS

PREFACE

Like other varieties of narrative, literary history has fallen on an age of neglect, disuse, and atrophy; there may be larger and more impressive reasons, but a simple one is this: historical trends grow out of and are founded on observed similarities among writers. But the way in which a particular writer resembles others of his species is precisely the least interesting thing about him. Particularly when he has a great number of predecessors, to whom he relates not only directly but through second and third parties, his indebtedness being not to an individual or two, but to a number of disparate figures in a number of different cultural strains (and this is inevitable in a museum culture like our own), the very idea of "history" becomes absurd. A narrative of American verse which culminates in the advent of Ezra Pound is enough to fracture the mind; after James Russell Lowell and Edgar Lee Masters and Edna St. Vincent Millay, where does *he* fit in? Pound was a master over history in that he deliberately picked and chose from among its materials to make his own mythology, his own technique, everything that's distinctively his. He doesn't "fit in" a line of American poets, or any other collection of poets who march in a line.

History drags us down dusty turnpikes, past every green and fragrant byway off which flourishes, a quiet and fugitive flower, the true self of the writer whom one wants to discuss. Particularly in discussing a mature art form like the contemporary novel in English, which exists in a cosmopolitan, multi-lingual culture, so many cross-

influences are possible, and "influence" itself becomes such an active
concept (implying almost of necessity a deliberate choice on the part
of the recipient), that one cannot possibly line up authors in the old-
fashioned ranks and files. Whether it's an impulse from Laforgue or
Bunyan that comes flying in at a tangent, it raises hob with the idea of
history as an ordered temporal sequence of comparable phenomena.
The Oxford History of English Literature explicitly admitted its
share in this defeat by entitling the volume which succeeded a series
of century-titles (16th, 17th, 18th, 19th) simply *Six Modern Authors*.

Conceivably time in its flight will simplify the 20th century—modern or post-modern, we don't yet have a proper name for the age—
as it has done with all the others. But I venture to think its literary
history will always be hard to write, simply because it's been such a
voluminous and eclectic era. The sheer weight of literature has grown
as startlingly as the English-speaking population; apart from the
multiplication of garbage, the pressure of numbers has produced an
impulse to variety, a compulsion to originality, growing out of nothing more complex than the need to avoid beaten paths. Foreign writers with foreign points of view have been domesticated in English to
an amazing degree. As Ibsen was without question the greatest English dramatist of the early century, Kafka has certainly become one of
the greatest English novelists of mid-century; and thus, reflexively,
by a kind of backward belated influence from his Continental followers, a name like Kierkegaard enters English literary discourse. Or
Vico, or Heidegger.

Tempora mutantur, nos et mutamur in illis. Since Joyce began to
publish, more than half a century has elapsed, and every modern
decade seems to compress more change within it than a dozen earlier
ones. Massive changes have taken place within a few decades in matters of sexual frankness; and as they've taken place generally along
lines adumbrated by Joyce, it would be reasonable enough to claim
for him a share of responsibility for the change. But documenting
anything like this thesis would be difficult, if not impossible. Vic-

torian prudery was collapsing seventy-five years ago, under blows from Freud, Zola, Rossetti, Havelock Ellis, Elinor Glyn, and Oscar Wilde, as well as Joyce; apart from exterior attacks, Victorian morality wilted with the decay of social groups previously stiff in its support. By the end of the 19th century the Nonconformist conscience, fading steadily from its heroic days under more bizarre titles in the 17th century, had been radically weakened; and the World Wars would do still more to render the old decorums ridiculous. D. H. Lawrence and Henry Miller pushed forward on the literary level a set of value-shifts that were fundamentally changes of manners, changes that would no doubt have taken place whether novels were written to reflect them or not. Giant forces like the decay of Protestantism, the ruin of bourgeois idealism, the advent of cultural relativism, vulgar Freudianism, and even more vulgar journalism all worked together, by permutation and combination; and trying to untangle any one man's part in them is like trying to distinguish the wool of one particular sheep in a blanket woven from the fleece of hundreds. About all we can discuss as Joycean constants are technical innovations in the art of story-telling, and in the use of language; and, at first glance anyhow, these don't seem to be overwhelming topics.

Why should we be interested in the way men choose to tell stories? There appears no limit to the number of ways stories can be told, and no reason to tell them a new way except that they get boring when told in the old way. But this is a potent energy. Pressure from behind (you must do something new) combines with lack of direction or compulsion (what specifically you do is altogether open except that the more genuine it is, the better) to make of prose fiction an indicator particularly sensitive to the drifts and waverings of the imagination. And that crucial word "genuine," precisely because it's impossible to define publicly, but appeals instantly to an inner sense, contains the crux of a giant and always pressing problem. The novelist is responsible always and only to the full consciousness of his time. Great as Dickens was, nobody can write Dickensian novels today without artsy and tricksy overtones showing through, sooner rather than later. Ezra Pound's commandment to "Make It New" was redundant; it is explicit in the very idea of "making," which from the dawn of literary history has lain at the root of the words *poet, poetry, poem.* Yet the thing which is made can be seen only in the light of that category which is defined by its predecessors.

So the novel, like any other cultural artifact, changes under a double impulsion, to be new, yet not-new; to meet our expectations and to surpass them as well; to be recognizably of the genus but distinctively a new species. And in this grumbling, grudging, slow shift, as of silt-beds falling, rising, and eroding through geologic time, the outline of things alters so steadily and gradually that we are amazed to see over a period of time how they have changed.

In this process predecessors can play many roles, as Harold Bloom has reminded us with a good deal more pomp and circumstance than I find useful here. Let the word "influence" mean whatever its various appearances will justify, for us it is more sinuous and various than six titles will encapsulate, or sixty. Not because we are sly or knowing fellows, but because we are ourselves influenced, in our concept of influence, by those who have exemplified it for us. If Yeats, Joyce, Eliot, and Pound had not been such inventive borrowers, if the idea of "imitation" retained still that stiff and doctrinaire meaning that it had for the 18th century, we of today surely shouldn't find discussion of influence and imitation half so difficult, or half so appealing. Apart from all the ambiguities of originality and ironic distancing, and perhaps more important in the case of an immediate predecessor, there are the temerities and timidities involved in "inviting comparison." A figure of influence is always surrounded by an aura of incitation and dread—like a new bicycle, like an unbroken horse. And a writer like Joyce is particularly fearful, because he writes so largely in gaps, unexpressed implications, and unresolved ironies, that nobody has even read him more than provisionally. New structural patterns, new levels of allusion, new elements of relatedness have kept turning up steadily in the more than fifty years since Joyce's major novel *Ulysses* was first published. The book is infinitely more complex now than it was in 1922. Partly this is because the sort of questions we ask about it have been changed by our experience of other art-forms, other novelists—not excluding those whom Joyce himself influenced. The very shape and tempo of life as we experience it have changed, underlining some new patterns in the arabesque and erasing others. Out of this arrangement of emerging and retreating images, there is hardly any way to make a sequential history.

So I have not tried to draw this sprawling, disorderly subject into a proper historical straight line, but simply freed the subject to take its own shape by flowing where it seemed to want to go. On the other side, the principle of economy also applies; all discussions of "the modern novel" begin perforce by discarding 90 percent of the specimens, and there is no reason to multiply them when all perceptions are tentative. Afloat as we all are on swift and eddying streams of change, it ill behooves any of us to make categorical declarations about where the permanent benchmarks are going to be.

I am grateful to several undergraduate classes at the University of California, on whom some of these ideas were first tried out, and to the John Simon Guggenheim Foundation for leisure to assemble them.

AFTERJOYCE

CHAPTER ONE

JOYCE

THE SUBJECT of fiction-after-Joyce widens even as one tries to pick it up—widens and becomes ever thinner, not to say flabby, like a Dali watch. In the simplest chronological terms, what novel of the last fifty years is *not* a post-Joycean novel? Even novelists who thought Joyce an influence for evil and his work a black hole of negative energy have been forced by that energy to consolidate and draw apart, to formulate counter-positions which without his potent presence they might never have conceived. But this is the least of it. The positive influence of Joyce has proved wide, deep, and enduring. Only one novelist of his day, Franz Kafka, has exercised an influence in any way comparable to Joyce's. Lawrence, Proust, Mann, Gide, Faulkner, Hemingway, and the scattering of their lesser contemporaries are simply not in the comparison. Literary criticism is famous for going on and on without reaching any definitive conclusions: one point, over the past fifty years, has proved itself absolutely. Joyce did not sound the death-knell of the novel, as he was once said to have done; he was not the sterile if splendid termination of a development, but a fecund and various influence on developing talents of many diverse sorts. There was no predicting this before it happened, but with the benefit of hindsight it is now obvious and inescapable.

Yet the story of his coming to power within the literary imagination of our time is far from a simple one. Any post-Joycean novelist in the loose chronological sense is also a post-Kafkan, a post-Freudian, a post-war novelist; he cannot have remained immune to the continuing deep influence of Dostoevsky; the art of the moving pictures will not have failed to influence his sense of structure; he must have lived through several periods of "modernism" in art and music and into that questionable beyond for which we are still trying to find an appropriate name. Joyce's influence thus worked either directly or indirectly in combination with many other influences, and what looks most like influence may be simply coincidence. Every novelist who lived after Joyce is no doubt a post-Joyce novelist, but none is simply that. Our subject thus consists of a relatively firm center, where certain specific technical or spiritual debts to Joyce's example can be demonstrated; around this core it consists also of a much larger and gassier band of shifting and overlapping energies, where reactions to Joyce or his followers, or to trends of which he formed only a part, diffuse into something moist and vague called a climate of opinion. It will be hard to avoid this shadow-zone altogether, but better to start with the concrete and specific where it can be found, and work out from that center. At the center of the center is of course the intricate fact of Joyce himself, and the angle from which he entered into the tradition of English fiction. This is a different story for each of his four major books of fiction, but a few generalizations may be useful before we shorten focus.

James Joyce was an Irishman, but in a way of his own that strongly influenced both the sort of books he wrote, and the shock-waves he spread through England and America. Passionately devoted to the memory of Charles Stuart Parnell, he grew up in the era of cynicism and recrimination that followed the great leader's fall. Thus from early youth he despised England and the English—meaning by the nation not simply a political institution, but also an attitude of speciously judicious, pseudo-reasonable, placid superiority, to which he was apt to attach the name of Gladstone, the prudent impostor. It was of course Gladstone's liberalism and the nonconformist conscience which allied with the Catholic bishops of Ireland to bring down Parnell. Yet the English language and the culture that had been established over the centuries in that language were precious to him as an artist, and he could not forgo them, though he could not fail to modify them more radically than had any predecessor since Milton. Ambivalent toward English and the English, Joyce was equally ambivalent toward Gaelic and the Irish. He saw his countrymen at their best as heroic outlaws and gallant failures, quixotic warriors of the spirit; yet he also saw them in the large as a race of underhanded cowards, quick to betray and turn upon their own leaders. He saw guttersnipe Ireland clearly and pitilessly, as only Sean O'Casey has done since ("the rabblement of the most belated race in Europe," he called it); but Joyce saw it from the perspective of a *déclassé* aristocrat who found in the rigors and the high austerities of his art grounds for a more than social hauteur. He declined to appear to learn Gaelic, finding it a mere political shibboleth and a threat to his art, which was rooted in English; but he knew a good deal of it nevertheless. Irish peasant humor and folklore, Irish fable and myth, he left contemptuously to their devotees; and yet he was, in his own way, ineluctably one of them. Irish blarney and sentiment he saw chiefly as masks for servility and toadying. The Irish novel of rural humor, as cultivated by Lever, Lover, and Carleton, he tended to equate with the loose Irish poetry of Moore, Davis, and Ferguson, and both with the ineffectual speechifying of Daniel O'Connell, the 19th-century "Liberator" whose eloquence never liberated a foot of Irish soil. Joyce associated himself with a more severe and dangerous spirit—that of Parnell, who did not seek to persuade but to demand, and whose will, till it was broken by treachery, was steel. As Parnell replaced mild, bumbling old Isaac Butt, so Joyce felt that a younger and fiercer generation lay behind Parnell; as Gerhard Hauptmann picked up the torch from Ibsen, so Joyce represented himself as the "third minister," standing by the door and ready to take over. The sense of menace in these images is very potent, and it underlines the fact that Joyce, quite exceptionally among English and especially Irish

authors of his day, did not think it befitted his character to entertain
or ingratiate. In Shaw and Wilde and George Moore there was always a touch of the buffoon, in Yeats of the amateur magician. Joyce
was not quite the intellectual cutthroat that Hulme, Lewis, and Pound
pretended to be, or were; but his chosen weapon was "the cold steel-
pen," and his chosen nickname "Kinch the knifeblade."

Englishmen laugh generously with and at a comical Celtiberian,
who sees his natural function in entertaining them; they do not take
comfortably to an Irishman whose literary models are those writers
of cold and forbidding comedy, Dante Alighieri and Henrik Ibsen.
Joyce not only rejected the traditional roles of an Irishman (though
of course it is an Irish tradition to reject those roles), he struck directly across the great tradition of the English novel, which is moral
and social commentary. This was not apparent at the beginning of
his career; after *Ulysses,* however, uneasiness rose to the surface, and
its orientation was predominantly social. Katherine Mansfield thought
of "wet linoleum and unemptied pails," Virginia Woolf of "a queasy
undergraduate scratching his pimples"; and Professor Mahaffy, with
a true Dublin instinct for the jugular, said that *Ulysses* simply proved
"that it was a mistake to establish a separate university for the aborig-
ines of this island—for the corner-boys who spit into the Liffey." In
their several ways these are all social, not literary, judgments, and
they all testify to Joyce's disregard of the middle-class novel of manners, morals, and money—the novel which is chiefly concerned with
producing a prudent and ingratiating alignment of these three
ingredients.

The "great tradition" of the English novel is a straight, consecutive sequence of novelists dealing in broadly the same way with
broadly the same themes. From Richardson and Fielding to Smollett
to Jane Austen, George Eliot, Dickens, Trollope, and E. M. Forster,
with Scott and Meredith on the near periphery, the themes consistently involve a balancing of property values, social values, and ethical
values, centering on the climactic decision of a marriage, and treated

by means of interwoven, temporally consecutive narrations. Enthusiasts for this tradition have sometimes given the impression that it is the overwhelming force in the English novel during the 18th and 19th centuries; in fact, the variants and deviations, if less homogeneous, are almost as numerous as the exemplars. Defoe, for instance, never quite fits into anyone's categories, nor does Sterne; *Castle Rackrent* and *Wuthering Heights,* the Gothic novels of Walpole, Lewis, and Maturin, *Frankenstein,* the novels of Peacock, Butler, and Conrad, all stand in the shallows, if not on the bank, of the mainstream. On the Continent, what is the mainstream in English is clearly the exception; there is no way to fit *Elective Affinities, The Charterhouse of Parma, A Sentimental Education, Germinal, A Rebours,* or *Il Trionfo della Morte* into the great bourgeois tradition. Yet in England, as late as the last years of Victoria, it is fair enough to say that the middle-class novel of love, class, and morality is the central literary phenomenon; and Joyce's decision to cut across it was a major factor in his personal and artistic definition. Early readers persistently supposed he was trying to manipulate sympathy for his characters, and doing it clumsily, whereas he was not only indifferent to sympathy and antipathy within a middle-class frame of values, but increasingly dubious whether characters in literature are or can be characters at all.

In discussing first reactions to Joyce, anyone writing in the 1970s finds it hard to avoid, as one must, looking beneath the surface. That a critic with the wordly experience of Edmund Gosse should have been shocked to the point of physical pain by the mere appearance on a page of words like "fuck" and "bloody," seems practically parodic, but so it was. In fact, it was Joyce's perfect artistic indifference to moral and social taboos, rather than any determination to violate them (which could have been construed as an indirect form of homage), that appalled genteel literary taste in England. Once this indifference was sensed, readers tended to become extremely suspicious of a cold and silent negation they felt lying in reserve, that might saturate even an apparently neutral passage with sinister or blas-

phemous significance. George Roberts demanded a dictionary defini-
nition of "simony" before he would imperil his salvation by printing
"The Sisters," a quiet, mysterious piece which had already appeared,
without serious damage to the moral fabric of the community, in the
"pigs' paper," edited by respectable George Russell. Joyce's position
was not unlike that of Cardinal Newman, who could not help seem-
ing to Charles Kingsley a man of infinite duplicity and devious mental reservation, simply because he was so much more long-headed—
he knew more and reflected more about the implications of what he
knew, before he opened his mouth.

Large structures of thought underlay the polished surfaces of
Joyce's prose, as of Newman's; they were suspected long before they
were seen. The literary parallel once again is with Ibsen, Dante, and
perhaps Flaubert. The conclusion, though trite, is important: Joyce
built his fiction on Continental rather than English models. Writing
to his brother from Rome in 1906, he reports on a program of English reading which includes Gissing, Arthur Morrison, Hardy, and
Thackeray, but concludes, in anticipatory discouragement, "Without
boasting, I think I have little or nothing to learn from English novelists." In much the same way, a few years later, T. S. Eliot would
find that he had little or nothing to learn from his immediate predecessors in the art of English verse, and so would turn to Jacobean
dramatists and French symbolists. The structure, the diction, the
range of variations and effects possible within the conventions of
English as they were understood had been exhausted: both men
looked abroad.

A major element which Joyce learned from Ibsen (to put the
matter quickly and simply) was the art of an action which starts forward but circles back to examine its own premises. We see this para-
digmatically in *Ghosts,* which advances its pretext-action fewer than
twenty-four hours, but reaches more than thirty years back into the
past to make plain why that pretext-action can never be completed.
From Flaubert, Joyce learned the enormous potential of a thin or
transparent character, who can be made the vessel of fictional effects

that he understands hardly or not at all. Indeed, as Flaubert's career advances, we see his "characters" get thinner and thinner, till Bouvard and Pecuchet are mere comic-strip outlines behind which looms, everywhere present but nowhere avowed, the immense, disabused mind of their creator. The same development is evident in Joyce. From Dante, Joyce learned the uses to be made of an exoskeletal structure, one which does not grow out of the characters either in the form of an intrigue or as a web of circumstances they unwittingly spin, but which is imposed on them as an artifice from the outside. A fourth diffused and complementary influence doubtless derived from Wagner, whose presence was widely pervasive in the latter part of the 19th century. The practice of telling a story and intimating an attitude through incremental repetition of leitmotifs entered Joyce's art as early as the *Portrait,* and became as important to him as it was to Proust or Yeats. It involved the reader in a radically new exercise, demanding precisely that he *not* be caught up in the present of a scene, but allow the remote use of a phrase or theme to resonate in his mind like an intellectual diphthong.

Each of these concepts which I have so wildly oversimplified Joyce absorbed slowly, combining it with many other ingredients, and putting the slowly forming technique into practice only gradually. A sharp eye will note that, while Joyce studied the novelists, good, bad, and indifferent, modern and traditional, in the hope of learning something from them, the authors who worked most deeply on his imagination were not generally writers of prose fiction. There is no fixed list of these literary ancestors, but Dante and Ibsen can hardly fail to head a provisional accounting; we may add Homer and Shakespeare and Vico, Swift, Flaubert, Blake, and Defoe, maybe Mallarmé and James Clarence Mangan. For a man who read as much as Joyce, it is not a very long roster; and within it are only two writers of prose fiction. It was thus, if not inevitable, at least very probable from the nature of his study and the cast of his mind, that he would do something drastic to the dimensions of the novel as he found them.

But even before Joyce came into conflict with the traditions of

English and Irish fiction over the dimensions—that is, the mode—of
the novel, his habits of structuring and developing a story brought
him into conflict with established taste. The combination of mean or
squalid materials, deep insights into them, and scrupulous artistic
workmanship pointed him toward an art which combined two ex-
tremes—a scrupulous reproduction of the everyday and a visionary
insight. The traditional English novel dealt with the middle range of
experience, treated in a middle style within the boundaries of good
middle-class taste. Joyce in his fiction undertook to sink below and
rise above those levels. Like Dante's, and for that matter Rabelais's,
his grossest comedy was rooted in the divine, and the middle range
of things he largely ignored or bypassed.

Given this set of attitudes, Joyce could not possibly have been interested in apportioning moral praise or blame on the usual novelistic
grounds of sympathy and antipathy. This is an easy game of make-
believe, played by the author with the relatively simple devices of as-
signing good lines to favored characters, allocating sensitivity, and
manipulating point of view, till the reader automatically finds Blifil
hateful, Parson Adams endearing, and Jane precisely deserving of
Mr. Bingley as a matrimonial partner just appropriate to her degree
of fictional merit. From Joyce's point of view, this is shooting fish in
a barrel. He looks at character, and the first premises of character,
in a longer and colder perspective; increasingly, he is dubious that alleged individuals have enough character to be considered individuals at
all—they are simply repeating patterns and formulas established long
ago. In fact, Joyce has shed or will sooner or later shed the Christian
assumption that each of us has an individual soul, for which we are
individually responsible, with reward or punishment (real or mimic)
being assigned on the basis of our custody. Our choice is between
continuing to revolve pointlessly on the wheel of life or somehow
getting off it. This is not necessarily *the* modern world, but it is one
of the available modern worlds, and it raises hob with traditional
19th-century notions of prose fiction, its structure, and its function.

A few words finally about his personal character, for that too enters
the story. James Joyce was from the first a colossal egotist, convinced
of his own genius and ready to sacrifice to it anything and anyone—
so ready to do this that he was often unable to see that he was demanding of others any particular sacrifice at all. He was generous to
the point of improvidence, and a vindictive, relentless prosecutor of
grudges. His mind was obsessed with structures, and he discovered,
imagined, or created systems of correspondence, not only through his
books, but also, to less happy effect, throughout his life. It is true
that the plots and betrayals and malignant coincidences that he was
perpetually discovering occasionally proved to be real; but more often
they were the result of irrational obsession—a paranoia, in other
words, as genuine as Rousseau's, and perhaps grounded like Rousseau's in the immense, painful work of self-analysis to which he devoted his life.

For Joyce, whose talent lay in seeing *through* things, in sensing
that luminosity of objects which Rebecca West has attributed so beau-
tifully to Ibsen, there was no line (any more than there was for
Blake) between paranoia and insight, between public and private
vision, between microcosm and macrocosm. When Stephen Dedalus
taps his brow and says (echoing Blake specifically), "in here it is I
must kill the priest and the king," Private Carr is infuriated. He
thinks Edward the Seventh has been insulted. Certainly he is wrong,
but no less certainly he is right; through Stephen, Joyce, like Blake,
is a prophet against empire. Had this been understood in 1904 or
even 1922, it would probably have seemed to be megalomania; from
the present perspective, there appears a good deal more to be said
for it.

In any event, it is a major aspect of Joyce's impact on the English
novel that he was a self-centered, inflexible, and unitary personality.
This wasn't simply a matter of his implacable exile, of his refusal to
confer "respectability" on his ménage, or of his ferocious struggle
over nine years against the castration of *Dubliners*. In the decision

to write *Finnegans Wake* in the style and on the scale which it had from the very first, he was supported by no literary opinion and by no prudential consideration whatever. On the contrary, he broke over it with friends, family, admirers, and devoted supporters. He simply had to write this book in this way; and, undeterred by good advice, ridicule, semi-blindness, family griefs, and a thousand other practical obstacles, he did so write it. It was a process of self-vivisection, as he declares in the *Wake* itself:

> this Esuan Menschavik and the first till last alshemist wrote over every square inch of the only foolscap available, his own body, till by its corrosive sublimation one continuous present tense integument slowly unfolded all marry-voising moodmoulded cyclewheeling history (thereby, he said, reflecting from his own individual person life unlivable, transaccidentated through the slow fires of consciousness into a dividual chaos, perilous, potent, common to allflesh, human only, mortal) [pp. 185-86].

The books of Joyce were written out of his lacerated consciousness, and they put the reader inside that consciousness with a peremptory violence which has only one parallel in the last seven hundred years. When Dante wants to show a glutton in Hell, he brings forward, not Lucullus or Apicius or someone whom we might recognize, but Ciaccio, a next-to-anonymous street-corner loafer of his own particular half-acre of downtown Florence. A fact in Dante's consciousness is a fact for the world; he imposes it. In the same spirit, Joyce brings into his epic novel the staff of the British consulate at Zurich in 1918, because of a squabble over a few francs and a pair of pants. He made his books out of his life and into his life; a reading of them was radically incomplete till Mr. Ellmann told in notable detail the story of that life. But any reading is still incomplete, because nobody can ever put as much time into Joyce as Joyce did. His demand on readers was, proverbially, absolute.

In following out this monomania, Joyce enrolled himself among the literary heroes—those rare and special spirits like Milton and

Blake who survived the scorn or indifference of their own time, and imposed their vision of life on posterity. This is a dream of glory congenial to everyone who has ever felt misunderstood; and at a level of remoteness and unreality which doesn't make us uncomfortable, we rejoice in it. But it is a forbidding act to follow. Joyce's eminence as a legend has not only earned him disciples, perhaps outnumbering his readers; it has also placed him on the shelf where stand the dusty busts of those too demanding to be imitated except in fantasy.

His example of independence was all the more striking because of the state of the English literary world at the time when he exiled himself from it. In Ireland very strikingly, but scarcely less so in England, it was a world of cliques, clubs, and narrow cenacles. Writers clustered together. Publishers were of course powerful, but restricted at least in their power to say a final "no" by the fact that there were so many of them. More potent in their limited sphere were the editors of reviews. On the whole, and with rare exceptions here and there (Professors Dowden, Saintsbury, and Quiller-Couch come immediately to mind), one doesn't get the impression that the universities had much to do with the making of contemporary literary opinion. Literary society was centered in London and Dublin; and to a degree quite exceptional in English history, it was directed by men of letters.

A man of letters is by definition an amphibious creature. He generally has some modest standing as an author in his own right; but his main commitment is to the field of public opinion and its unfenced neighbor, public relations. Hostile portraits of the man of letters are those of Jasper Milvain in Gissing's *New Grub Street* and Mr. Nixon in Pound's "Hugh Selwyn Mauberley." But Joyce in the library scene of *Ulysses* has given his own view of this society, as Stephen Dedalus steps cautiously through a cluster of editors, publishers, literary civil servants, and opinion-makers, plus the inevitable hangers-on. In London the fringes of literature were even thicker than in Dublin. Men like Frank Harris and Sir Walter Besant and Leslie Stephen and John Morley and Edmund Gosse and George

Meredith and Sidney Lee and Lytton Strachey and Ernest Rhys and
Max Beerbohm had practically nothing else in common, but they
all lived and worked in the publishing "world," in the semi-literary,
semi-business ambience for which a good English undergraduate education seems to fit men so admirably. The early century was the period when the great English collections, series, reference-books, and
summas were being completed—one thinks of the 11th Britannica,
the DNB and the OED, the English Men of Letters series, Everyman's Library, Bohn's Library, and a hundred lesser enterprises, all
of which needed, and paid for, laborers in the vineyard. It was also
a great period for reviews, of which a grossly perfunctory listing
would include *The Speaker, The Spectator, The Tatler, The Athenæum, The National Observer, The Bookman, The Savoy, The Satur-
day Review, The Fortnightly Review, The Literary World, T.P.'s
Weekly, John o'London's Weekly, The Academy, Men and Women,*
and so forth and so on. In addition, most of the London and several
of the Dublin newspapers carried regular literary sections and sup-
plements, copy for which was supplied by free-lance reviewers.

So much literary journalism surely implied a thriving literary marketplace, and indeed this was the fact. Yet it also implied vulgariza-
tion. It was not the worst books that had trouble finding a market in
literary London or Dublin, it was very often the best. In Dublin the
patriotic clique, with its strongly clerical and moralistic cast, set itself
consistently and resolutely against any literature which showed Irish
people in a less than ideal light. In England the censorship, though
generally less formal, was just as effective. The middle-class attitudes
of the average reader made it hard for even a slightly demanding or
unconventional author to gain a hearing. George Meredith complained all his life of neglect by the larger public; so did George Gissing; so did Joseph Conrad; so did Henry James. Most of these men
won a measure of popular success in the end, but only after long
struggles, frequent deprivations—and sometimes on the basis of
work far inferior to their best. What grated most was not the diffi-

culties they faced, but the ready acceptance of frank and unashamed trash. Publishers welcomed it, and the influential lending libraries circulated it; polite opinion sniffed, but the lowbrows avidly devoured rhetorical romances by such as Elinor Glyn, Marie Corelli, Mrs. Henry Wood, Miss Rhoda Broughton, Mary Elizabeth Braddon, Maria Susanna Cummins, and other weird sisters. At least in certain circles, it was an age very tolerant of florid and artificial rhetoric. Poetry and journalism flourished alike, with a really glorious lack of self-consciousness, on high-sounding clichés. Normal fictional prose, as written by otherwise respectable authors, was a stiff and artificial *lingua franca* only mildly diluted from the worst excesses of Lord Lytton. The ludicrous artificialities of Victorian melodrama, which provided Shaw with a lifetime of material to counter or parody, continued well into the 20th century to hold the boards, not just in the provinces, but in London and Dublin as well.

We must not overstate. Following Virginia Woolf, it has become customary to distinguish sharply between the social and exterior fiction of the Edwardian era, and the new psychological inwardness of the fiction which followed—within which Joyce's fiction must clearly occupy a leading position. But the break is not all that sharp. Within English fiction itself there are predecessors—Henry James, George Meredith, Samuel Butler. And on the Continent, the Virginia Woolf rule does not apply at all; in Chekhov, Maupassant, Huysmans, Jacobsen, D'Annunzio, not to mention Paul Bourget and Turgenev and even the "coarse, comprehensive, prodigious Zola," there is no deficiency of psychological analysis. Moreover, the Continent was starting to encroach upon the insular English, and to be better represented there than ever before. It was the men of letters who did most to help with this process. In 1899 the first edition of Arthur Symons's *The Symbolist Movement in Literature* served to introduce Yeats and English poetry generally to techniques and concepts far more advanced than the language had hitherto known. In 1889 Henry Vizetelly had been fined and jailed for publishing Zola in translation, but within a few years first Dostoevsky and then Chekhov were appearing in increasingly competent English versions. Both proved hard for English readers to digest, and Dostoevsky particularly aroused fierce resistance because he appealed too directly, too violently to the basic emotions. Yet it happened often that authors who deplored Dostoevsky, and prophesied that his books would lead to the downfall of the English novel, were found within a few years to be imitating them directly.

What all this suggests is that English literary opinion, and a great deal of English literary practice at the turn of the century, was controlled by inertia and timidity, the fruit of consensus. It was due to receive some terrible shocks within the first two decades of the 20th century, but in good part it was asking for them, and in part, after preliminary difficulties, managed to welcome them. Nor is this to say that honest and honorable work wasn't done in the old tradition even at the time when, overall, it was stagnating. *New Grub Street, Esther Waters, Howards End, The Old Wive's Tale, The Forsyte Saga* are fine books. Yet there is no denying that the novel before Lawrence and Joyce shows many signs of having reached maturity as an art form, of having used up most of its first premises as implied in a particular subject matter and mode of story-telling. It was rotten-ripe for a revolution, strong evidence of which is the fact that one happened.

Looking for a moment beyond literature—which is, after all, only one of the several artistic fields in which the revolution took place—we can briefly describe it as a clash between smooth, or continuous, and broken surfaces; and as such it can be observed in painting, in sculpture, in music, in poetry, on the stage. Within a decade or two of Victoria's death, Stravinsky begins to fracture melody, Picasso and his Cubist friends start to break up the surface of a painting, Pirandello begins to crack through stage illusions, Pound and Eliot start fragmenting their verses, while Brancusi and Duchamp-Villon are moving sculpture, perhaps a little less abruptly, into the sphere of the non-representational. Of course, "non-representational" in this context is a word which bears all too clearly the mark of 19th-century presumptions. The works referred to, like the fiction of Joyce and Kafka, do not fail to represent; they do fracture the exterior surface—that is, the illusion of being in the presence of an object, a person, or a scene—by distorting it in a perceptible way or putting it in a significant context. In "traditional" fiction it is the stream of a story, a narration, that balances the reader on each fresh moment of revelation, as the story moves forward; the reader exists, within such a fiction, in a moment of ever-advancing time, and reacts at his best—with astonishment, dismay, anguished anticipation—as he is caught up in the moment. Modernist writing is (or was, for we are now into something else) relatively static as far as events go; one would go mad reading Proust, Kafka, or Joyce to "find out what happens next." The story gets, and is intended to get, nowhere; at least, where it gets is relatively unimportant. Its point is the process by which it gets there— that is, the incidental revelations available through a retrospective rearrangement of its episodes. Instead of moving steadily forward, the reader of a modernist fiction reads back and forth, comparing, contrasting, analyzing, and reassessing his response to what he understood one way when it was first presented but must now see "in a different light." His consciousness, freed from the obligation of responding to the vicissitudes of the moment, thus intertwines and interacts with that of the narrator and those of the characters, in a way which contains elements of irony. Since he is in effect recomposing and reinterpreting the novel as he reads it, there can be no authoritative correct reading for which the author vouches in his directives or explanations. Introductions, descriptions, and formal analyses tend to disappear from modernist fiction as contributions by the author, precisely because they are assumed to be so largely the responsibility of the reader. There is no inherent or organic connection, I think, between stream-of-consciousness technique and modernist fiction; but the principle of laying out apparently unrelated details and inviting the reader to see a pattern in them is common to both.

Joyce, however, did not move immediately, or at least not openly, against the central fortifications of traditional fiction, and it was quite a while before anyone sensed that in his first prose publication he had moved against them at all. For a book which had so much trouble being born in the first place—which was refused, quibbled, and paltered over by publishers for nine exasperating years, and twice aborted after being set in type—*Dubliners* had a surprisingly mild reception when it appeared, under Grant Richards's imprint, in 1914. Obviously the war distracted attention from Joyce's sour, static sketches of Ireland in the days of Edward the Seventh; and in the ten years between conception and birth, English taste and standards had changed radically. The war and the ghastly fact of mass killing may have coarsened taste; the mere fact that Zola had been published twenty years before, without moral detriment to the community, rendered the *Dubliners* stories safer. Finally, the technical novelties and spiritual insights of *Dubliners* were not in any sense on the surface; they became apparent only after a good deal of study, which hardly began till the 1940s. It was more than a quarter-century after *Dubliners* first appeared that Messrs. Levin and Shattuck began extending the exegetical procedures developed for *Ulysses* by arguing that there was an *Odyssey*-parallel in the earlier book as well. Then, one at a time, starting with "Clay," the individual stories were explicated; and it began to be generally sensed (not without considerable uneasiness) that there was more to them than met the eye. The work of exegesis and textual analysis was carried on almost entirely by American students. This is in line with the publishing history of the original text, which was largely ignored in England, but in America passed quickly from the house of B. W. Huebsch to the cheap reprint series of the Modern Library, and in that incarnation sold more than 60,000 copies. American readers were intrigued by the surfaces of the *Dubliners* stories long before they had any reason to suspect covert allusions or hidden meanings; the love-hate relationship toward the old country evidently appealed to significant numbers of Irish-Americans. British readers, with less reason to feel nostalgia or relief at the thought of the Dublin slums—with a sizable literature about their own slum-realities—tended to take the stories of Joyce as those of an Irish Arthur Morrison or Israel Zangwill, as a *Limehouse Nights* from across the Irish Channel. So far as *Dubliners* charmed readers on either side of the Atlantic, the story that did so was "The Dead," about which H. E. Bates was vociferously enthusiastic as early as 1943. That was the first break in a profound British tradition of silence about *Dubliners;* it came almost thirty years after the stories first appeared in print.

One can indeed represent *Dubliners* as having been dragged into the mainstream of Joycean studies through the influence of the other works, which demanded exegesis and commentary more urgently. From *Ulysses,* which was largely unintelligible without exegesis, the habit of mind spread backward to the earlier works. Yet the collection of stories has a retrospective value in the tale of Joyce's literary advent, by virtue of its very colorless and neutral reception. Harry Levin, in his influential early study of Joyce (1941), spoke of the *Dubliners* stories as having passed easily and naturally into the prevailing mode of short fiction:

> It is hard to appreciate the originality of Joyce's technique, twenty-five years after the appearance of *Dubliners,* because it has been standardized into an industry. This industry is particularly well equipped to deal with the incongruities and derelictions of metropolitan life. Its typical products are the shrewd Parisian waifs of *Les Hommes de bonne volonté* and the well-meaning nonentities who blunder through the pen and pencil sketches of *The New Yorker* [p. 31].

From where we stand now, James Joyce as an artist does not look much more like Helen Hokinson and James Thurber than he does like Jules Romains; but it is both important and true that after a full quarter-century on the literary scene he did. An observer as shrewd as Mr. Levin judged that the polished surfaces of *Dubliners* were designed to reflect coldly and impersonally the characteristic mannerisms of the urban flotsam. It was only later, when critics started worrying about chalices and simony, about parallels with Dante and Job, and the possibility that Maria might be the Virgin, a witch, or (worst of all) both, that something beyond surface realism was seen to be involved. The experience of a collapsing surface which turned out to have been a mask for some sort of covert second meaning timed to reveal itself after more or less delay, was integral to many early readings of Joyce.

A Portrait of the Artist, with its combination of romanticism and irony, and its sustained passages of expressive prose, was the first book of Joyce's to exercise widespread fascination over readers. The Stephen Dedalus mystique was one which Joyce had long practiced, and the value of which he knew; on the other hand, much of its power came from the contrast between Stephen's aesthetic aspirations and the squalor out of which he had to work his way. The further fact that Joyce had to cut down his novel from the much longer *Stephen Hero* made for an uneven and apparently fragmentary narrative texture, which tested the reader's powers of integration, and gave pause to publishers who were afraid of getting over their readers' heads. In fact, each of these three elements was made a cause of complaint against the *Portrait.* The aesthetic themes were complained of as too narrow, too professional; on the basis of that complaint, a 1917 reviewer ventured to say categorically of Joyce, "it is doubtful if he will make a novelist." The book's lack of morality, or more precisely of gentility, was a cause of objection even while it was appearing in serial scraps in *The Egoist;* the printers simply refused to set certain sentences generally involving excretion. This was not so much virtue on their part as fear of legal consequences; after the suppression of Lawrence's *The Rainbow* in 1915, printers and publishers alike tended to be prudish in self-defense. But even after the *Portrait* had been published in America, and appeared in an English edition, English readers and critics complained of the book's squalor. Finally, its narrative fragmentation, which had very much upset Edward Garnett when he read the manuscript for Duckworth, proved less of an obstacle for readers than had been anticipated. This doubtless was related to a new, impressionistic habit of reading introduced mainly by Dostoevsky, in which calendar time was largely usurped by psychological time. Several years might thus be silently passed over in a chapter heading or a mere set of asterisks, while ten crucial minutes of emotional decision were described in close detail. It is, of course, a technique of the movies as well, where without preliminaries or explanations it is possible to change focus in space and in time and to obliterate transitions. Ordinary readers of the *Portrait* adjusted without effort to the difficulties which had so disturbed Garnett—which is not to say that, in his own terms, he was not right about the *Portrait*. The hell-fire sermons, which take up more than a tenth of the entire book, are far out of proportion to the rest of the novel—unless one measures that proportion psychologically. The final pages splinter into isolated and laconic entries in a diary, which is anticlimactic unless one estimates its purpose as the detachment of Stephen Dedalus from what has, after all, been the world of his past, and the preparation of his mind for a launch into the future. Many early readers found the music of the *Portrait* "wild" and unconventional; but the presence of music, both verbal and intellectual, they had no trouble in recognizing.

As nobody has failed to observe, the *Portrait* belongs to a class of novels which is perfectly familiar, and quite well defined; it is a Bildungsroman, like *Wilhelm Meister, Richard Feverel, A Sentimental Education, The Way of All Flesh, Confessions of a Young Man.* What was special about Joyce's book was the peculiar expressiveness of the prose, its unmediated action on the reader's sensitivities. For example, the hell-fire sermons, with their relentless pounding on the child's nerves, their terror and yet their monotony, were allowed to act in exactly the same way on the reader. What was blurred and incomprehensible to the boy was not explained by an omniscient author for the comfort of the reader: Athy's riddle went unanswered; smugging in the square passed without commentary; the word "Lotts" scrawled on an alley wall stood blank on the page to suggest what it would. At quite the opposite extreme, Joyce's prose constantly brushed the reader's imagination with tenuous suggestions of correspondence and associative imagery. The persistent imagery of birds and flight was very easy to see, and its recurrence made its importance evident. But the book continually teased its readers to find symbolic significance in images and fantasies of which the meanings were by no means clear. The importance of the little old man in the National Library—who reads Sir Walter Scott, and about whom Stephen has a dream or a fantasy associating him with incest and Davin—was not obvious, yet in a book which omitted so much, he must have had significance to be included. The book thus floated, to a considerable degree, on its prose style. What wasn't clear in it—transitions, proportions, allusions, symbolic connections, deliberate privacies—was carried by the vivid, expressive writing. Like *Dubliners,* the *Portrait* was at first read unsuspiciously, which is to say superficially; this was natural enough, since there was little overt evidence in the book that it was meant to be read in any other way, and the 19th-century view of fiction was that the author must take a relatively wholehearted attitude toward his hero. Especially in the Bildungsroman, the hero may suffer from exterior difficulties or faults of immaturity, but he does not generally endure lack of sympathy on the part of his creator. That there were serious ironic reservations on the part of Joyce against Stephen Dedalus as an artist was not, therefore, immediately apparent to readers of the *Portrait;* it was not until 1948 that Hugh Kenner, reading back from the later books with characteristic assurance and narrowness, denounced the character of Dedalus, especially in the last chapter, as "insufferable." The point has been pushed a little further, in Ellmann's diagnosis of the rhythms of the *Portrait* as "masturbatory"; it has been disputed, qualified, compromised. But the upshot of the process is that, as with *Dubliners,* the *Portrait,* when read retrospectively from the later books, proved richer and more complex, more ironic and less romantic than it had at first appeared. It also became more of a labyrinth or a puzzle—a labyrinth without an exit, a puzzle without a solution, on occasion—than novels have traditionally been.

Good novels, like good writing of any sort, respond to analysis, yielding pattern after pattern of meaning or implication or verbal design; we talk about them, loosely, as "inexhaustible," but that is partly because the critics, unexhausted, are always approaching them with fresh questions. But when the patterns start clashing on one another so violently that they cannot be held within a single perspective, disquiet sets in. If one were to read the *Portrait* as Mr. Kenner proposed, the novel became the story of the making of a frigid pseudo-Byronic prig, and a reader might well ask why he should follow, with the sympathy obviously expected of him, the making of such a disagreeable fellow. The answer was, evidently, that one must then read *Ulysses,* and after that *Finnegans Wake,* to see the completed image of Stephen Dedalus, portrayed in the richly comic light which alone represented Joyce's terminal vision. This may be true in one sense or another, but it makes hash of the *Portrait* as a coherent literary unit, and it is especially discouraging for those readers with the bad luck to read it between 1917 and 1939, when they couldn't possibly appreciate what the whole thing was about, since the *Wake* hadn't yet been published. Of course there are ways to work out these difficulties, as there are ways to guess what the bat-and-incest themes are about, and why Simon Dedalus hesitates over the name of a Cork bartender: "Here you, Tim or Tom or whatever your name is, give us the same again here." But these solutions take us very far from the experience of reading a literary fiction. Literary biographers, literary detectives, and literary problem-solvers have no reason to complain when Joyce sets before them intricate rebuses involving details from his personal life, allusive particulars from his remote reading, and unresolved contradictions of attitude from his own subconscious. Readers of fiction in the traditional sense can be excused for not having sensed immedi-

ately that Joyce had started a whole new ball game. The "wild" music of the *Portrait* really was wild—not just by Irish contrast with civilized England, nor by 20th-century contrast with stodgy Victorians, but
because it involved a new sort of animistic logic, an intuited structure
of the mind and therefore of the world. Like Blake, Joyce had turned
the world of Locke upside down; but he did not explicitly say so, perhaps because he only gradually became aware of what he was doing.
All this was to be seen or sensed in the *Portrait,* though not in *Dubliners:* but chiefly as back-interpretation from the two last fictions.
And while this roundabout vision was forming, the *Portrait* throve
on its impressionistic prose—throve in America more than in England, and more in the free literary climate after the war than before
or during it. The book, it will be remembered, deals with a sequence
of events from roughly 1885 to 1902—a period remote to the point
of antiquity from the jazzy 1920s; and its allusive, evocative technique enabled it to suggest vulgarities and indecencies without using
language or imagery which would shock the liberated sensibility of
the twenties.

Thus, both Joyce's first two books made their way irregularly but
impressively, by an original process of ingratiation and fascination—
only later by a process of challenge. They appealed chiefly through
lyric prose a good deal more emotive and imagistic than that of the
customary novel, but also more sharply contrasted with language expressing repugnance and disgust. Words like "swoon," "languor,"
and "ardent" as they applied to Stephen Dedalus and Gabriel Conroy
were balanced by words like "foul," "sickly," "mouldering," and
"squalor," as they applied to the rest of Ireland. This rather bifocal
view of the world evidently appealed more to Americans, with their
sense of social alienation, than to British readers with their somewhat
stronger sense of social intimacy, and their relative indifference to
Bohemia.

Though Joyce's first three books were written over a quarter-
century, from about 1897 to 1922, the first two appeared almost si-

multaneously in 1916, and the third started to appear in periodical form fewer than two years later, early in 1918. With the publication of *Ulysses,* the antagonist aspect of Joyce, which had been suspected but muted in the first two books, came to the fore. The printing of *Ulysses* in the *Little Review* was sabotaged by printers before it was forbidden by the police and the editors fined. Thereafter, no printer in the English-speaking world could be found to print the volume, and its very importation into the Anglo-Saxon world was made illegal. By the standards of the time when it was published, the book was clearly obscene—I use the word without odium, and with full recognition of its oddity in a culture which has accepted Petronius and Rabelais as classics. The book shocked, and was intended to shock; the American judge who held its importation legal did so on the tenuous grounds that it might be emetic but was not aphrodisiac. Of course, he was perfectly correct in his decision, and the book now is neither emetic nor aphrodisiac, nor for that matter obscene. But in its day it distinctly and deliberately violated deep-seated conventions of propriety—which is in effect the meaning of obscenity. In addition, it was very long and in passages deliberately tedious; it was often obscure, and sometimes impenetrably so. It seemed to have little or no moral point. Its many different styles were often parodic, and so called attention to the presence of the author in a way that was felt to be exhibitionistic and undramatic. Accurate though some of these terms may be, they sound like, and are, extremely superficial criticisms to apply to *Ulysses;* by now we have gone far beyond the categories of judgment that they imply. But they were and are the traditional terms for judging novels on the literary Rialto, where a book was and largely is expected to be titillating but not disgusting, entertaining, easy to read, true to life, and morally improving. *Ulysses* clearly challenged all these judgments and demanded that readers deal with it in other terms.

The book's relation to epic tradition gave early critics a first handle to clutch. Seeing that it was a diminished, unheroic version of the

Odyssey, with Bloom the advertising man serving as epic hero, provincial Dublin equaling the whole Homeric world, and a single day foreshortening universal history, they tended to exaggerate the "protest" element of the book. It was thought to represent, in a mood between horror and dismay, life in a world without heroism, religion, or meaning—"an explosion in a sewer" was Paul Elmer More's memorable phrase, which on mature reflection he modified by expressions such as "details of tumescent filth" and "verminous darkness." Indeed, there was an element of truth in this view, as there was in the opposing position that Joyce's imagination was essentially Catholic in its structuring of the world, and that he was one of the most "orthodox" of contemporary writers, as contrasted with an essential heretic and barbarian like D. H. Lawrence. What was missing from this cross-fire of criticism (and Joyce himself mildly protested the omission) was any general recognition that *Ulysses* was in any degree a comic novel. There were important and understandable reasons for this oversight; among others, Joyce's sense of humor, like Ibsen's and Swift's, had a broad streak of cruelty that made it hard to recognize. Thus, in the first general casting-up of the book, comedy was a natural element to be overlooked, and its disappearance threw many otherwise intelligent assessments out of balance.

These rather large discussions of what the novel was about—of what it meant in terms of a philosophical statement about the universe—made up the mainstream of commentary upon *Ulysses* during the first few years after its publication. There were of course secondary streams of critical commentary. The book's alleged morality or immorality was debated with much vehemence and little insight during the 1920s; and there was a minor flare-up of this polemic after its official admission to the Anglo-Saxon world in the mid-1930s. Then its stream-of-consciousness technique was described and traced to its origins, while Marxist criticism viewed the book with gloomy satisfaction as a giant landmark thrown up to indicate the end of bourgeois individualism. All these discussions took for granted—rather complacently in the light of the detailed explication which followed them—that the book had in fact been read. In a gross way, no doubt it had. But relatively few of the early commentators worked earnestly or at length on understanding the novel's details. The great flood of this work—and the first warnings against doing too much of it— started to appear only after the war. For example, it was not till the late 1950s that a significant study appeared (by W. M. Schutte, 1957) on Joyce's use of Shakespeare in the novel; and it was about the same time that articles on specific episodes, individual figures, and detailed passages of the book began to appear.

Probably Stuart Gilbert's book on *Ulysses,* which was well understood to be Joyce's book as well, accounted for the timing of the great explication-wave. Appearing first in 1930, *James Joyce's Ulysses* laid out authoritatively and in vast detail the first principles of Joyce-exegesis; and it made fully apparent, for the first time, the amount of study and cross-comparison that would be required to read the book with a first approximation of adequacy. Along with Frank Budgen's book *The Making of Ulysses* (1934) and Miles Hanley's *Word-Index to Ulysses* (1937), the book that went under the name of Stuart Gilbert made clear that before one could really talk about what *Ulysses* meant, there was a lot of work to be done in defining simply what it was. Most of this work has been simple, old-fashioned *explication de texte;* and it is still going on. It began with analyses of Joyce's reliance upon large old Dublin institutions like Thom's *Directory* and the *Freeman's Journal* (as, for example, by Richard M. Kain in *Fabulous Voyager,* 1947) and has culminated in several volumes of annotation—extensive, incomplete, inaccurate, but certain to expand and improve over the years—like Weldon Thompson's *Allusions in Ulysses* (1961, 1968) and Gifford and Seidman's *Notes for Joyce* (1974). Since all existing texts of *Ulysses* are extravagantly inaccurate, it seems inevitable that the next step in *Ulysses*-scholarship will be the reconstruction of a new text, based not simply on the best available version, but on a careful study of the surviving manuscripts, typescripts, and proof-sheets. A new text may of course involve some readjustment of hermeneutics based on the old one, but at least the new processes will be founded on something closer to bedrock than the present mud and water. And then we can look forward to the variorum.

It is important to repeat that reading Joyce has been largely a process in reverse. One starts by making broad surface responses, or asking heavy confident questions which take a good deal for granted; one ends up scrutinizing the text for very small indications indeed. The text is constructed to give way beneath the reader's feet; later passages call into question, quite as often as they explain, earlier ones. This is the essence of the method, which doesn't aim at laying out a story before the reader, like toothpaste on a brush, but at entangling, engaging, and teasing his mind, by giving him enough or almost enough materials to make for himself one or several or many retrospective patterns.

The scale of *Ulysses*-interpretation has inevitably diminished with the passage of time. In part, this is a simple consequence of the fact that no limited quantity of material can reveal an unlimited number of major patterns. Even Mr. Ellmann's recent book *Ulysses on the Liffey,* which seems an exception to the rule, really proves it. For the interpretive patterns which Mr. Ellmann discovers with extreme ingenuity, and enforces with a truly structuralist disregard of positive evidence, are really substructural patterns—fascinating enough, and maybe even present, but dependent more on the special perspective from which they are discerned than on any reader's natural response to the text.* This consideration doesn't, and isn't intended to, amount

---

* A "natural" response to a text may of course be simply a naïve, i.e., a stupid one. Critical theories aren't to be dismissed simply because they don't jibe with nincompoop readings. Yet there's a line to be drawn here somewhere. An art critic discussing a painting is not entitled to describe as its *structure* a set of relations that can be seen only by looking at it through green-tinted glasses—unless, of course, the painter has somehow indicated that that's the way to see it, or unless the critic is able to persuade us that it's a better and more interesting picture when viewed in this way. Two sepa-

to a derogation of Mr. Ellmann's book; it's simply a factual observation that, by the early 1970s, most of the gross observations regarding *Ulysses* had been made, and the gleaners were at work—some, clearly, more ambitious and perceptive than others, but most engaged on matters either minute or peripheral to the book's major impact. No one can ever be quite sure that a revolutionary new interpretation of *Ulysses* will not appear tomorrow, and everyone can predict with perfect confidence that minor adjustments, revaluations, and recasting of critical balances will continue for a long time to come. For though the book itself can hardly change now (except by re-editing, as noted above), readers can and will; and, seeing the book with new eyes, they will see in it, of necessity, new proportions and colorations.

As for where *Ulysses* has found its resting place among Anglo-American readers, that is hard to say, even roughly. For some readers it is certainly very close to a sacred text; for others, it is a forbidding and exasperating bore. The book is perhaps respected and feared more widely than it is liked; it is certainly read *in* far more often than it is read *through*. Because it is a wonderful book to teach and a test for young and strenuous minds, a good many of its readers are probably to be found in the academies. As a "modernist classic" the book has been excerpted in anthologies, placed on phonograph records, adapted to stage presentation, and converted against fearful odds into a movie. It has been widely translated, too, into such tongues as Hungarian and Japanese, as well as the standard European languages. No history of the novel, no discussion of modern literature (even when written by a man like Mr. J. I. M. Stuart, who clearly finds Joyce utterly uncongenial and largely incomprehensible) can afford to ignore the central importance of *Ulysses*.

And yet . . . and yet . . . though it's a colossal monument, *Ulys-*

---

rate questions are likely to get mixed up in the latter judgment: whether the critic has written an ingenious and attractive argument, and whether he has made the artwork under discussion seem more ingenious and attractive. A final basic question to be asked about the whole process is whether a work of art is necessarily more attractive as it is more ingenious.

ses remains an enigmatic one. It has not been accommodated to the tradition of the English novel or to the cut of the usual department of English, far less the common reader. Very frequently it finds its place in a course on the European Novel, or on World Literature as a whole; or else it is set apart for study in a course of its own. People who become involved with *Finnegans Wake* tend to specialize in that one book alone; *Ulysses* is not quite so all-absorbing, but it is a hard book to teach or study (or simply to hold in the mind) in combination with any other novels—or, for that matter, with any other works of literature. And this is not just because it's an outsize novel, large physically, intellectually, artistically. It is also because *Ulysses* contains a streak of that visionary insight which goes beyond fiction and works against it. It is a novel, to be sure, especially in its first chapters; but as it develops, it transcends and subverts the novel form entirely. Apart from calling it a book—as we call the writings of Apuleius and Rabelais, not fictions, but books—we have no proper terminology for this sort of writing, and no place to put it in a curriculum or a categorization, except in a box of its own.

A special and formidable problem with the interpretation and "positioning" of *Ulysses* is the proximate presence of *Finnegans Wake.* Joyce's mind was extraordinarily of a piece; it developed (like Ibsen's) by a kind of inexorable exfoliation, in response to a deep inner logic. It is not just the blazing noon of hindsight which enables us to say assuredly that *Dubliners* implied the *Portrait,* the *Portrait* led necessarily to *Ulysses,* and *Ulysses* could only have been followed by the *Wake.* The logic of the development could be explicated in a nutshell. The sour smells and lowered horizons of *Dubliners* demanded a perceptive and intricate consciousness which could make artistic use of such an environment; the analysis of that consciousness in its slow and painful growth (against the environment, but also through use of it) is in the *Portrait.* The exercise of that full-grown talent, first in the outside social world, then increasingly in the darkening world of night and introspection, is the theme of *Ulysses.* Full submergence in the universal subworld of the collective human semi-consciousness remains for the *Wake*. The last book—surely not by accident—repeats with symphonic amplitude the situation and basic themes of the very first short story.

Such rigorous intensity of single-minded purpose is a quality in itself; it serves also to backlight elements in the early work, which show up more vividly when seen in the light of what they later became. *Finnegans Wake*, whether greeted with awe or revulsion, made evident the distance of Joyce's mind from the common mind of the common reader. (Even if one accepted that the *Wake* revealed to every one of its readers his true self, it was a true self from which those habits of mind making him a common reader had long ago alienated him.) To the author's great though unreasonable disappointment, the *Wake* never gained mass readership; even among readers of Joyce to this day, the book is sometimes ignored—as if elements of the previous career could somehow be discussed without reference to this large, untidy problem. That Joyce's career seemed to end in a gigantic enigma, a labyrinth more inconceivably labyrinthine and in some ways more inelegant than anything seen in literature since *The Book of the Dead,* could not help reflecting back on the path which had brought him to this end.

None of these observations can preclude the possibility that the *Wake* may ultimately be judged, by those capable of making such a judgment, to be Joyce's greatest book. The fact is that it has been published now (as a whole for thirty-five years, but in selections for fifty) without transcending, in the minds of more than a small clique, the status of a curiosity. It may be a great curiosity: it has certainly proved to be an inaccessible one. Joyce's career comes to an end with the production of a book that cannot be read, but must be deciphered. Exegetical aids, critiques, concordances, summaries, seminars, and cenacles have of course helped the limited circle of Joyce addicts to find their way through the winding paths and out of a few of the dead ends. But, speaking broadly, the *Wake* provides the first exam-

ple in post-Reformation Europe of a major book by a recognized major author which was so alien to its potential readers that their knowledge of it had to come through a priestly caste of interpreters, or else
had to remain superstitious altogether.

The reasons for the obscurity of the *Wake* are well known and
easy to summarize. The book is written essentially in English, but in
English distorted by a variety of puns from other languages and mis-
spellings made, some with, and many without, discoverable reason.
The characters are not simple, but contain, and can convert without
warning to, other analogous characters, to animals, or to inanimate
objects. The "plot" is rudimentary, but narrated without any effort at
consecutive, sequential representation; in accordance with the theme
of the book, it stutters, stammers, and repeats itself. The range of allusive erudition is enormous, encompassing both the polite and the
popular, indeed the vulgar, cultures; there is a great deal in the book
which is private to Dubliners of the late 19th century, and even more
which is private to James Joyce personally. The key to some passage
is often found to lie in a particular event, individual, or social fact of
the author's private biography. The patterning of the book, as distinct from its plot, is inconceivably complex. Cycles and correspondences, parallels and analogues are thick almost beyond tracing. The
book *can* be deciphered, and with great pleasure, preferably by a
small and dedicated group, possessing a wide scattering of languages,
who are ready to ruminate the text very slowly indeed, generally
phrase by phrase, but sometimes word by word or syllable by syllable.
Yet even such a group, meeting regularly over a period of months
and years, must have, again and again, the unsatisfied sense of having
passed over certain words without getting any notion of why they are
there or why they are as they are. Behind this dissatisfaction is bound
to lurk a nagging suspicion that the text as we possess it contains
many corruptions which are the product simply of accident or some
intermediary's ignorance. Joyce was half-blind when he wrote the
book; many of his amanuenses and typists knew no English, and

would have hesitated (rightly) to apply such knowledge if they had had it. Lacking that accepted norm for spelling words which enables us to recognize common forms and identify them, even when they look like, and are, something else, the creators of the *Wake* committed many errors—how many it is of course impossible to say, and perhaps Joyce, if he knew of them, would not have considered them all errors. He wanted the *Wake* to be a frowzy, entangling book, and so it is. A study of the book's many layers of composition shows that Joyce generally began with a relatively simple and straightforward English prose statement, which he steadily enriched, distorted, and entangled with new levels of allusion and significance. In the process, he allowed changes to slip in which not only contribute nothing to the meaning of the passage but sometimes obscure it, and distract from whatever other meanings it may have.

Reading the *Wake* properly is thus a superhuman task. It involves not only reading the printed text and understanding its encyclopedic complexities, but tracing its development through the pre-texts, and disentangling the accidental from the significant. The laziness and complacency of readers is commonly and often rightly blamed when inventive and original literary work fails of its effect. Good writers know that what is absorbed without effort is as effortlessly forgotten, and they build deliberate difficulties into their work. From the author's point of view, when one writes under the aspect of eternity, as Joyce evidently did, it matters relatively little if five or ten generations of readers, after wrestling with the text, give up on it (with rare exceptions) in frustration, if not despair. This means only that the audience has not grown up to the author's conceptions. But the practical consequences of having an unread and almost unreadable book as the supreme achievement of the most talented prose writer of his day are bound to be complex. A first, primitive reaction is, of course, to deny in varying degrees that Joyce was a great writer at all, the usual formula being that he had great talents but misused them. (The distinction between "use" and "misuse" tacitly but perceptibly assumes the standards of contemporary society as a norm—whereas it is exactly from the sleep of contemporary society that Joyce asks us to wake that we may put on the dimensions of all the buried Finnegans within us.) There is no logical way of refuting this position, except to point out that its pragmatic Gladstone prudence imposes on the visionary artist an impossibly contradictory set of demands. Joyce's art is the art of seeing through, of going beyond. He looks past ideologies, conventions, and intentions, beyond morals, manners, character, and individuality, to the visionary substructure of human life: by which I mean the primitive instinctual patterns and tropisms by which life is and always has been controlled. To ask that such a vision be conveyed in conventional literary forms, tailored to the measure of semi-conscious minds in search of diversion, is like asking for the universal solvent to be delivered in a plastic teacup. The forger of an art which deliberately transcends prudence cannot be judged on merely prudent principles.

If there's no doubt, then, that Joyce was a great writer, there's no doubt either that the qualities which made him great also made him write more and more difficult and finally almost impossible books. The career is of a piece. We cannot have the virtues which made Joyce a supremely potent figure in modern literature without the faults (if faults they be) which made him all-but-unreadable.

The conclusion of these many rather superficial considerations of a superficial subject is simply that Joyce's literary reputation has been surrounded by a *cheval de frise* of question marks, such as surrounds the repute of no writers other than perhaps Blake and Lawrence. It is only natural that different groups—such as the Irish, the Catholics, the Americans, the young, the professional writers, the scholars, the women, the semantic structuralists, and the social realists—should see Joyce under the aspect of their own particular phobias and fixations; this is often a case of the strong finger of prepossession at work on the wax nose of perception. But the whole question of Joyce's achievement, and its position in the rest of the cosmos, has been left up in the air—not through anybody's fault, not in a way that this or any other study can pretend to resolve. For the question is not simply of what *Ulysses* and the *Wake* are, nor simply of what modern man is, but of what they are and what he thinks he is. In relation to that fantasy, is Joyce's achievement—vast as it undoubtedly is—eccentric or essential? The prudent, platitudinous, evasive answer to that question is of course that time will tell. But time will tell only if it is made to talk by the literary conscience of the day. What Joyce himself did has been before us for a good while now, not just in the passive capacity of material to be judged, but in the active and substantial character of an agent which prompts and provokes and pre-empts, incites and forbids and interacts with the subtlest and most ambitious minds of the age. Joyce lives; and after thirty-five years, the time is perhaps ripe for a preliminary statement that will try to answer two plain questions. Where? and How?

CHAPTER TWO

THREE THEMATIC
INTERLUDES

T HE GREATER PART of any responsible discussion of a great author's "influence" is bound to consist of biographical specifics,
even intimacies. One follows B's awareness of A's presence
through the various uses to which he put what he knew of A's writings, or the various efforts he made to escape the incubus of A's presence, or the various ways in which, under the guise of performing
one such activity, he accomplished the other. But in the case of Joyce
at least, there's a slightly different way of laying out the cards. It is
to discuss quickly, using only a limited number of examples, a few of
the main devices-patterns-structures that he applied to prose fiction
and that others applied after him. On the surface at least, the transaction is no more complex than the spread of a new axe-shape among
primitive peoples, or the adoption of a new shovel-design. Of course
there is no such thing as "mere technique" in fiction, where a fresh
narrative angle or a new way of sectoring experience has been known
to have revolutionary consequences spreading far beyond the art itself. Still, at the preliminary stage of things, it may be worthwhile to
treat Joycean influence in this hasty and superficial way, for the sake
of perspective, and to give an idea of the various levels at which, over
the years, that influence has operated.

PARADIGMS AND GRIDS

The first real shock-waves of Joycean influence began to spread across the literary pond with the publication of *Ulysses,* and they struck first, not novelists, but a poet, T. S. Eliot. Through the good offices of Ezra Pound and the mediation of *The Egoist,* where he served as editor after 1916, Eliot had been aware of Joyce's presence since about 1914; he approved of the *Portrait* and, in the *Athenæum* for July 4, 1919, spoke some hesitant and equivocal words in behalf of *Ulysses* as it had been appearing in *Little Review.* In August 1920 he and Joyce met face to face; and while the encounter wasn't any triumph of personal warmth or social tact, it was enough to seal a sort of literary alliance. Joyce had various of the later episodes sent to Eliot, in addition to those he had already seen in *Little Review;* and Eliot responded in a characteristically indirect way, when he wrote to Joyce (May 21, 1921) that the book was a splendid thing, and "I wish for my own sake that I had not read it." He was of course in the process of writing his own greatest poem.

Whether *Ulysses* had such overpowering influence on *The Waste Land* that the latter is in effect a parody of the former is a point that need not be decided here; Joyce thought it did, but he was touchy in these matters, and even if he was right, hardly anyone connected the two works till many years after both were published. The basic fact that *Ulysses* made a tremendous impression on Eliot is beyond question, and nobody did more to make it clear than Eliot himself. His friends were amazed; for the first time in their experience, he was openly enthusiastic about a contemporary book. He not only talked up *Ulysses* among his acquaintance, he wrote, in November 1923, a most influential notice for *The Dial,* under the heading "Ulysses, Order, and Myth"; this statement served for many years not only as a landmark of Joyce criticism, but as a credo for advocates of myth as a structural principle in modern writing.

In fact, Eliot's essay in *The Dial* applies more directly to the use of myth in *The Waste Land* than to the use of myth in *Ulysses*. The Grail legend as interpreted by Jessie Weston really serves as a structural principle on which Eliot hung (with the help of Pound) his observations of contemporary London. To a much greater extent, *Ulysses* takes its own direction, throwing off parallels with the *Odyssey* as it goes, rearranging the episodes as the author chooses, and changing their tonalities to accord with a complex rhythm of his own. At the supreme moment when the *Odyssey* might actually work to order the world of June 16, 1904—on the matter of uniting Stephen with Bloom as Telemachus is united with Odysseus—the parallel wilts into insignificance. Still, Eliot's essay lent intellectual stiffening to Joyce's reputation, and offered a formula under which some of the book's forbidding complexities could be subsumed for a while. It did not adequately define the relation of *Ulysses* to the *Odyssey,* but in declaring that relation the key to a new definition of literary structure, it pointed in the right direction.

As Eliot enunciated it, however, there was nothing particularly new about the notion of using a myth or a classic story to shape a body of contemporary material. The French, with their long neoclassical tradition reaching back to Corneille, Racine, Regnier, and Scarron, had been recasting classical stories in modern guises (or pouring contemporary materials into classic molds—the terminology is interchangeable, the process much the same) for hundreds of years. Even in English we note the mock-heroic, pantomimic, burlesque, and parodic genres as almost all resting at least one foot on a literary paradigm, whether mythical or simply literary. The genre known as "imitation," which flourished during the 18th century, comes even closer to the kind of relationship that Eliot evidently saw as original in Joyce's dealings with Homer. Finally, we must recall that larky, over-ingenious man George Meredith, for whom Joyce rarely failed to find a word of respect. What's notable about Meredith is that he found a way of countering the weight and rigidity of the great classical stories which did not commit him with equal but opposite inflexibility to parody and burlesque. In *The Egoist,* for example, Meredith equivocates jocoseriously with several parallels from classical mythology—Perseus and Andromeda, Iphigenia and Agamemnon; but the basic underpinning for his fiction comes from a humbler narrative, lying directly under everyone's nose—the tale on the willow plate. The effect of these different parallels is to extend the import of Meredith's basic story, to universalize the comedy at Patterne by making it both loftier and more vulgar than the actors can see at any one time. We see the characters in Meredith as we do those in Joyce; but we also see through them, to a dimension of which they are only momentarily and partially aware. It is this rather exceptional quality which gives Meredith particular standing among the literary ancestors of Joyce.

Thus it is easy to find a variety of precedents for Joyce's use of Homer in his novel, though not many of them took the form of prose fiction, and none of them shaped the intimate structure of the imitating work, episode by episode, in precisely the exoskeletal way that we find Homer being employed by Joyce. But then we do not find anybody else using classical materials in precisely this way, either among Joyce's contemporaries or among his predecessors. To be sure, *Ulysses,* seen with the historian's hindsight, falls into quite an impressive group of works created during the 1920s which made various uses of classical themes and imitative, allusive techniques. Nineteen-twenties' neo-classicism was a hectic but authentic international phenomenon which is still looking for its historian. A preliminary and very perfunctory accounting of its episodes would include Gide's *Thésée,* Stravinsky's *Oedipe* and *Apollon,* Pound's *Homage to Sextus Propertius,* O'Neill's *Mourning Becomes Electra,* the metamorphic phase of Picasso, Rilke's *Sonnets to Orpheus,* Valéry's *La Jeune Parque,* Cocteau's *Infernal Machine,* in addition to *The Waste Land*

and *Ulysses*. Somewhere in the background of all this activity, we are bound to recognize the new vitality conferred on classical studies by the Cambridge anthropologists working hand in glove with Jung and the comparative folklorists. But of course the mere use of classical and mythological materials constitutes a very flimsy bond among authors: if we are to have any sense of Joyce as exercising an influence in this matter, we must push a little closer to the way in which he made use of mythical materials, some of the specific effects he gained by using them.

Here the field confronting us is diminished at once by 50 percent, for the plain reason that (with rare exceptions duly noted, as for David Jones's *Anathemata*) the immense pan-mythical resonances of *Finnegans Wake* have had no major influence at all on subsequent writers. Verbally, of course, and in terms of its conception of character, the matter is wholly different, and the influence of the *Wake* has been tremendous. But not even writers like Anthony Burgess or Thornton Wilder, who I suppose would count themselves among the frank disciples, have tried very hard to emulate the multiple mythical veils of the *Wake,* the sense of one mythology lurking behind another. For one thing, the effect is hard to achieve without a rather forbidding atmosphere of authorial pedantry; for another, the structure to which it gives rise is so intricate and demanding in its own right that it diminishes and disembodies the foreground figures whom ostensibly it exists to serve. By illustrating both these consequences himself, Joyce may have cut short further experiment in this area; by doing the novel of the collective unconscious *par excellence* he preempted the fields of a dozen minor pioneers, and reduced them, as an alternative to being minor followers, to doing something else altogether.

The *Ulysses*-procedure of maintaining a running parallel with a single, specific myth (or, alternatively, of maintaining an overlay of myth above fable or vice versa) has continued as a working technique of fiction, but not generally with Joyce's effects and never on

Joyce's scale. For one thing, Joyce was not much interested in the short-range comic effects to be gained by "humanizing" gods and heroes of antiquity (giving Hercules a pot-belly, or representing Helen as a blowsy matron). To a remarkable degree, he treated Homeric Greece and 1904 Dublin not as comic contrasts, but as congruent impersonal shapes. Homer may control a particular episode as a whole, but not so decisively the material within it. This is the case in the "Oxen of the Sun" unit of *Ulysses,* where the Homeric points of contact within the episode are neither expressive nor supportive. The birth of Purefoy's baby and the development of English prose style dominate the unit; various Irish bulls come up in the course of the discussion, and the word "oxen" is actually pronounced at a crucial juncture. But on the whole, there is little interaction between Joyce and his Homeric "original" in the details of this chapter. Here, as in "Scylla and Charybdis" or "Nestor," the Homeric incident acts as a container into which Joyce pours just about whatever he wants; and this point is confirmed by a study of his procedure in composing, of which we have evidence in his typescripts and proof-sheets. He was constantly adding to his first versions, till his final draft exceeded his first one in volume, generally by as much as 30 percent; but it was only exceptionally that his additions bore in any way on the Homeric parallel. Frequently he seems determined to sink it out of sight under an influx of extraneous material.

To compose in this way, however, one has to be working to the large scale, and in episodes as strongly marked by change of style or point of view as those of *Ulysses;* the ordinary novel, having no equivalent for those eighteen sharply marked units, has to work for its effects on the short range and through character. I find no massive fictional achievements to illustrate this point (and undoubtedly the lack of such works represents a critical point in itself), but relatively modest performances will illustrate the main idea. John Updike's *Centaur* counterpoints a nostalgic version of life in Olinger High School as of 1947, with life on Mount Olympus. Three of the book's chapters (numbered 1, 3, 9) are predominantly mythological with rural-Pennsylvania details showing through; the other six are predominantly Pennsylvania with mythological overtones. Most of the parallels depend on positioning, reinforced by alliteration: Zimmerman, principal of the school, is Zeus; his mistress, Mrs. Herzog is Hera; Doctor Applegate is Apollo, his maiden sister Hester is Artemis; Al Hummel the garage mechanic is Hephaestus, his generous wife Vera is Venus, and so forth and so on. Some of the parallels seem rather forced: Minor Kretz, the proprietor of a hamburger joint, is said to be Minos, and Mrs. Passify the postmistress is Pasiphae, but neither of them does anything to carry out the assigned role. Peter/Prometheus the narrator has an uneasy premonition that they may be, or may have been, married; but this is the mythology imposing itself on his imagination—in the life of Olinger, there's no reason to think that Minor Kretz and Mrs. Passify have anything to do with one another, and though there's a Minotaur in the book, it seems to be Minor Kretz himself, who is thus keeper of the Dædalian maze and the monster inside it, husband of Pasiphae and also her monstrous offspring. Characters shift their mythological identifications from time to time; as the author points out, Deifendorf is sometimes a centaur, sometimes a merman, even Hercules. Episodes recur in radically diminished and foreshortened form: the sibyl is a voice in a bottle in a dream, the story of Marsyas is hinted by a blurred print in the doctor's waiting room, the story of Python by the doctor's discarded stethoscope which lies on a table "like a slain rubber serpent." Downtown Alton is to be connected with Athens, the city of Athena, because Foy's department store boasts a neon sign that includes the figure of a blinking owl.

This is much the same sort of anti-allegorical mobility with which Joyce often enlivened and varied his classical parallels; and Updike, like Joyce, uses the sense of mythical presences to give dignity and a sense of universality to a scene of deliberate meanness, ugliness, and squalor. If *The Centaur* falls short of Joyce's work by a good deal, the chief reason may be a soft weight of self-pity and self-consciousness, to which the classical parallels actually contribute—because they are bits and pieces in the first place, and because their connection with the Olinger story is primarily decorative and dependent. It's perfectly comprehensible that Updike, wanting to avoid the univocal rigidity of allegory, deliberately diffused and disorganized his classical references; it is the basic weakness of the novel that, with a set of indigenous materials that needed some long-range stiffening, he made so weak a gesture toward providing it.

The fact is that for assorted reasons—good, bad, and hard to judge—most recent novelists approach the mythologically braced fiction with a kind of bad conscience, as if ashamed of the cross-cultural correspondence-game. Apart from the fact that an increasing number of readers cannot play it, for lack of the basic vocabulary—the classics are losing currency as an idiom almost faster than the Bible—mythology as such implies a belief in final answers and public truths that sits ill on the contemporary story-teller. It isn't just that the mythological novel pretends to reward the industrious and well-prepared reader (who is not necessarily the best reader) with a plum which is itself imaginary; but that it puts the author in the position of dispensing ultimate wisdom of a quasi-religious sort. Something has to be taken off the mythology—an aura, an attitude; it has to be subject to question. One sees mythology being used in a new, equivocal way, for example, in Beckett's *Molloy,* where for a brief, evanescent moment we almost get an Oedipus configuration. But it fades, declines to assert itself, and drops away. Instead of a fixed backdrop, framing the fable, myth is simply a momentary veil, perhaps illusory, perhaps not, drawn across the surface of the story. It is part of the pantomime.

Bruce Morrissette made explicit, what a careful reader could hardly help noticing, that Alain Robbe-Grillet had scattered hints and suggestions of the Oedipus myth under the surface of *Les Gommes,* but the author himself carefully avoided giving the myth enough substantiality in itself, or a sufficiently intimate relation to the main narration, to let it be strongly felt. It doesn't help the story along, or support it with complementary "meanings"; if anything, it distracts. Meanwhile M. Robbe-Grillet cheerfully augments the confusion by denouncing all forms of myth, including such modest offenders as anthropomorphic metaphors and pathetic fallacies, as forms of untruth with which he disdains to involve himself.

In similar, or even more confusing fashion, Iris Murdoch has worked into *The Unicorn* various elements of lore from the bestiaries, involving unicorns. They relate or can be related to the violent, intricate story taking place in the foreground; but the different elements are not systematically related to one another, and any set of coherent connections that one makes between myth and fable is strictly provisional. Sometimes the myth is simply a back-formation from the fable, as for example in *Le Voyeur,* where in a crucial moment of the action, the central character Mathias discovers that he has simply fulfilled an ancient myth about a monster rising from the sea to devour a maiden. An older use of paradigmatic structure would encourage the reader to think of Andromeda and the sea-monster, or Angelica and the Orc, or some similar piece of weighty antique machinery. Even if the allusion were handled lightly, its function would be heavy. But, as handled, the "myth" is merely a glint in a distant mirror, yielding Mathias only an instantaneous (though overwhelming) glimpse of his own outline. If Poe's "Annabel Lee" isn't properly a myth underlying a good part of Nabokov's *Lolita,* it could perhaps be called a paradigm—a foreknown outline-image of a main plot-configuration. So long as it functions to lend thematic or expressive support to the main action, and operates through the bonds of analogy, the paradigm or model can assume many guises, from passing allusion to fully developed allegory. Given "The Octopus" or "Ship of Fools" as a title, one has a basic metaphor to give shape to the details of the fiction that follows—and that, I suppose, is the minimal form of mythmaking out of which more elaborate shapes rise and to which, often enough, they reduce.

Joyce made use of the full range of these mythical and paradigmatic devices, from the simplest and most traditional to the most
complex and innovative; he also added another, qualitatively different, for which, in fiction at least, he had few precedents. This is the
formal configuration applied to a basic narrative but not integrally
or expressively connected with it, which could most simply be described as a pattern or a grid. Viconian cycles and circles, for example,
generally form themselves in Joyce's fiction without regard to the
motivation or even the conscious awareness of the characters; they
constitute a pattern which lies underneath the melodic line of the
"action," whether physical or psychological, like a figured bass. The
pattern, so defined, doesn't lend expressive or thematic support to
the action; on the contrary, it counters the development of the narration—as schemas like those of Yeats or Blake are perceived, almost
like diagrams in an instant of time—and so cancels the sense of progress and motion implicit in most narrative. Commonly, it doesn't even
deepen one's sense of the fiction, and doesn't seem intended to do so:
one doesn't see further and further into action or characters, and so
discover a pattern; the pattern is a thing apart, exterior to everything
except the author and his book. It is a shape into which the book's
events fall; one sees them through the pattern, as if looking through
a barred window.

Clearly, there are many variations in the use of such a device;
some of its roots seem even to lie in their apparent opposite—that is,
Joyce's peculiarly liberal definition of imitative form. "Sirens," for
instance, makes use of a lavish array of devices for imitating musical
forms and shapes, which were certainly in the author's mind and may
be in the industrious reader's if he chooses. But they have little or
nothing to do with Bloom's preoccupations, they are beyond the intellectual capacities of anyone present in the Ormond bar, yet they
are not explicitly attributed to the author either. They are simply
stitched into the pattern of events. To the extent that one is aware of
them, they stand between the reader and the events of the episode,

including whatever mental events befall the novel's chief character. The nominal personae of the *Wake* are no more aware of Viconian cycles than Molly when she says "O rocks!" is supposed to be aware of her metempsychosis through cycles of absence from and return to Calypso. The terminology of lattice or grid may serve to describe well enough the reader's experience of this device, for he sees the characters, when he is looking at them, through it; but when he is looking at the grid, he sees it through them. It is a device of depth in that it leads our eye into the infinite cyclical recessions of the past, but it is a device of fictional shallowness, because it may diminish characters, reducing them to momentary manifestations of an eternal principle or fragments of a three-dimensional mosaic that is bigger than all of them. The grid may have expressive meaning, or none at all; it may be a pattern growing out of the characters' actions or imposed arbitrarily on them; it may comment allusively or ironically on the story; it may represent an author's game of hocus-pocus with his readers.

Nabokov's novel *The Luzhin Defense* deals with a chess master; what more natural than that many actions of the characters should imitate moves on a chess board? Luzhin's marriage is a defensive castling, his final gambit a clear instance of suicide mate. This is a neat example, because the locus of the pattern is so obviously not in the minds of any of the actors, who define themselves as free agents yet play out the patterns of a game as seen from above. This seems very close to the Joycean use of pattern as imitative form; the point is again clear that the paradigmatic structure does not deepen our sense of character or plot, but usurps on, and diminishes it. In addition, the Nabokov instance has a strong element of puzzle-setting.

Geometrical figures, because they are enigmatic and unportentous, lend themselves particularly well to use as patterns or paradigms. Mathias, in Robbe-Grillet's *Le Voyeur,* sees and/or creates figure-eights wherever he goes. Seagulls form the pattern overhead, bits of string fall into it underfoot, iron rings on docks form it before his eyes, even his bicycle trip around the island falls naturally into two joined loops, a figure-eight. The murder which he may or may not have committed takes place on a blank page between Section 1 and Section 2; in the spatial context of the island and his trip around it, it takes place at the point where the line drawn in forming a figure-eight crosses itself, and in the first French edition that page is numbered 88. Mathias is of course an obsessed figure; what he is pre-programmed to see and do he sees and does. But some of these figure-eights never impinge on his consciousness at all, and most of those that he does notice don't tell us anything about his surroundings or him, except that there are a lot of free-floating figure-eights in the vicinity of both. In the classical economy of the novel, this kind of distraction would destroy a variety of author-reader relations, a shared trust which the author's proceedings and the reader's learned responses aimed to build. The new-style novel implies a measure of antagonism and mistrust to begin with; a fixed relation between author and reader is avoided, and the grid or pattern is a kind of pseudo-structure, serving to unsettle and complicate that relation. It is pseudo, not in terms of the author's beliefs, which may be utterly sincere, but in terms of the workings of the fiction, defined in the old way, of course, as action, character, representation. But as the reader's engagement with these old friends diminishes, so it becomes more involved with the texture of the author's construct—not with the author as public spokesman, but with the author's personal game.

The free-floating structure (which doesn't support, order, or express, doesn't instruct or entertain, but exists simply as a condition of vision) implies an impersonal and aseptic element in fiction, apart from that playing for impressions and effects and sympathetic responses which is the normal stuff of character-manipulation. Whether it is a pre-programmed condition of the seeing eye or an inherent shape of the reality that is seen, the mode of fiction allows to remain ambiguous. On one end of the fictional spectrum, this kind of unconcern shades easily into pretentious equivocations about reality—a topic on which practically nobody these days has anything responsible to say. Whether grid or deep shape, the afunctional or negatively functioning structure belongs appropriately to a variety of writing in which only a hairline separates the sacred from the cheap, the profound from the tricky. This is a kind of development in itself, taking the common form of annulling the distinction between literature and subliterature, between cliché and archetype, between comic-book and art, between philosophy and game. All are seen simply as varieties of structure, variously adorned but essentially the same.

Games, being frankly controlled by arbitrarily agreed-upon sets of rules, have a particular value for the novelist who wants to make us aware of how stylized and provisional our everyday perception of things ordinarily is. An interesting recent example is the use made by Italo Calvino of the Tarot deck in his *Castello dei destini incrociati* (Einaudi, 1973). A pack of cards provides the author with a structure, but a structure without any fixed outline or significance, amounting to no more than a shifting and flexible arrangement of a fixed number of variables. Fortune-telling in reverse is the basic device of the fable, in which a group of travelers meet at an inn and exchange their life stories by means of a Tarot pack, which they play out in linear patterns describing their individual stories, and which combine spontaneously to create a total pattern in which every card has at least two narrative contexts (horizontal and vertical). The necessity for this cumbersome if ingenious device is given as a mysterious, compelling muteness, which prevents the characters for the time being from speaking a word. It is at least one point of the exercise that the same card can have a variety of different meanings, depending on the context in which it is played. Structure determines evidence. In the last unit of the book, reserved for himself and his own story, Calvino underlines the virtuoso quality of his game by laying down cards to tell the stories of Oedipus, Lear, Hamlet, and the Marquis de Sade. Of course, "success" in these several enterprises has the effect of undermining belief in itself, as the more ingeniously a sophist turns one basic argument to serve a variety of momentary purposes, the less confidence we can have that it really serves any of them. Still, in emphasizing the degree to which our image of existence is formed of common counters into which each of us projects his own private meanings, even the monotony and speciousness of the book serve expressive ends. And there's no denying that it is a more skillful performance to construct a set of short stories out of a pack of cards than to write a set of vignettes out of which the reader must make his own game. That is the device of Edoardo Sanguineti's *Giuoco dell' Oca* (1967), the episodes of which can be shuffled, dealt out, and combined to produce an entertainment rather on the order of Monopoly.

In the guise of formal lattice-work on which the events of a fiction are hung out or compartmentalized, grids of time and space are common indeed. *Ulysses* as a twenty-four-hour novel is one of a regular class (other obvious examples are Victor Hugo's *Dernier jour d'un condamné*, Louis Bromfield's aptly titled *Twenty-four Hours*, Virginia Woolf's *Mrs. Dalloway*); and Claude Mauriac has squeezed the material of one of his fictions into the modest space of just 120 seconds. Apartment-house, hotel-room, and steamer-stateroom novels, accepting and emphasizing the pattern of partitions in a structure, gain thereby the effect of ironic juxtaposition. Michel Butor has hung a novel on a railway timetable, with its spatial and temporal divisions; and the novels of Thomas Pynchon are replete with geometrical shapes and logos, yo-yos and parabolas, which reduplicate and recur as on a screen set far behind the action of the capering characters in the foreground. But all these instances serve a purpose more or less functional—to express or echo a theme, divide or frame material, adumbrate a historical shape or meaning. And I suppose there is no way to draw an absolutely clearcut line between the grid that functions in support of the fiction and that which seems indifferent or hostile to it. Still, the point remains that these grids and paradigms to which a story is stitched, like needlepoint to a backing, seem more open than before about countering the story with which they co-exist. This is evidently a consequence of the new antagonistic, rather than ingratiating, attitude between reader and writer. The challenge that a book poses to its reader may be of the sort that Dorothy Sayers flings down when she tacks the investigation of a murder onto a web of intricate expertise about the ringing of church-bells, in *The Nine Tailors*. (And wasn't there, not so many years ago, a murder-mystery, the clues to which were to be deciphered through a close exegesis of *Ulysses* itself?) The popularity with mystery writers of such adventitious materials, which serve as an impeding grill for the reader to penetrate if he can, is wholly understandable. So, on the other levels, novelists who view themselves as frank illusionists, or define the world as maze or labyrinth, may be expected to make grateful use of the grill, not simply as direct impediment, but as counter-structure, or veil to be penetrated, or device of enticement. A rich example is Vladimir Nabokov's *Pale Fire,* where one story is implied rather vaguely in a poem (it is dull and inconclusive but probably true), another is imposed on it rather violently in the form of an interpretation (it is lurid but probably half-paranoid, at least), and still further bits and pieces of dramatic detail are allowed to leak through the unlikely format of an index. The narrative forms themselves are specious grids. The apparatuses of commentary and critical analysis are used, wholly against their own nature, wholly against their ostensible content—not like overlaid or underlying myth, to deepen the significance of the basic stories, but to entangle them with one another, roughen their textures, fracture their sequences, render them more difficult of access.

SURFACES, HOLES, BLURS, SMEARS

"All art is at once surface and symbol," said Oscar Wilde, memorably; but he neglected to mention that symbol itself may be just another form of surface. Nobody at this late date needs to be reminded that the art of the late 19th century was preoccupied with surfaces, but that symbols were simply another way to variegate and perforate them is less familiar. The repertoire of other modernist devices for making surfaces as such the objects of deliberate consciousness spreads far beyond Joyce, and for that matter beyond prose fiction altogether. It includes (in a brief summary) such devices as contrasting depths; a fragment from one context used in another; a discourse framed to imply, and to require for its completion, an unstated concept to be supplied by the reader; highly stylized, artificial, or two-dimensional representations; a meticulous surface realism surrounding a single anomaly or absurdity; discontinuity in the texture of the artwork itself—not just holes or gaps, but reflections upon itself, or self-negations; duplicities, like parody and self-parody; diaphanous representations of one order of experience, through which another order is felt; various forms of violence performed on linguistic conventions, especially diction and syntax; simultaneous contradictory points of view; anti-narratives and endo-narratives; *objets-trouvés,* collages, and minimalism; most varieties of *trompe-l'oeil;* intrusion of the author's authorial concerns, writing about the act of writing, etc.; any constructional technique that involves active, self-conscious complicity on the part of audience or reader; anti-functional form in general; blanks, silences, and non-performances; arbitrary or gratuitous obstacles; and a thousand other devices still awaiting their definitive taxonomist.

Right at the center of this move to transform surfaces from declaratives to interrogatives, Joyce deals with them differently in each of his major publications. The sketches and stories of *Dubliners* offer a series of cold and meticulous mirrors on various meager aspects of Dublin life; but they are mirrors troubled by a generally ironic and sometimes malignant intelligence which delights in covert intimations of its presence. The schoolboy who is fascinated by words picks intuitively on those three which defined, in the mind of the mature writer, the method of the book, the predominant sin of its characters, and the state of their society. The dead priest of the first story is a commonplace provincial tragedy—a man disappointed in life quietly dies in paltry circumstances, creating very little stir in the neighborhood. Yet there is a blur around the far-off cause of his downfall, the kernel of that load of guilt he has carried all his life long; and because it is not, and cannot be, cleared up, the whole surface of the story, lace-curtain Dublin, is suffused with the mystery and the magnitude of an unrecited myth. It is an eerie story of commonplace people in a commonplace setting with intimations of another point of view hovering darkly around them. And this is very characteristic of one way in which Joyce handles surfaces, reducing them to a thin curtain behind which something else is felt, if only another curtain.

The *Portrait* also fades and blurs its appearances at crucial moments; in addition, it blots out long stretches of dead time, concentrating like a Dostoevsky fiction on a few crucial minutes in which critical energies cross. And it runs the gamut of prose, from coarsely realistic to ecstatically lyrical, with a special fondness in the upper register for states of swoon and semi-trance. There are problems of fluctuating attitude toward Stephen, the church, Ireland, hazy intimations of contrary attitudes toward the young man's acquaintance; there is also a deliberate use of leitmotifs and recurrent, sometimes incremental, verbal patterns. Because the novel is so ostentatiously selective in its details, and sometimes conceals latent meanings in them, many readers have felt impelled to scrutinize all its details in search of occult meanings—their disappointment marking one more incongruity in their experience of the novel's surface. Yet on the whole, the *Portrait* is of all Joyce's books the most thingly. Of course it does without a lot of that across-the-board description typical of 19th-century fiction; its flats and props are sketched or implied, not drawn in detail, and a floating ingenue like E.C. is left as blurry as are the Dedalus brothers and sisters—of whom we don't even know the number. But these are economies natural to the development of an egotist. The record of the way the *Portrait* has been read supports the notion that its surfaces were, on the whole, trusted. "Trustworthy" is another matter; but trusted they generally have been.

Ulysses, on the other hand, gives away its surface pretensions almost from the beginning. On the very first page, Mulligan whistles a signal to someone in the Great Beyond, and is mysteriously answered; we never learn by whom. Parody-relations to the *Odyssey* and the dozens of different styles are just the start of it. There are enigmas of vacancy like Mackintosh, visionary reachings through the veil of present circumstance as in "Proteus" and "Nausicaa," literary allusions and parallels beyond number, internal thematic repetitions, gross incongruities of physical circumstance, blurs and smears of motivation—all inviting one to mistrust or see through the novel's surface as surface, and all leading up to the tremendous development of the last part of the book, the dematerialization of Stephen, Bloom, and Molly. They disintegrate, they are mythicized, astrologized, turned into emblems of themselves. The kind of experience that one can know with the five senses and discursive logic is parodied throughout "Ithaca," crumpled up, and thrown down the drain at the end of the chapter. Molly knows, Bloom knows, and in the end Stephen will know, not with the knife-blade of logic, but by another kind of animistic, instinctive mind, what it is to be a human being celebrating inwardly the religion of humanity. From "Penelope" it is only a short step to the *Wake,* where we have no sense at all of a surface being punctured or a logic being violated, because the basic structure of shifting and overlaid patterns precludes fixed surfaces or secure logic from being established. Although there's an oppressive sense of monotony in the *Wake,* of things repeating themselves endlessly in an infinitude of different guises, there's very little open space that one could describe as void—as there's no real surface to the novel, because we are already behind what we know in novels as surface, and, behind this behind, there's only more of the same.

What is distinctive about Joyce's handling of surfaces is not instantly obvious, and we can perhaps grasp a little of it by discussing *mere* surfaces. The phrase is inevitable, and in good part it is a consequence of familiarity breeding contempt. Most objects in everyday life—table, bird, horse, friend—we know simply and automatically from the surface, which, if not the thing itself, fairly represents the thing for all our normal purposes. Sure enough, when I get up in the morning I put on what looks like a pair of shoes and take the semblance of an egg out of the retinal image of an icebox; that's the full reality of the situation. But when I start living in these terms, without taking any of the handy and practical shortcuts built up over a lifetime, it's obviously shrink-time. In literature too, to emphasize surfaces as distinct from what they commonly stand for is to diminish or question them, generally to comic effect. Lane, the butler in *The Importance of Being Earnest,* mentions (while discussing the detrimental effect of marriage on the quality of champagne served in a household) the fact that he was once married. "I don't know that I'm interested in your private life, Lane," his employer remarks; and Lane, with equal cool, agrees: "No, sir, it is not very interesting; I seldom think of it myself." The passage, in its brevity, is paradigmatic: role takes over from self, stencil from three-dimensional representation. Capering emptiness is the traditional vehicle of satire from Candide through the hollow butts of Waugh (Paul Pennyfeather) and Huxley (Theodore Gumbril, junior) and on into comic ciphers beyond number—Watt, Malcolm, Benny Profane, Snow White, and so forth and so on. These aren't categorically fools or schlemiels or sacred innocents, though they often encroach on these several groupings; their essence lies in being non-persons, deliberately constructed to give a sense of their insubstantiality. And, fond as one may be of them, useful as they are in isolating particular features of modern man in the modern world, they don't seem to me to bear very close kinship to the kind of thin-surfaced, semi-transparent character in which Joyce's fiction abounds.

Allegorical neutralities on the order of Kafka's protagonists also stand well apart from the Joycean model. For one thing, they inhabit a featureless halfway world, neither as specific as Dublin, June 16, 1904, nor as diffusely pan-cultural as that of the *Wake.* The milieu through which they struggle has few benchmarks; characters are often without names, places are indistinct, and the characters (quite unlike any of Joyce's) know vividly, first that they don't know where they stand, and second that there's some better place where they should be standing. Thus they live largely outside the realm of time in a state of unappeasable anxiety, forever in the wrong. But that is a kind of fixed principle, an assured surface, in itself. As far as outside judgments are concerned, surfaces and appearances are constantly giving way beneath K and Joseph K; every apparent solution to the enigma confronting them is a more forbidding and excluding enigma. But as the outside does not really change, being forever alien, so their own insides (their pasts, their resources of accumulated feeling) are forever alien to them as well. Below their surface as compulsive questers there is literally no resource for the Kafka character, who is so crucified on the cross of the immovable present that he is not a window to anything.

This sense of the Joyce character's being a clouded glass, not to see or to reflect, but to be seen through, effectively sets Joyce's work apart from other players with artificial surfaces like, for example, Yeats with his masks or Pirandello with his theatrical peekaboos. Skewed social surfaces and collapsing social façades we're of course used to; depth psychology, in the sense of motivations lying below surfaces, even below consciousness, and gradually revealed by exploration or explanation, is equally conventional. What is special about Joyce's handling of surfaces is not exactly his social vision, or the thin transparency of his characters, but the fact that immense and alien systems can be seen through them. Not only alien, but contradictory identifications lie under the surface of a "character"; Bloom is not only Odysseus, he is a mountain-range, the Hill of Howth, an earwig, a sungod, and Ulysses S. Grant. In this very specific respect of portraying grotesquely primitive and even non-human structures within or beneath a modern character (Finnegan is an earwig, Finnegan is Wellington, Finnegan is Finn MacCool and a huge salmon in the Liffey), I think Joyce has had few followers. Ross Lockridge tried, rather timidly, something of the sort in *Raintree County;* Raymond Queneau in *Saint-Glinglin* struck much bolder anthropological discords in the course of building his comic circular structure; and Donald Barthelme has come very close to resurrecting HCE in the course of burying him in *The Dead Father.* One could, perhaps, add a few other titles to this list, but it would consist, however built up, of adventurous, peripheral figures and offbeat, interesting books. And if Joyce's influence on the modern novel in the matter of surfaces were confined to those authors who specifically imitated qualities of his fiction which are distinctively his, the list wouldn't be a long one.

But if we deliberately widen our perspective to see Joyce's work in context, I think we will find it peculiarly representative, in its dealings with surfaces, of two widespread, multi-form trends that look more contradictory than they are. These are the rejection of representation in favor of overt artifice; and the rejection of artifice in favor of vision. Both involve an act of penetration, of seeing through surfaces. In the first place one gets rid of detailed description, pictorial specificity, and that close imitation of surfaces which aims at achieving a persuasive sense of "truth to life." The work of art is an artificial arrangement which calls attention by its very exaggerations and formal structuring to the controlling mind of the artist. The artist is not nature's faithful hound, appealing to his audience to agree that he has followed her successfully; all she provides for him are a few commonplace materials, the more common the better, out of which he makes an artificial cosmos. It is then up to the audience to enter this new cosmos and appreciate its faceted and intricate structure, if they are able to do so. But the next stage is to transcend artifice as well, to push through artifice as easily as artifice had pushed away imitation, and to the same effect, of entering so far as possible the presence of pure vision—vision as an act wholly stripped of particular experience.

The path of preparation had been long and gradual. In Huysmans the novel first turns backward and inward, leaving the vision of pullulating mass societies to pursue processes of fester and decay minutely recorded by Zola, and instead making an artificial world out of an isolated individual's perverse tastes and appetites. Beyond, outside, he sees nothing—only, in the traditional imagery, a dark ocean of doubt, a vague light of faith. But the poets and musicians had been there before, had pushed beyond. The cult of void, purest in Mallarmé and his friend Jean Lahore, but apparent also in Wagnerians and pseudo-Wagnerians like d'Annunzio and Maeterlinck, prepared modernism to see through the thin veil of things lit by the weak light of the sun, and into the sphere behind of night, unconsciousness, dissolution, and the sole self. Seeing in the abstract is nothing but seeing the act of seeing, but this is more like seeing everything; for sight is an act performed not just with the eyes, but with the reflexes and synapses of the brain, with the jumbled memories of the psyche, with the instincts and tropisms and fantasies and silt-like residue of the entire consciousness of the race. So that Joyce, like only Flaubert among the other novelists, can be seen as an ancestor of the minimalist or nothing-novel (like Beckett's *The Way It Is*) and of the encyclopedic or pile-up-the-details novel (like Dos Passos's *USA* trilogy or Farrell's *Studs Lonigan* marathon). And this is a consequence primarily of a triple view of surfaces, as things to be seen, things to be manipulated, and veils concealing or only vaguely suggesting what the mind, from inspecting its own processes, intuits as the essence of things.

Finally, in this very perfunctory discussion of fictional surfaces, one is under obligation to mention a particular development, if not innovation, of Joyce's which might as well be known as the uncertainty principle. In the classic names of unity, economy, and precision of effect, traditional fictions had not been very tolerant of unresolved blurs and ambiguities in crucial areas of their moral or social patterning. So long as plot amounted essentially to intrigue, this was natural and almost necessary; characters in an intrigue who don't know who they are or what they're doing can throw the whole operation out of kilter. When all conflicts must be resolved, and all energies balanced off at the end of the book, it won't do for the reader to be left in the dark about essential ingredients.

Suspended but ultimately resolved confusion is a device as old as story-telling; deliberately unresolved narrative doubt may be playful provocation, as it often is in Sterne, or "serious" enticement to the puzzling mind, as it generally is in Joyce. It implies a certain indifference to motivation, as if one couldn't and didn't really have to know the inner causes of behavior, which is determined in any case by patterns, roles, and archetypes. But it isn't simply limited to the narrative, or the motives of characters in it; the uncertainty extends to the signs and signals of which the narrative itself is composed. Checkerboard narrative by itself is flat and obvious, and as old as the Middle Ages when it was sometimes called *entrelacement*. In modern crosscutting, the significant part of an action taking place in an ostensibly dramatic context may be a wholly undramatic and secondary element; it gets its importance by chiming on an undramatic and secondary element of a vaguely analogous action taking place at some distance. This produces what Nabokov, in the 1970 preface to *Glory*, elegantly describes as "the echoing and linking of minor events, . . . back-and-forth switches which produce an illusion of impetus." The example he cites from that novel is "an old daydream directly becoming the blessing of the ball hugged to one's chest," and it is an example interesting chiefly for the pains the author has taken to keep it from being obvious, or for that matter perceivable. The old daydream of Martin Edelweiss is to clasp Sonia, which in fact he does, in roughhouse not romance, some time after he stops a soccer ball by hugging it. (There's a further overtone, if overtones are the name of the game, in his hugging an Alpine cliff that he had been driven to climb by inarticulate impulses of self-testing.) In any case, there's not a word in the ball-clutching scene to suggest that any of these other preoccupations of Martin's are even remotely present to him. In fact, it is not Martin Edelweiss who grasps the flying ball just in front of the net; it is "the custodian," and only after "the custodian" has stopped it does Martin Edelweiss kick it downfield. "Custodian" is Continental sports-jargon for a soccer goalie, but Martin in his relation to Sonia is not the custodian of anything—quite the contrary, he is the eager forward, whose ambition is only to score. The effect of "impetus" which Nabokov describes involves a deepening zig-zag, not impetus in the narrative sense, but inner impetus, another term for which might be ironic pressure. And to know that this sort of weasel is loose in a fiction creates extraordinary anxieties in readers who have the traditional touch of chicken in their complexion.

In the novel as game all surfaces are naturally suspect. The one sure assumption is that the significant element will not look significant, at least not in the way that it finally proves to be significant. But this phrasing suggests a larger puzzle-design, a set of formulated questions to which we are denied answers. Uncertainties in the surface of *Ulysses* are built into the social details of the novel even more randomly. The financial transactions between Mulligan and Dedalus are a mass of exact and detailed confusions from which it's impossible to extract the basic information of who owes exactly how much to whom. The domestic geography of Dublin and environs, the physical dimensions of Bloom, the sexual history of Molly, on these and a thousand other matters, we have a great deal of information out of which we can make little sense. There are hundreds of personal allusions which, without biographical intervention, we could never discover; there are hundreds of others which, even after years of exegetical work and biographical nosings-about, we still cannot explain.

In Beckett, of course, this and many other varieties of equivocation are raised to a fine art; in Borges and Robbe-Grillet the very surface of things is a series of enigmas; popular novelists like Anthony Burgess and John Fowles feel perfectly free to leave unresolved blurs, confusions, equivocations on the surface of their fictions. There is a great variety of reasons for doing so. The modern novelist often has a bad conscience about make-believe, and deliberately calls attention to his own fraudulent proceedings; exegetical complexities are often successful in enticing or challenging readers; variations in surface texture give flexibility and relief to a fiction; impressionistic and

elliptical modes of discourse are fun in themselves; a hallucinated observer who drifts between reality and obsession provides rich fictional
material. Of course none of these materials or impulses is peculiar to
modern authors; what is novel is that modern readers have accustomed themselves to accept less authorial guidance, less explanation,
and to be satisfied with a much lower level of "comprehension" than
fiction used to involve. This can all be seen as part of a relatively new
definition of imitation which (metaphorically speaking) paints on
the retina not the canvas, trusting four shapeless blobs and a smear to
resolve themselves for an acute eye into crows over a cornfield.

Cincinnatus C. in Nabokov's early novel, *Invitation to a Beheading,* is visited in his cell by his mother; she proves, after much
camouflage-patter, to be the one person in his entire world who is in
any way real; and the flicker of that recognition is enough to bring
the jailer, raging, into the cell to terminate the visit. But not before
she has had occasion, talking idly and nostalgically, to mention some
little toys with which children used to play, called *nonnons.* Grotesquely distorted and uncouth, they could nonetheless be paired off
with a special distorting mirror, in such a way that the two distortions
complemented and offset one another. There is a kind of object that
is only to be seen with a certain sort of vision, a kind of vision that is
good only for a certain object. The analogy applies to Cincinnatus,
who is trapped in a world where everything is contrived and decep-
tive; but it applies also to the particular novel, and to the surface conventions of many modern novels. In the early days of their acquaintance, Cincinnatus speaks to his fellow inmate M'sieu Pierre (but he
is really the headsman in disguise) of some hope, certain hints, someone else too who is concerned with escape.

"This is curious," said M'sieu Pierre. "What are these hopes and
who is this savior?"

"Imagination," replied Cincinnatus.

This is a put-off, but it is also the bare truth, as the novel's last scene
implies. The parable has an extensive application.

LANGUAGE

Because it is so vast and so obvious, Joyce's influence on the language of fiction invites one to clichés. Cliché or no, however, it is true that in *Ulysses* he reaffirmed standards for precision and economy of diction not seen since Swift; that he widened the range of fictional language to encompass scholastic notions of ontology at one end of the scale and foul-mouthed guttersnipery at the other. He also required language to be more intimately and intricately imitative than it had ever been before—playing games not only with literary history and music, Ireland and Israel, Shakespeare and Vico, but with the vulgarities, inanities, sentimentalities, and pomposities of vulgar speech in its many aspects. These parodic ineptitudes are underlined by the steely polish and elegance of the prose when Joyce is really making it work. Like Flaubert, he formed and filed his sentences to bring out the exact rhythm and emphasis he wanted, he chose words for their precise bite and sting, and he made them chime chords and discords across the full span of the novel. Unlike any English novelist of whom I'm aware, he worked himself into the texture of specific words by listing them on separate sheets of paper as they suggested one another in long association-strings, then built them one at a time into his fiction. However subtle the lines of connection, he trusted them to make themselves felt subliminally. In the same way he stitched puns and metaphors of which even a careful reader is rarely conscious along the central themes of his chapters: Molly's stockings are out of plumb in "Lestrygonians," and police constables goosestep; but in "Hades" people drink like the devil and think of the dead-letter office.

Joyce had relatively few direct followers in the extravagant in-

tricacy with which he wove his language-patterns; but the example
of artfully composed prose as a prominent and independent texture
in fiction—as substitution for character and fable if not an actual impediment to them—had not been so clearly set since Peacock and
Meredith. As Joyce's example was more various than theirs, so it appeared less idiosyncratic and exercised more influence. Wherever one
finds, in modern fiction, writing that seems aimed at rousing admiration for itself rather than attracting sympathy to the characters or
opening a clear window on a scene, one can suspect the influence of
Joyce. There are good grounds to feel ambivalent about this.

Yet on the contrary tack, one of the major operations that Joyce
performed on language was to disintegrate it, which is to say that he
saw it not only as a fine surgical instrument, but as a pile of miscellaneous garbage. The changeover began to be striking in the last part
of "Oxen of the Sun," and in the *Wake* atomization of the word proceeds farther than practically anyone else has been willing to follow.
The profound effectiveness of this process is beyond question; sustained reading of the *Wake* works within the mind from the inside
out like a strong drug, producing a troubled sense of blind and desperate strain, as of deep-seated habits being violently disturbed. The
book operates on one's dream-life to devastating effect, and disturbs
one's speech-patterns; it is a harrowing of the linguistic subsoil, and
reading it is submission to a form of verbal sadism. Many artificial
dialects have this effect to a much lesser degree: the quack-talk of
Sam Pollit and his brood in *The Man Who Loved Children;* "Jabber-
wocky," Nabokov's polyglot fantasies; the coagulate romanesco of
Quer Pasticciaccio Brutto di Via Merulana; Lucky's thinking-speech
in Godot. The *Wake* stands in a dark and unspecific way behind
them all, as deep exploration of a territory in which no one but Joyce
has been more than a brief sojourner.

One can only indicate a few of the many aspects from which the
language of the *Wake* could be considered in its working on modern
prose. Being rooted in vulgar and colloquial diction, comic-books,

pantomimes, popular song, low jokes—the mere rags and tatters of language—it struck with particular force upon writers in tongues like French (men like Queneau, Céline, Vian), where formal standards of polite speech had long gone unchallenged in literature. In José Lezama Lima and his follower Severo Sarduy, we find violent and macabre combinations of metaphors, sadistic fantasies, popular superstitions, and philosophical abstractions woven together in a high-pitched, free-floating narrative that constitutes, like the *Wake,* its own essential subject. In authors as diverse as Grass, Gadda, Nabokov, and Beckett (to name only a few), the *Wake's* cosmopolitan puns, distortions, and flirting decorations have loosened standards of verbal niceness, and encouraged a kind of Pangloss dialect by making clear that the dead metaphors of modern tongues need no more than an imaginative twitch to revive and begin capering.

Like Milton, Joyce had an instinct for animating the dead languages that lie buried in our own, and for rousing us to their presence. While murdering a lot of fictional clichés, he roused moribund words and phonemes to new life, stirring tired phrases and faded formulations to fresh vitality. One can find traces of his liberating influence in the prose of not particularly distinguished stylists, from Henry Miller to Jack Kerouac, from Fernand Céline to Claude Mauriac. A whole massive unit of my book has been pre-empted by Vivian Mercier in his study of the New French Novel, which he views as lying under the predominant influence of Joyce. And this influence he defines primarily, though by no means exclusively, as linguistic in nature. Under other circumstances, there might be reason to quarrel with this or that nuance of Mr. Mercier's *The New Novel;* in the present circumstance, there's little more to do than point to his study as an indispensable supplement to my argument, or a preliminary to it. Finally, apart from the whole business of direct influence via imitation, the *Wake's* language has provoked theoretical reflection by linguistic theorists and the developers of speculation about print and ultra-print cultures. For better or worse, it has moved men like Marshall McLuhan to far-reaching considerations of the nature of language and its future in a technological age.

Less vivid than these aspects of *Wake*speech, but perhaps also less superficial, is a dimension of Joyce's last dialect, a character to the writing—hard to define, but for all that not to be dodged. The *Wake* was written in blood. I like to think we would know this by looking at its pages, without consulting Mr. Ellmann's biography—and that we shouldn't be put off this perception by the undeniable, intimate presence on every page of high and low comedy. For it's a fact, and a special fact. The *Wake* is the product of do-it-yourself vivisection; it is not an aesthetic arrangement or a criticism of life, but in a special sense life itself. And so everything I've said about its language so far is at least peripherally wrong, being beside the point or insignificant. The book isn't a story or a fiction; I can't make much sense of it as a symbolic action; it doesn't narrate much because it doesn't represent much. More than most English prose, it is put together on musical principles, and so is concerned less to mean than to be. But, more centrally, it is the writing of a man for whom writing itself is in question, because he has seen through too many of his own poses and attitudes. Writing is filth, guilt, bad conscience; the book itself (*Finnegans Wake*) is represented by a smeary rag of paper, covered with henscratches and buried in a dunghill. A good deal of the *Wake* is, in the literal sense of the word, self-abuse. Humphrey's guilt is built into his back in the shape of his hump; Shem's shame is ineradicable, because he is a sham.

Opaque and elaborately contrived though it is in general, the language of *Finnegans Wake* reflects lucidly the agony that went into its creation—the sense of a priestly vocation missed, fouled and corrupted by the dirty tools of a dirty language, under the direction of a weak and dishonest mind. In this holy sense of the calling and shame over the betrayal of it, Joyce has no follower except Samuel Beckett. For both, great artists as they are, language is only a secondary and ungrateful instrument of composition.

CHAPTER THREE

WOOLF AND FAULKNER

STREAMS OF CONSCIOUSNESS

S TREAM OF CONSCIOUSNESS" is by now a hackneyed term, and imprecise of application. Yet Joyce's early influence was very liberally involved with this device, and the subject is not to be dodged simply because its outlines are fuzzy and its core commonplace.

As a literary style, there is nothing distinctive about "stream of consciousness"; it differs from other literary styles in degree, not in kind, and could be described simply as an extension of Henry James's principle of using a limited narrative consciousness and concentrating on it very closely. But James, though he formulated a persuasive rationale for this method, did not by any means originate it, nor did he ever try to render his chosen consciousness through its own formulations or pre-formulations. That too had been done by novelists without any particular theoretical underpinnings, before Joyce and for that matter before James. Lawrence Sterne is a familiar example; short passages of Tolstoi are sometimes cited; a semi-serious comparison is often urged with the erratic ejaculations of Alfred Jingle in *Pickwick*. Apart from these presumed, and at best partial, anticipations of "stream of consciousness," there is a full but ill-defined tradition among 19th-century novelists of what the Germans call *erlebte Rede,* and we know simply as indirect discourse—writing in which ostensible third-person prose is tinged with the verbal or mental mannerisms of a dramatic character. In a novelist like Giovanni Verga, who tells the story of a village through a kind of choral, communal prose, using a version of Italian strongly flavored with primitive Sicilian, we come very close to a direct rendering of consciousness as it flows now in divergent and now in confluent streams. And then of course there are the direct and full-fledged "predecessors of Joyce"— Dujardin, whom he lavishly acknowledged; Dorothy Richardson, whom he did not; Poe and Dostoevsky, to whom Gide attributed so much of the credit; and the psychoanalytic movement in general, which placed so much emphasis on the flow of imagery, the currents of hidden intention buried below, or in the interstices of, a sequence of conscious concepts. The philosophy of Bergson, the example of Proust, even the influence of Robert Browning, contributed to diffuse the abstract notion of stream of consciousness through the intellectual atmosphere long before Joyce provided, in *Ulysses,* something like a test case of the method.

There are, obviously, two big dangers confronting any novelist who tries to paddle down the stream of a character's consciousness. One is the immense quantity of irrelevant trash that is bound to float on the surface; the other is the difficulty of rendering undercurrents that rise only intermittently and unexpectedly to view. These difficulties work together to violate the principles of economy and purity of effect to which writers and readers were once trained; the author can't explain, concisely and authoritatively, what's up with his character, but he must record shop-fronts, tram-cars, irrelevant passers in the street. He can't introduce a new character with a thumbnail sketch of his appearance, background, and moral habits; he must record accidents and surfaces as they occur. These are serious, even fatal, objections; and if the method were followed out rigorously, there's hardly any question that it would produce an unreadable novel. Joyce did not follow it rigorously. Even as we trail after Bloom's drifting mind through the flotsam and jetsam of midtown, midday Dublin, we are planted firmly in time and space by an occasional third-person, factually oriented sentence. And Stephen Dedalus's most acrobatic associational leaps are made easier for a reader to follow by carefully repeated verbal tags. To be sure, no book in English had ever pushed the method as far as *Ulysses* did; no book had made such demands on a reader—that he sift through packets of Joyce's private junk, leap across chasms of esoteric allusion, and balance himself astride a restive Homeric parallel. But these rather technical considerations were not what made *Ulysses* a test case of the stream method; no previous book, in English or on the Continent, had ever made use to the degree that *Ulysses* did of sex, digestion, and excretion as the matrices within which a character's meditations took place. *Ulysses* wasn't simply a "dirty" book, it was a "vulgar" book; it showed the "higher" activities of human beings as mixed with and growing out of the "squalid" ones, as if there were in fact no clearcut distinction between the two. Thus the book became a focus of resistance for readers who had accepted the method as such without question and without even much awareness, as long as its contents were relatively innocuous.

For example, Virginia and Leonard Woolf, in behalf of the Hogarth Press, declined for severely practical reasons to publish *Ulysses* when it was an outsize manuscript looking for a publisher; quite apart from the façade of those practical considerations, Mrs. Woolf's first and deepest response to the book was that it "reeked" of indecencies. When it finally appeared in volume form, her objections to its bad form remained the same, though concealed behind another inkscreen of allusive adjectives. In a single diary entry for September 6, 1922, she declared that *Ulysses* was diffuse, brackish, pretentious, self-conscious, egotistical, and mannered, besides being a misfire. Yet only the next day, under the influence of "a very intelligent review in the American *Nation*" (it was by Gilbert Seldes, August 1922, pp. 211-12), she wavered; *Ulysses* might be a work of genius after all, though of genius misguided. But the moment passed, while the need for protection remained; and on September 26, she recorded a conversation with Eliot in which they agreed that Joyce was a crude stylist and a destructive writer—making a clean sweep of things by adding that Dostoevsky was the ruin of English literature. The connection is characteristic of the age: Joyce and Dostoevsky are the barbarians of the new era, speaking continually about the unspeakable, and shattering the old harmonies with painful, blatant discords. It is, thus, a curiously negative picture that we get from the 1922 diaries (at least as they have been made public); and one is surprised to learn from a retrospective entry of January 5, 1941, that in fact Eliot had been rapt, enthusiastic about Joyce's novel. Obviously that enthusiasm—of which we get no inkling in the 1922 entries, but which Mrs. Woolf was able to recall vividly after Joyce was safely dead—had forced a reconsideration on her. She had approached the book, as she said herself, "with her back up"; she was jealous of Joyce and afraid of him. One catches a glimpse behind the façade from her remark (*A Writer's Diary*, p. 28) that she composed *Jacob's Room* with a secret sense that Mr. Joyce must be doing the same thing at the same moment, and doing it better.

The timing is crucial here. Mrs. Woolf was actually reading proof on *Jacob's Room* at the very moment (September 1922) when she was recording in most detail her hostile reactions to *Ulysses*. But she had seen the first four chapters at least of Joyce's novel much earlier, in 1918, and her 1919 essay on contemporary fiction (reprinted in *The Common Reader*) shows that she had read the *Portrait* and was following serial publication of *Ulysses* in the *Little Review*. She was thus well acquainted with Joyce's work long before *Jacob's Room* was begun; whether or not that breakthrough novel in her development was directly influenced by Joyce, she certainly recognized it as occupying the same general area of the literary landscape. They were at one, and it must have bulked large at the time, in rejecting the Arnold Bennett novel of plot, formulated character, and social observation. But Mrs. Woolf was oppressed by the sense of Joyce's giant egotism, and frightened by the hard surface of that scholastic structure which he offered in place of the traditional intrigue. She must have felt uneasy about replacing one rigidity, one formalism, with another. And so she absorbed Joyce slowly. The contrast between *Jacob's Room* (1922) and *Mrs. Dalloway* (1925) is for the most part a contrast of nuances and degrees of assurance. It can't be described as sweeping; and yet there's no question that the later novel has much greater fullness of texture, a less arch and mannered way of suggesting the interstices that both books perceive in the apparent solidities of "human nature."

Jacob's Room implies something close to a pun in the title. The novel is about the room—the space—occupied by Jacob during his life; it ends on a vacancy, with his mother and his best friend sorting through the litter left in his room after his death. En route, we have had a biography of sorts, as intermittent and discontinuous as that of the *Portrait,* but with the major difference that everything in the *Portrait* is seen through the eyes and mind of Stephen Dedalus, colored by his moods and related to his developing concerns, while Jacob, though observed by a variety of people, sees hardly anything or anybody himself. Instead of Jacob, who is an enclosure, a vacancy with a name, we see a great deal of the authoress. She is seen, not simply in her various lectures—on perception, on disparity of character, on letters and communications, on illusions—but more importantly in her tight control of the representation. From the first page of the book, she exercises a peculiar mannerism of clipping and trimming the dialogue, and for that matter the action, to a bare minimum. She is fond of throwing us a mere scrap of a conversation and dismissing the rest of it as inconsequential—a practice which makes her assertion that character is mysterious and unknowable seem a little *voulu.* "If she would just get out of the way a bit [we think] and let us listen to her young man talk or think for a few uninterrupted minutes on a topic of some importance, there'd be a lot less mystery about the human personality."

Though a natural reaction, this isn't necessarily right. Jacob Flanders seems to be an enigmatic young man: people comment on his silences, on the weight of his presence; they are fond of him, without being able to say why. What opinions he is represented as having (enthusiasms for Greece and *Tom Jones,* without apparently knowing

very much about either) seem to be callow and wholly inadequate to
make up a personality. There may be no mystery to him at all, as there
is no mystery to Richard Dalloway; though then, the mystery becomes
why people care about him so extraordinarily. Or there is perhaps
such a deep mystery to his character that it is hidden even from Jacob
himself. We are delighted with a fine Dalmatian puppy or Russian
wolfhound, and don't demand that he favor us with a display of philosophical discourse or moral feeling, to justify our sense of sympathy.
Jacob is young and responsive to people and places, almost on the
level of unthinking instinct, yet he can also be almost obtusely mascu-
line; and in the end, there is something about him "which can never
be conveyed to a second person save by Jacob himself." Reflecting on
this intertwining of seer, seen, and circumstance, Mrs. Woolf gives
to a deliberately ordinary scene the vibrant, felt quiet of a Vermeer
painting:

> Moreover, part of his [scene] is not Jacob but Richard Bonamy—the
> room; the market carts; the hour; the very moment of history. Then
> consider the effect of sex—how between man and woman it hangs wavy,
> tremulous, so that here's a valley, there's a peak, when in truth, per-
> haps, all's as flat as my hand. Even the exact words get the wrong ac-
> cent of them. But something is always compelling one to hang vibrating,
> like the hawk moth, at the mouth of the cavern of mystery, endowing
> Jacob Flanders with all sorts of qualities he had not at all—for though,
> certainly, he sat talking to Bonamy, half of what he said was too dull
> to repeat; much unintelligible (about unknown people and Parlia-
> ment); what remains is mostly a matter of guess work. Yet over him
> we hang vibrating [pp. 120-21].

Of course it's folderol to talk of Jacob himself conveying anything to
a second person, since as we all know he is nothing but a texture of
words woven by Mrs. Woolf. As such, he has more of the negative
and fugitive qualities of Frederic Moreau than the bardic intensity of
Stephen Dedalus. He is in effect an unknown soldier, a silhouette of
potentialities; and the final vision of the book, a pair of worn shoes,
conveys very fully the pathos of emptiness when the indefinable has

evaporated. But the book's hovering technique has as yet little in common with anything in Joyce.

By contrast, *Mrs. Dalloway* moves us authoritatively within a couple of minds, distant yet resonant, and keeps us there for the greater part of the novel. Human character is still a mystery, still a relationship of hovering and hesitant surmises about an action lying far below the level of opinions and articulate speech. But we see it from the inside reaching out, instead of vice versa. The presence of the authoress is much diminished, partly perhaps because the feminine point of view is already represented, partly also because the narrative scale has been drastically reduced. Instead of a lifetime, the book occupies fewer than twenty-four hours of fictional time. But in addition the authoress has simply erased herself and foregone her essays; while giving the surface of the novel a continuity of its own (clocks and the sun continually strike the hour), she allows the overtones of circumstance and social combination to vibrate subsurface. Finally, *Mrs. Dalloway* is a much more rootedly urban novel than *Jacob's Room;* the random intercrossing of paths and fantasies makes up a thicker social texture than anything in the earlier novel.

Like Jacob, Mrs. Dalloway is a person of great charm and relatively little mental prowess (the subtleties of the obtuse were Virginia Woolf's favorite theme). Whether it's Armenians or Albanians that her wooden husband is going to Do Something About she can't quite remember; and what the Equator is she simply doesn't know. This is rather ostentatious mindlessness, quite the kind of elegant vacancy one would anticipate from a preliminary appearance of Richard and Clarissa Dalloway as stuffed shirts in *The Voyage Out*. Clarissa isn't critical of persons, any more than she's retentive of basic ideas. She refuses to judge Hugh Whitbread whom everyone else finds a stuffed shirt; he is, after all, kind to his old mother and remembers his aunts' birthdays (though he is really greedy about food). Peter Walsh calls her, by way of insult, the perfect hostess; and in her own thoughts she agrees. Different people, she thinks, are scattered across London,

living isolated and separate lives; it is her gift to bring
gether, and another name for the parties she likes so much
life.

This could be the portrait of a silly, superficial society
Mrs. Woolf takes no special precautions against this formula, except
that of filling Mrs. Dalloway's consciousness so full of other things
that the formula is clearly irrelevant and ridiculous, even if true. Clarissa is, for example, in love with London, delightedly responsive to
its parti-color particulars; she is full of the past, and that special sum-
mer at Boulton when she had to decide between Peter Walsh and
Richard Dalloway; she is responsive to people of all sorts, and frankly
loathes Miss Kilman and Sir William Bradshaw; it is in no way in-
credible that she should feel all day long resonances of the desperate
unhappiness of Septimus Smith, whom she never meets and only
hears about late in her party.

The chords of sympathy, and for that matter antipathy, are perhaps
as mysterious as any mystery of personality; but the result of their being felt is a full rather than empty human presence. *Mrs. Dalloway*
makes one feel that life is a gallant celebration, not (as it appears in
Jacob's Room) a sad and perhaps insoluble puzzle. This may be simply a consequence of Mrs. Woolf's dealing with a heroine rather than
a hero. Her feminist feelings, for all the public discounts she placed
on them, ran deep. One can't help noting the parallel between Mrs.
Dalloway and Mrs. Ramsay of *To the Lighthouse:* they are both as-
semblers and healers of people—self-sacrificial, illogical, emotionally
rich. They are also both doomed; in a first version of her novel, Mrs.
Dalloway was to perish after her party, as Mrs. Ramsay dies immediately (in reading though not in fictional time) after hers. The addition of Septimus Smith made the development of *Mrs. Dalloway*
more spacious and the denouement of the novel more subtle.

It is at least a curious and maybe a significant observation that the
inner monologue which Joyce made popular was almost immediately
applied by others to cases of abnormal psychology, though Joyce him-

self never attempted to turn it in that direction. There are lunatics in *Ulysses*—Denis Breen is nearly if not quite insane, and Cashel Boyle O'Connor Fitzmaurice Tisdall Farrell is certifiable though harmless. But Joyce never ventures inside them, he simply renders their mannerisms from the outside. Actually, apart from Poldy, Stephen, and Molly, we see the inner consciousness of only a few Dubliners, mostly in the "Wandering Rocks" episode and only momentarily in each instance (Father Conmee, Mr. Kernan, Master Patrick Dignam, jr.). One reason is no doubt that a lot of unremarkable streams of consciousness flowing together are bound to produce a confusion. That's not alien to the effect sought by "Wandering Rocks," but elsewhere it would hardly do. And on the other hand, a really distrait and disoriented personality would be too much for the general economy of *Ulysses*—none of the main figures is distracted, and the peculiar notes of madness would create discord elsewhere. But in Septimus Smith, wandering back and forth across the borders of sanity, Mrs. Woolf tapped a splendid resource of Joycean or Jamesian method.

The alternative formulation is necessary because "stream of consciousness" is inherently such a loose and impressionistic term. Mrs. Woolf, though she sees life intermittently through the eyes of Septimus Smith, and counts on us to appreciate and correct for the distortions of that particular vision, does not try to reach into the stage of pre-articulate response, or suggest that "normality" itself incorporates visceral responses. What she writes is therefore a variety of indirect discourse; and while she intimates the terrified uncertainties of the paranoid mind, she never fails to formulate them in perfectly constructed sentences, using concepts of perfect lucidity. Indeed, she does not try to go beyond the standard hallucinations and established formulas of paranoia; nor is there any reason why she should. Within the pastel shades of her palette, Septimus Smith is quite strong enough as he is to convey the breaking of that thin ribbon of things which, for Mrs. Dalloway, barely holds the day together.

Just as with Bloom, the stream of her consciousness is fed from a

spring of impressions and diffused through a labyrinth of associations. As Bloom, toward the end of "Nausicaa," wanders off into a
thin, transparent mood which almost enables him to reach through
the veil of things, so for Mrs. Dalloway everything is subject to question because imbued with a hidden meaning at which we are bound
to guess. Sir William Bradshaw, with an explicit irony rare in Virginia Woolf, notes of Septimus Smith that "he was attaching meanings
to words of a symbolical kind," and judges this "a serious symptom,
to be noted on the card." In one of the few semi-explicit borrowings
from *Ulysses,* an airplane skywrites an enigmatic message over London, as on that June day eighteen years earlier Wisdom Hely's sand-
wichmen wound their reptilian way through Dublin. Things seem to
move every so often toward a meaning, accidental or occult; yet at the
same time, the fragility of the sense-continuum is overwhelming, so
that objects always possess the quality of glass or soap-bubbles. On
this score, as on so many others, Mrs. Woolf's novel reminds us of
Pope's *Rape of the Lock.* Both are passionately *London* works; a Clarissa is the peacemaker and reconciler in both; and there is about both
the same aura of glittering sunlit civilization threatened by dark violence on one side, shading off into affectation and foppery on the
other. Mrs. Woolf's social spectrum is narrower than Joyce's, and so
is her imaginative spectrum; the intricate intellectual mosaicwork of
"Proteus" is beyond her reach, as is the deliberate obscenity of "Circe."
But in *Mrs. Dalloway* she has absorbed as much of the Joycean novel
as she could use, socialized and yet poeticized it, and turned it very
much to her advantage. I think it not wholly accidental that she in
Mrs. Dalloway and Eliot in *The Waste Land,* especially the first versions, both responded to the "barbaric" influence of Joyce by mingling with it a strong element of decorum and civilized nuance from
the subtlest and wittiest of 18th-century poets.

In Mrs. Woolf's later novels, one does not feel the same measure
of Joycean presence, though for most of them she retained the technique of semi-dramatic monologue and many of the same themes.

The central enigma recurs of an unintellectual figure among clever in-
troverts and phrase-makers; the thinness of the material universe and
the indefinite and shifting quality of human character are constant
modalities. Like Joyce, Mrs. Woolf abandoned in her later writings
the kind of naturalism and particularity through which, as through an
iridescence, some hidden signatures shine or seem to shine. In *The
Waves,* for example, we follow six closely related and carefully contrasted personalities, who across the span of their lives speak mono-
logues expressing both the stage of existence in which they find themselves, the peculiar slant of their separate natures, and a common
groping after the special value or meaning of their existence. The cyclical pattern is akin to Joyce, as the interpenetrating personalities
might be congenial to him, but the prose puts the book in another
cosmos entirely. Though as artificial as *Wake*speech, it is far less
tangled, far more rhetorical, and less "deep." In declamations of almost exaggerated formality, elaborately metaphorical, carefully allusive, and sparsely strewn with particulars, the characters discuss and
expose themselves. That they all speak the same dialect, whatever
their age, sex, or character, suggests their underlying identity, but it
is more like the dialect of philosophic discourse and analysis than that
of mythic insight. For all its ingenuity of metaphor, it is fading toward neutrality.

The crest of Mrs. Woolf's fictional work—*Mrs. Dalloway, To the
Lighthouse, The Waves*—is intermittently vibrant with complex and
nervous responses to the texture of experience. These are not the materials of psychic or correspondent structures; they are not proper
thought, nor fully arranged sense response, but attitudinal gestures—
tropisms, to borrow Natalie Sarraute's word, invented primarily to
deal with Mrs. Woolf. While these half-conscious responses are lively
and various, they serve partially to define character, or at least some
of a character's characteristic responses to experience, including experience of self. But like the lyric impulse generally, this sort of perception is irregular at best: and one can't read through *The Years,*

that drab chronicle of an empty and sterile family, without being aware of a deep exhaustion. It isn't simply that the characters drift into anonymous senility without ever rising above a set of platitudes and catch-phrases toward which the author cannot manage a defined point of view; the structuring of the novel itself is loose and indifferent. It is as if, in the absence of tight formal pattern, her insight into the materials of fiction diffused and lost contour altogether.

Between the Acts, a posthumous publication, confirms as it redeems these judgments; as if drawing itself together for a last, splendid effort, it is as compressed and intricately cut as a diamond. For one thing, the novel deals with an afternoon, not fifty years, with a few central figures and a scattered, secondary supporting cast, not with a dozen different actors. The scene is festive (a rural church pageant contrived by Miss La Trobe), the occasion grim (we are on the eve of World War II); the mishaps of amateur theatricals form interludes of grotesque comedy, lacing together grimmer episodes and more gruesome perceptions in the audience. More important than this new structural complexity is a sense of the deep past, ridiculously represented in Miss La Trobe's doggerel pageant with its sketchy, pathetic chronicle of English history, but also echoed in the *Outline of History* that Mrs. Swithin is reading. The past is present and shines through the absurdities of dramatic, as of social, convention; the several acts of the pageant form an interlude, not only between the ominous rumblings of war, but between the acts of Giles's and Isabella's fighting and reconciliation—and the whole thing is seen or felt as a single process, natural and terrible.

There is a festive Shakespearean universality about the way everyone is admitted to the circle of *Between the Acts*—the very old and the very childish, the vulgar, the snobbish, the shy, the stupid, the humble, the village idiot—all have parts to play, and so, to its own amazement and dismay, does the audience. Shakespearean too is the novel's mocking representation of itself and its own action, under the guise of a rural pageant much too ambitious for its own limited repertory of props and talents. Inevitably, it is the despair of its author; yet she knows, like Duke Theseus, that "the best in this kind are but shadows; and the worst are no worse, if imagination amend them." Such is the playfulness of this sunlit comedy; but Mrs. Woolf has slipped into her idyllic English afternoon a brief moment of perfect horror. When Giles, jealous of his wife and haunted by presentiments of war, walks away toward the barn, he comes on a snake struggling to swallow a toad—one animal unable to breathe, the other unable to die. In a rage, he stamps on both of the beasts, bloodying his tennis shoes. For the rest of the afternoon, he wears them, almost as a badge of the world beyond comedy. No preachments are made, no symbolic significance explained; it is simply an ugly blotch on the day, cruel, beastly, ineradicable. (*To the Lighthouse* has a parallel scene, where the pilot's boy catches a fish, cuts a chunk out of its side, and throws it back, living, into the water.)

Thus the texture of *Between the Acts* is richer, more ironic, and more elaborately patterned than anything else in the canon of Virginia Woolf. Both the life represented and the writing about it are emotionally rich. The book does not overtly resemble anything in Joyce; it does not, like *Mrs. Dalloway*, remind one of Ulysses in its incidents or its prose rhythms. But in its play of surfaces against depths, absurd against grotesque, and ancient patterns against the motions of individual character, *Between the Acts* is the most essentially Joycean of Mrs. Woolf's books. This isn't in any real sense a matter of influence, but simply of one author making use of fictional dimensions first occupied by another—congruence, perhaps, not influence.

It was something of an accident that publication of *Ulysses* coincided so closely with Mrs. Woolf's readiness (demonstrated in *Jacob's Room*) to make use of interior monologue as a way of tracing the thin, irregular line between consciousness and experience. But it was no accident that she chose the inward streaming of *Ulysses*—as opposed, for example, to the outward fracturing of the "story," or the intimation of parodic or mythic dimensions—as her special device. *To the Lighthouse* and *The Waves* exhausted most of that limited *donnée*. But for her last novel, where she deliberately reached through the veil of fiction toward the vein of poetry, she went not farther away from Joyce but deeper into him. Whether she would have defined her undertaking in this way hardly matters, and influence in the demonstrable sense isn't even alleged. The strength of his example is shown by her ability to disregard mannerisms, formulas, techniques, machinery—and yet make us feel that she has seen into her subject and through it, as Joyce did with his.

Across the Atlantic, it's customary to point to Sherwood Anderson as not only the first major author influenced by *Ulysses,* but the channel of influence upon other writers, particularly Dos Passos, Wolfe, and Faulkner. *Dark Laughter* (1925) is the chief piece of evidence for this view, and a curious, conglomerate document it is, compounded equally of autobiography, pallid but determined eroticism out of Whitman and Lawrence, and some ventures into stream-of-consciousness prose. Only the latter items betray—or, rather, advertise—a Joycean influence. The basic narrative builds on a contrast between mechanical, commercial civilization leading to impotence, and the sensual, unfettered life of blacks and uninhibited white proles. "Bruce Dudley" having abandoned his original name of John Stockton, his original wife Bernice, and his position on the fringe of the middle-Western middle class, finds peace for himself in the unstriving anonymity of the folk, and persuades Aline, the unfulfilled wife of a go-getting parts supplier, to share that peace with him. The myth, in other words—or perhaps one should simply call it the cliché—is that of the noble savage; and this is not very Joycean. But Anderson himself thought his chief indebtedness to *Ulysses* lay in the prose; and this is right. Particularly in the retrospective inner soliloquies of "Bruce Dudley," sense impressions are woven together with fragments of memory and inchoate desire into a discourse strongly reminiscent of Bloom's in "Lotus-eaters."

Bruce lay lazy in bed. The brown girl's body was like the thick waving leaf of a young banana plant. If you were a painter now, you could paint that, maybe. Paint a brown nigger girl in a broad leaf waving and send it up North. Why not sell it to a society woman of New Orleans? Get some money to loaf a while longer on. She wouldn't know, would never guess. Paint a brown laborer's narrow suave flanks on the trunk of a tree. Send it to the Art Institute in Chicago. Send it to the Anderson Galleries in New York. A French painter went down to the South Seas. Freddy O'Brien went down. Remember when the brown woman tried to ravage him and he said how he escaped? Gauguin put a lot of pep in his book but they trimmed it for us. No one cared much, not after Gauguin was dead anyway. You get a cup of such coffee for five cents, and a big roll of bread. No swill. In Chicago, morning coffee at cheap places is like swill. Niggers like good things. Good big sweet words, flesh, corn, cane. Niggers like a free throat for song. You're a nigger down South and you get some white blood in you. A little more, and a little more. Northern travelers help, they say. Oh, Lord! Oh, my banjo dog! [p. 80].

Down to the last awkwardness, naïveté, loose association, and dream of easy glory, this is the mind lazying—an American mind in an American setting, dandering and dawdling at its barbaric ease. Such a passage makes clear that the unlikely marriage of Joyce and Lawrence in Anderson's writing grew out of a common and deep-seated hostility to rational consciousness. This link needs little explanation as it applies to Lawrence and Anderson; but hostility to the conscious mind is also latent in the last pages of *Ulysses*. It is figured in the dead bones of the factual catechism in "Ithaca," in the gelatinous maunderings of "Eumaeus," and in the oozings of Molly's ductless but fertile brain. Whether Sherwood Anderson ever read far enough in from either end of *Ulysses* to sense more than hazily the movement of Joyce's thought is disputable; but his Adamic American imagination apparently converted Joyce's incipient Buddhism, without much effort, to admiration for the spontaneous sensuality which his always vigilant Puritanism attributed to others, not without a touch of envy. His sense of structure was far less rigid and complex than Joyce's, and on the whole relatively little of *Ulysses* rubbed off on him.

Even smaller and more superficial was the scent of *Ulysses* that penetrated to John Dos Passos and Thomas Wolfe. Except for the intercalated Newsreel and Camera's Eye sections of *USA,* which perhaps owe something in their general conception to the "Aeolus" episode of *Ulysses,* one could read Dos Passos's entire trilogy, not without fatigue, but with little sense that Joyce ever existed. The three novels consist of interwoven biographies narrated mostly in standard third-person prose; there is little sense of overall pattern and none of mythic substructure. Even the Newsreel and Camera's Eye features seem to have wearied the author after a while; in the later pages they are sparse. Indisputably they distract, as would so many bundles of social statistics, from whatever interest the mingled biographies have managed to generate.

Thomas Wolfe, on the other hand, having essentially a portrait of himself as artist to compose, leaned more heavily on Joyce's first novel than on his second. Like Dos Passos, he was wholly immune to any lessons of verbal economy that Joyce might have taught him, but a number of disparate verbal mannerisms suggest a duplication of Joycean effects. These are strongest and most noticeable in the first novel, *Look Homeward Angel,* where interior monologue (for example, old Mr. Gant's in Section 7 or Eugene's in Section 20) plays a considerable role. Sections 14 and 24 are clearly patterned on the "Wandering Rocks" episode of *Ulysses,* describing Altamont in the same irrelevant, ironic simultaneities that Joyce used to convey the flavor of Dublin. The latter section has in it overtones of "Aeolus" as well; and it makes use of buried literary quotations, after the Joycean manner, to genuine comic effect. *Of Time and the River* is more perfunctory in its nods to Joyce. The book is divided into units under the names of various mythological figures—"Telemachus," "Proteus," "Antaeus," "Faustus," "Jason," and so forth—but these analogies are only impressionistic, not integral to the structure of the narrative. At one point, normal autobiographical narration gives way to a writer's diary, after the manner of Stephen Dedalus, but without the same

rationale to suggest the dissolution of a persona, its fading and with-
drawal. Eugene Gant returns from his dip into diary-writing as substantial and methodical a story-teller as ever. These disparate units of
Joycean imitation achieve, as scenes, different degrees of success or
failure; but as a group they are more like pastiches than integral parts
of Wolfe's vision. Whether it was his gift or a disease preying on
that gift, the flood of verbal yeast which was under some control in
the first novel got out of hand in the second, and drowned most traces
of Joycean art in the foam of its grandiose rhetoric.

How to use Joyce without swamping him or being swamped by
him was evidently the problem these early followers faced. The most
interesting instance of these tentative, ambivalent dealings is undoubtedly that of William Faulkner. But, departing momentarily
from the company of the great and the near-great, it may be useful
to see, from the example of a lesser novelist, how one could in fact
be victimized by the contagious power of Joycean mannerisms, and as
late as 1947. Ross Lockridge's Civil-War-and-rural-Indiana romanzo,
Raintree County, is awash with Joycean mannerisms and overtones.
As Lockridge conceives his imaginary landscape, it is thickly popu-
lated with the pale ghosts of its previous inhabitants, and a trick of
double-exposure syntax enables the author to backward or forward instantly from one end of the 19th century to the other. Verbal recollections of Joyce are almost too numerous, especially in those dramatic
interludes (modeled on the "Circe" episode of *Ulysses*) in which
characters act out their hallucinations. But none of these influences
cuts very deeply under the surface of the novel. The mythology remains mostly rhetorical and exclamatory, to the point of being hard
to distinguish from the Fourth-of-July oratory which the novel affec-
tionately mocks; no real figures emerge from the fabled past to penetrate the screen of words thrown up about them. And the jumpy narrative, which leaps across decades in mid-sentence, systematically
collects all the climaxes of all the narrations at the end of the book,
so that within a few pages the hero wins the Fourth-of-July race of

1859 and learns of the post-war deaths of his mother and sweetheart. This carefully managed and cross-cut narration comes at last to seem forced and arbitrary, because it isn't authenticated by any really long perspective, or required by the basic materials. Yet at the same time, it casts long shadows over the bumpkin-comedy aspects of the book, which might have done very well without such portentous competition. Being so adventitious, the Joyceisms can't help being felt as pastiche.

Muting and managing Joyce were thus the heavy problems for his early imitators, and no one felt their urgency more than the youthful William Faulkner. Unlike Virginia Woolf, he grew up with Joyce, so to speak, in his hand. The relation dated far back in his personal history, so that in some respects he may have had to make himself conscious of it; in addition, he was a deeply reticent man, and (evidently as a defensive strategy) much given to representing himself as a primitive American artist, naïvely unconcerned with the subtleties and the traditions of his story-telling craft. But no man who grows up with Mallarmé as a literary ideal is to be accepted at face value as an unself-conscious primitive. On various occasions, in interviews or under questioning, Faulkner denied that in his early days of apprenticeship he knew much of Joyce or Joyce's work. It was in the atmosphere, of course; other people had described it to him, but he hadn't read *Ulysses,* for example, till long after he wrote *The Sound and the Fury* (1929). These are perfectly natural responses of a man who cherished his individuality; and indeed, the record suggests that Faulkner had to struggle harder to liberate himself from Joyce than to accept or absorb his influence. But various facts suggest an impulse from Joyce much stronger, more specific, and earlier than Faulkner himself was ever ready to confess. He certainly knew *Ulysses* earlier than he let on; his personal copy of the book was dated "1924," and while this may have been a careless or a deliberate error, Faulkner's wife reported that on their honeymoon (June 1929), she read *Ulysses* through twice under her husband's instructions. Sherwood Anderson, who as we have seen was influenced by *Ulysses* in the writing of *Dark Laughter* (1925), was lending his copy of the book around New Orleans during the period of his greatest intimacy with Faulkner, in that same year. Furthermore, Faulkner may have become aware of Joyce's work even earlier, through the influence of his friend and literary mentor Phil Stone, who apparently subscribed to *Little Review* during the years when the first version of *Ulysses* was appearing serially in it (1918-20), and who customarily encouraged Faulkner to read widely in "experimental" writers. In the mind of a young man whose tastes as an adolescent were already directed toward Continental authors, who took Gautier, Mallarmé, Wilde, Beardsley, and Eliot with the greatest seriousness, it is inconceivable that Joyce's most conspicuous novel have remained *terra incognita* as late as 1930, when Faulkner was already more than thirty years old.

But the specific evidence of acquaintance with Joycean techniques is less compelling than the pattern of that influence as made evident in the early novels. Joseph Blotner summarizes some of the tricks and devices that Faulkner adapted from Joyce in the course of *Soldiers' Pay*:

> He employed interior monologue and associated devices in a way that suggested James Joyce. He set up the thoughts of the characters in the form of a play script and called one of them "The Town," much as Joyce had done in the "Circe" chapter of *Ulysses*. After a comment by Reverend Mahon about Mrs. Powers, he gave Jones's responding thoughts in parentheses, using phraseology which suggested similar ruminations of Leopold Bloom on female anatomy and wiles. One section of Chapter Seven consisted only of sequential summary statements by characters, some drawn from "The Town." Joyce had used discrete statements in this way for the "overture" to "The Sirens" chapter of *Ulysses*. Tricks of phonetic spelling suggested Joyce's rendering of characters' perceptions of sounds in the "Circe" chapter . . . [p. 429].

This is in general a fair statement of the case. There are a few other parallels, amounting on occasion to little more than the imitation of a Joycean tic. Experienced Gilligan and naïve Julian Lowe have some slight kinship with the familiar tandem of Bloom and Stephen; after the death of poor, mindless, mutilated Mahon, most of the other characters drift apart in a determinedly anti-romantic conclusion to the novel. A minor figure like Robert Saunders bears comic relationship to Paddy Dignam, jr.; and a lyric, atmospheric description like that beginning "Niggers and mules" at the beginning of Chapter 4 is clearly modeled on the "Noon slumbers" passage of "Proteus." There are little touches of narrative pace—crucial incidents withheld (Emmy's crushing Jones's hand in a door), ironic juxtapositions, abrupt yet unmarked transitions within and between scenes—which would confirm a sense of Joyce if one approached them with the Joyce parallel already in mind. Yet as a whole, Faulkner's novel is not Joycean in either theme or style. The almost wordless figure of Lieutenant Mahon, a massive, unmovable rock in the stream of time, fills the center of the novel; he can hardly fail to remind us of Benjy, who will occupy a similar position in *The Sound and the Fury,* but for such a figure there is no parallel in Joyce at all. Around his unmoving figure the characters range themselves in response to various motivations and impulses, but not in accord with an underlying pattern, least of all a mythological one. The book fulfills "normal" narrative expectations by moving in time; its structure involves no sense of the cyclical. In all these ways, therefore, *Soldiers' Pay,* even as it confirms Faulkner's early acquaintance with Joyce, makes clear that mannerisms and surfaces were what the young Faulkner chiefly imitated. And much the same argument could be made regarding *Mosquitoes,* which an early reviewer commended, rather condescendingly, on the ground that the writing was occasionally good when it wasn't Joyce. It is a study of ephemerids, with more contempt for its characters and more esthetic lecturing than the author can quite control; and again it is through mannerisms that Joyce's influence makes itself most clearly felt. The final stroll of Fairchild, Gordon, and "the Semitic man" through the Storyville section of New Orleans evidently owes something to Bloom's escorting of Stephen through Dublin's Nighttown;

the narrative is divided into semi-static, discontinuous time periods; even the name of the boat, "Nausikaa," reverberates with Joyce's contempt for literary garbage. But the basic tone of the novel, determined by its character as satiric social comedy, is closer to the youthful Aldous Huxley than to Joyce.

Faulkner's two apprentice novels are very different indeed from one another, but alike in showing clear awareness of Joyce and a set of superficial or fragmentary responses to him. *The Sound and the Fury*, which shows fewer traces of direct influence or imitation, is in fact much closer to the techniques and structural energies of a Joycean novel. The book makes much more thorough-going and consistent use of stream-of-consciousness techniques than did any of Faulkner's previous novels; those streams are choked and barricaded in more elaborate ways, and more intricately dappled with thematic repetitions. Under its surface, never quite explicit but increasingly felt as the novel progresses, is a mythical parallel (a parodic crucifixion, descent into hell, and resurrection) which can be treated either as a central narrative pattern in itself or, more interestingly, as a shadowy counter-structure to the contemporary fable. The energies of the reader are completely involved in piecing together fragments which, when assembled, tell a bitter tale of futility and circularity. Like *Ulysses, The Sound and the Fury* is relatively indifferent to the moral note, which is simply a way of saying that good and bad intentions don't count for much in the book's economy. The doom of the Compsons is deeper than any villain can spin out or any savior redeem. At one pole of the unmoving axis on which the book spins stands Mr. Compson's desolate assurance that "no battle is ever won. . . . They are not even fought. The field only reveals to man his own folly and despair, and victory is an illusion of philosophers and fools." At the other end is the bitter shape of that order which brings peace to Benjy, when he is driven around the monument on the left- rather than the right-hand side: "The broken flower drooped over Ben's fist and his eyes were empty and blue and serene again as cornice and façade flowed smoothly once more from left to right; post and tree, window and doorway, and signboard, each in its ordered place."

More than anything else, it is the field of centripetal-centrifugal forces in violent self-contained conflict that defines the greatness of *The Sound and the Fury;* the book could be described as a series of private, defeated furies united in a common doom. Having no use for the trappings of epic, and little interest in mimetic tricks or parodic parallels, Faulkner wrote a far tighter and more economical novel than *Ulysses* had been. For example, the furious little man with the traveling show who tries to split Jason Compson's head is remotely comparable, as a blind, comic menace, to the Citizen; but he is dealt with in outline and held to narrow compass. Quentin Compson, in the complexity of his mental processes and the layered, allusive quality of his mind, is comparable to Stephen Dedalus, but he takes no time out to exercise on the Indian clubs of literary criticism, as in the "Library" scene. His thinking on time is as pointed and functional (fictionally speaking) as Stephen's meditations on space and body, in "Proteus." *Ulysses* had made some play with scrambled or undefined identities or different persons passing under the same name; Faulkner, as a man obsessed with temporal repetition, makes his reader discriminate between two Quentins, two Maurys, and no fewer than three Jason Compsons—yet holds these various confusions strictly subordinate to a passionate historical complexity in his own mind, which doesn't allow or require him to say a word of incidental explanation. Without the postscript done for the Portable Faulkner at the instance of Malcolm Cowley, we'd be able at best only to guess at that complex; and even with it, there are gaps, contradictions, anomalies. The postscript is as close as Faulkner could come to those intricate schemas that Joyce wrote for *Ulysses*—gigantic graphs of raw materials, assigned as by a superbly perceptive, and often witty, computer to the various episodes of the book. But it is not very close; essentially it is a summary of Ur-history and background narrative, which *The Sound and the Fury* takes for granted. Some of it is rele-

vant, much of it irrelevant, or at least relevant only as setting a mood
or establishing a set of general pre-conditions. Joyce's novel is more
pointedly, more ostentatiously, exoskeletal than Faulkner's—which is
to say simply that Faulkner has built from the bottom up and the inside out in turning Joycean techniques to his own purposes. He was
not only a less informed but also a less formal artist than his great
predecessor; certainly in *The Sound and the Fury,* he worked under a
greater head of emotional steam, toward a more shattering, intimate,
and personal experience than Joyce in many parts of *Ulysses* was at-
tempting. Faulkner's masterpiece isn't, therefore, in any sense a
Joycean imitation, though it's clearly a book which, without the example of Joyce, would not have taken anything like its present form.
When Faulkner said that in writing it he had put the entire question
of publishers and publication out of his mind, he meant something
more than editors and audiences; a whole set of structural devices and
narrative conventions went with them, as he stripped his novel down
to the basic themes and the techniques essential to bring them living
forth. That so much evidence of Joyce's presence remains is surpris-
ing; but it simply confirms that the Joycean influence wasn't for
Faulkner either a passive or an adventitious thing; it was built, so to
speak, into the structure of his fictional vision, into the way he defined consciousness, into the way he wove a web of past circumstance
into a tissue of present action.

For example, Benjy is, beyond all question, the central pivot of
The Sound and the Fury, not just because of his nature but because
of his positioning. Around him all the other lives in the book revolve, to him the reader is constantly referring back his later experi-
ences in the novel. His mental arrest, though different in all sorts of
ways from the deadly stasis in which Stephen Dedalus is frozen during the first three units of *Ulysses,* functions similarly in the novel.
He is the screen through which the reader's mind must penetrate;
but, more than that, he is the hopelessly marred materials out of
which full humanity must be built—built by the reader, in the course

of putting the novel together in his head. Benjy's consciousness is in
fact less a flowing stream than a crossword, cross-referenced puzzle,
a Dædalian maze. Simply by positioning him at the head of the novel,
Faulkner converted into instant advantages most of the inherent defi-
ciencies of "stream-of-consciousness" method. But in so doing he
imitated, in a way that can't be described as "imitation" simply because its essence is boldness and audacity, the pattern of Joyce's fictional construction. No doubt this is one reason why Faulkner's novel
has seemed, like Joyce's, to stand a little apart from other fictions, as
involving the reader more radically, to the hazard of his equanimity,
in a perilous personal enterprise.

After *The Sound and the Fury,* traces of Joycean structure and
verbal device fade gradually from the work of Faulkner. Indeed, there
is a pronounced mythical structure underlying *Light in August,* and
both *As I Lay Dying* and *Absalom, Absalom* make sustained use of a
monologue which, if not fully interiorized, is at least given a heavy
coloring of individual manner. But none of these novels reminds us
decisively of Joyce; they are a working—eloquent, funny, impas-
sioned—of indigenous materials that Faulkner needed no specially
Joycean techniques to handle. Occasionally in later years, when he
tried to draw his artistic calculations *very* fine, Faulkner fell back on
fictional mechanisms as a substitute for the kind of unitary passion he
generated in *The Sound and the Fury.* The solemn machinery of *A
Fable* represents his most notable failure of the sort: as apparatus
without dynamics, it can stand for Joyce's exoskeletal structure-
making at its dryest. But the greatest of Faulkner's novels is less an
example of Joycean influence or even inspiration than of Joyce's
liberating effect on an indigenous and independent inspiration. Even
apart from the masterpiece that resulted, it is one of the most interesting examples in literature of influence accepted and converted into
the direct opposite of itself. Thus it became a substantial influence in
its own right; and one can read a fully achieved novel like William
Styron's *Lie Down in Darkness* without feeling (despite its epi-

graph from Joyce) any impulse to look beyond Faulkner for the root of its inspiration.

As already noted, stream of consciousness finds one of its richest uses in randomizing what the reader will eventually rationalize. Consciousness in fiction is not a stream on whose surface we float, but a moving semi-transparency through which we try to look for underlying principles of order. In a real sense, the streaming of consciousness has taken the place, as a working element in the novel, of that dramatic action which used to be the means by which (or the obstacle against which) characters made evident something like their "true selves." It is a screen of ostensibles out of whose several indications the reader, guided by the author, works to construct a "final" definition of character or pattern or meaning. This is the traditional reader's progress, from first impressions, through indirections, incongruities, and difficulties, to a "deeper understanding." In this development, the stream of consciousness serves partly as motive agent (it supplies the details out of which we are to construct the final image), but more as wilful impediment. Perhaps this function helps explain its tendency to get thicker and more turbid, till from daydreamers we come to night-dreamers, from individual half-consciousness to collective unconsciousness, from children, paranoids, and primitives to idiots, cretins, and agonized, anonymous awareness, buried facedown for eternity in freezing mud. Starting as it does very close to what used to be the terminus of fictional revelation, the stream of consciousness has to be thick and reluctant lest it drain us too quickly out of the area of "character" altogether. What we come to see through the moving transparency may determine whether individuality is not simply a shallow illusion, and fiction consequently a desperate and somewhat childish device for focusing on shadows and appearances. A few novelists have confronted rather cheerfully this dilemma toward which stream of consciousness hurries them; the majority have been less sanguine about putting the thin veil of their art to the test.

CHAPTER FOUR

SAMUEL
BECKETT

S AMUEL BECKETT'S connections and contacts with Joyce are so many, so early, and at the superficial level so obvious, that enumerating them seems almost superfluous. Scratching a little deeper, looking a little harder, we find the gap between the two men growing not only wider and wider but defining itself in ever-sharper terms of antithesis, so that on certain scales they seem diametrically opposed. To reconcile the yin and the yang of this most familiar of comparisons involves us in a mass of discriminations and simultaneous identifications not easy to sort out.

To start on the most primitive level, Beckett is Irish as was Joyce; but there is no sign that the politics of Irish independence ever disturbed Beckett as they did the writer who was eighteen years his senior. For Beckett, Parnell is simply a historical name (if it ever occurs in his writings, the occasion has escaped me); the dispute over Gaelic, the hostility to England, the program of Sinn Fein, all are exactly nowhere in Beckett's economy. Joyce's fictional world is the city and suburbs of Dublin, and all his writing is rooted in the particulars of that community and its history. Beckett makes only vague, distant, and occasional allusions to Ireland in his fiction. Names of characters apart, a couple of hundred words deleted from his four-hundred-page trilogy would efface every recognizable vestige of Ireland and the Irish. Irish folklore and Irish humor hardly exist in Beckett's world, even for purposes of parody or sardonic comment; a figure like the Citizen, who swaggers grotesquely through the "Cyclops" episode of

Ulysses like a one-man anthology of Irish giants, is quite outside the range of Beckett's perception. All his life long Joyce was in conscious exile from Ireland; he used the word and the concept of "exile" again and again, and being away from Ireland was a major part of his life. Beckett could much more properly be described as a Parisian who was born in Ireland; he is at home in the 15me arondissement, and has spent little time yearning for the delights of Clanbrassil street.

Again, Beckett is an unbeliever as was Joyce; but unbelieving out of a Protestant, not a Catholic, background. Priests and the priesthood seem to have had little impact on his imagination, by contrast with the tremendous impression they made on Joyce's. All his life, Joyce enacted and re-enacted the role of priest, filling his books with parody-rituals, mock-sacraments, epiphanies, benedictions, vestments; more deeply, he was preoccupied with the incarnation, both as a metaphor for his own art, and as an image of the world as he saw it, ostensibly thick and thingly but really luminous with spiritual significance. Reading the signatures of things like Boehme, he aspired with his art, with his insight, to express their inner nature. Beckett is much closer to wholly mythless man; the philosophical problem which preoccupies him is the relation or non-relation between the mind and exterior reality, and to this problem ecclesiasticism, with all its trappings, is wholly irrelevant. Joyce sees through the exterior tegument of the world to a meaning hidden behind its physical texture; Beckett, in traditional Protestant fashion, hears inner voices. They do not seem to say the traditional things to him or to his characters, but they guide both along that quest or pilgrimage which is the oldest and most traditional of Protestant metaphors for the spiritual life. In their different unbelieving ways, both Joyce and Beckett are haunted by the doubt that the God in whom they disbelieve may exist, probably as a secret, malignant force concerned chiefly with tormenting His creatures.

Joyce's background of reading was primarily literary, in a sense peculiar to the late 19th century, when hierophants like Mallarmé and Maeterlinck held sway over the imaginations of men. In his early admirations, he was strongly marked, as already noted, by Ibsen and Flaubert, D'Annunzio, Wilde, Hauptmann, and Yeats; yet his principal model as a prose stylist was the severe and ceremonious, yet relatively old-fashioned, Cardinal Newman. For Beckett we can compile no such list; whether for temperamental or historical reasons, he missed the aesthetic movement altogether, preferring (so far as can be determined) to study thinkers rather than stylists. In his early prose particularly, he is not above using an occasional exotic reference like William of Champeaux, very much as Joyce makes use of Joachim Abbas; but the later style of Beckett is harder, dryer, flatter, more stripped than anything in Joyce. Along with the specifics of time, place, and particular reference, circumlocutions and metaphors drop away; the later art of Beckett depends on utter simplicity of diction and grammar, frequent repetition, carefully controlled rhythm. If he can be assigned a master in the art of prose, it is no individual, but an 18th-century assemblage which could include such figures as Swift, Defoe, Archbishop William King, and maybe David Hume.

Other differences and parallels can be summarized more swiftly. Joyce was fascinated by music, Beckett is chiefly interested in abstract painting. Though Joyce knew many languages and incorporated most of them in his writing under various guises, he did not on the whole compose in foreign tongues or translate much of his own work into or out of English. Beckett, less polyglot than Joyce, frequently composes in French and translates into English, or vice versa. French as a language has thus had more of an influence on him than any individual language ever had on Joyce; and there are interesting arguments that the severe discipline of French composition has hardened both Beckett's style and the tenor of his thought—even that it enabled him to escape from Joyce. As there is less linguistic archeology in Beckett than in Joyce, so there is nothing to correspond with the elaborate pattern of Viconian cycles which Joyce built into his books. They are less elaborately structured, overall. Joyce's mosaic method of composition implied an obsession with pattern, and with completeness of pattern, such as we don't find in Beckett to any degree. So far as Beckett concerns himself with pattern at all, it is with incomplete pattern; his circles are never closed, his lists are always bogus, when he plays games they cry aloud in advance their own meaninglessness. The depth of Beckett's morbidity is sometimes obscured by his extraordinary comic touch; the comic inspiration of Joyce is sometimes swamped by the gigantic structural complexity of his books.

Joyce, in brief, was a man who aspired by a process of addition to put everything into his volumes; Beckett, working by a contrary arithmetic, has steadily subtracted more and more from his books, emptying them of substance, and working toward the cold and dark of a naked consciousness, aware only of itself, confronting the absolute zero of non-experience. Every one of Joyce's books is in its own way a *summa*—the *Wake* most of all; Beckett's writings all aspire to the condition of *nullas*—questioning, thus, the nature of their own existence in a manner more radical than Joyce ever attempted. Joyce's undertaking may have been megalomaniac, but it was not absurd, did not involve a contradiction in terms. In a celebrated formula which emerged during a dialogue with the abstract painter Georges Duthuit, Beckett once expressed his commitment to "the expression that there is nothing to express, nothing with which to express, nothing from which to express, no power to express, no desire to express, together with the obligation to express" ("Three Dialogues with Georges Duthuit," *Transition,* 1949). Any expression which refuses to analyze more explicitly than this the nature of that "obligation" which is its only *raison d'être* exists perforce in a state of absurdity; and in this respect, Beckett departs most radically of all from Joyce. Beckett's is an implosive imagination at odds with its own premises; Joyce gives us the feeling of infinity.

The formulation of this contrast is based pretty largely on Beckett's own sayings; and it suggests a sort of anti-Joyce dialectic, as if

Beckett, who knew Joyce intimately over many years, and was, of all
the people subject to Joyce's influence, most deeply involved in the
creation of the *Wake,* had decided early on to stand that gigantic
structure on its head. He had to go the other way, and radically—
through impotence, ignorance, and all manner of denial—on the
chance that this road was not the dead end that it appeared. What
affirmations he could squeeze out of this stony soil, though scanty,
might be expected to prove pure. And though he seems to have entered on this path with the sense of drawing back into a completely
private cul-de-sac, it has proved unexpectedly populous; his self-
imposed, self-defined Thebaid has attracted fascinated commitment
from those who like to see the problem of existence driven down to a
strict equation, factored further into its simplest elements, and so
unwaveringly confronted.

Beckett himself embarked on his fictional program (if that phrase
doesn't over-formalize the process) with obvious hesitations and misgivings; and the pace at which he pursued it has been curiously uneven. To consider only the major fictions, *Murphy* appeared in 1938,
Watt was written between 1942 and 1945, *Mercier et Camier,* to
which he devoted 1946-47, never worked itself out to his satisfaction.
The miraculous years were those between 1947 and 1950, when in
solitude and utter concentration he produced not only the trilogy of
novels, *Molloy, Malone Dies,* and *The Unnamable,* but the play
that made him famous, *Waiting for Godot.* After this breakthrough, the pace of his production slackens radically; there are no
more novels, one more full-size play (*Endgame,* 1955), but then
one-acters, curtain-raisers, sketches, and relatively short bits and
pieces of narrative prose. Mere quantity of production is the least of
all considerations in dealing with an artist like Beckett; but the pace
of his work and the manner of his approach combine to reinforce the
impression that he advanced on his formidable themes slowly and
indirectly, wrestled with them furiously during a brief period of total
concentration, and has teased and shredded them since, no less in-

tently, but from a greater distance. The core of his problematic has always been the extravagant, almost vindictive isolation of Beckett's characters from one another, from the resources of history, society, and their own past—even from their own minds. In fact, we wrong them even to talk of them as "characters"; for though there are in the various books entities called "Murphy," "Watt," and so forth, these are mere verbal parcels of convenience; their ingredients are jumbled together as provisionally and insecurely as the contents of a grocery bag. It is their disintegration, continuous from work to work and continuous in that context as nothing is within the individual fictions, that makes for the fascination of Beckett's *oeuvre*.

The first of the major books, *Murphy*, seems closest to being a "normal" fiction, having a sort of intrigue, a distinct locale, and several personages who surround the central enigma and try with comic ineptitude to interact with him. But Murphy himself, with his icy eyes and utter indifference to all others and everything other than his own mind, is one of the coldest and least human of Beckett's isolatos. His favorite exercise is to strap himself naked in a rocking-chair, and rock himself—like Rousseau, in the famous fifth Reverie—into a state of complete self-possession. The path on which he thus sets his foot, in secrecy and alone, coincides with that which constitutes his brief and modest public career—when, with spectacular success, he becomes custodian in an institution for the feeble-minded. To his charges, at least, he is perfectly attuned; and the height of his rapport with them is reached in the marvelously comic chess game which he plays with the mild little schizophrenic, Mr. Endon. The game is played on both sides, not to check or mate the king, not to capture pieces, but on the contrary to evade and delay as long as possible contact between the opposing forces. Disengagement is the aim of the game, on the board as in life; and Murphy all but successfully accomplishes this difficult objective. The highest and most satisfying level of his mental activity is described as that which involves most complete autonomy for the mind—the achievement of a dark containing

> neither elements nor states, nothing but forms becoming and crumbling
> into the fragments of a new becoming, without love or hate or any in-
> telligible principle of change. Here there was nothing but commotion
> or the pure forms of commotion. Here he was not free but a mote in
> the dark of absolute freedom. He did not move, he was a point in the
> ceaseless unconditioned generation and passing away of line. Matrix of
> surds [Grove Press, p. 112].

Behind this complex panoply of metaphorical disguises lies the concept of chaos, perhaps as figured in the concept of Brownian motion;
as a "matrix of surds," or womb of irrationals, Murphy instinctively
moves toward madness as a state of ultimate satisfaction. The only
flaws he can find in the "dungeon in Spain," which is the madman's
cell, are those imported by the healers, so-called. Left to themselves,
Beckett has Murphy imagine—not without a measure of ironic distance—that the insane would be happy as Larry, short for Lazarus.

The full consequences of this view are not worked out because of
what passes within the fiction for an accident; the gas leading to the
heater in Murphy's attic goes on, there is an explosion, he is killed. If
the exact cause of this significant episode in the book is never made
clear to us, at least some of the contributory circumstances are. The
gas-connection is ramshackle, improvised by a pot-poet in a desperate
hurry; the gas has an odd way of going on and off of its own accord;
and Murphy, being absorbed in his own mind, is completely oblivious
of vulgar practicalities. Still, it seems significant that the gas which
kills Murphy (our hero, if only in the sense that he is not a paper
cutout like everyone else in the book) is identified etymologically
with chaos, while the cretins, among whom he feels so much at home,
are identified etymologically with Christians. Van Helmont, who invented the word "gas," had in mind an allusion to "chaos"; and the
word "cretin," deriving from a Swiss patois, distinguishes the idiot,
as a "Christian soul," from animals. Murphy, whose erudition,
though always marginal and exotic, is rarely bogus, has hit his chosen
nails on the head. To be a Christian (using the word in an ethical, not
a sectarian, sense) is, by the lights of this world, to be a cretin; to

abandon oneself to one's mind is to accept chaos, and thus the equivalent of taking the pipe. Behind idiocy, behind ecstasy, the overwhelming appetite of Murphy is toward the dark and the void of
non-existence.

A plot which runs the protagonist so directly and eagerly toward
the large black hole which awaits us all, and which most of us would
take some pains to avoid, needs no motive energy to move it forward,
but rather brakes to hold it back. *Murphy* is the best example prior to
Godot of a literary action used to postpone rather than advance the
movement of a development possessing its own inertia. Since he has
no real function in moving forward the story (it gets where it is
inevitably going without any of his efforts), the author is free to
embroider intellectual and stylistic curlicues on the margins of the
tale—which he does with the owlish solemnity of an insane scholar.
Some of this fancy-work sounds, and no doubt is, Joycean; but its
function in the economy is different. Joyce is going somewhere, and
uses his verbal decorations to enrich and forward his theme; Beckett
is going nowhere, and uses his decoration to delay his arrival there.

The subzero temperature of *Murphy*'s major theme is partly mitigated by the drollery of its manner, and many readers have found it
the most accessible of Beckett's fictions—partly, perhaps, because
they take it at about three-quarters of its basic potency. *Watt,* on the
other hand, has a less inevitable line of development and a more
highly developed, exasperatingly efficient set of time-killers to prevent
its arriving where it is not in any case very likely to get. Under some
compulsion of which we know nothing, Watt takes service with an
inaccessible Mr. Knott; after serving for a while, in a capacity not
easy to summarize under any particular head, his successor arrives,
and Watt knows it is time to depart, which he does. Some of this
story is told by Watt to Sam, a fellow-inmate in an insane asylum:
there is no reason to avoid the supposition that Sam is Samuel Beckett. The story contains no characters who think it either possible or
desirable to become acquainted with Watt; he himself does not know

what he is doing, or why, nor does he know who or what he is. To be sure, he is eager to find out, and in the effort to understand a situation will run unflaggingly through all the permutations and alternatives of which the situation allows. He is a spectacular extrapolator; and from the simple circumstance that Mr. Knott's chaotic food, when not eaten, must be given to a hungry dog, is capable of deriving an enormous, utterly repulsive, and abjectly unfortunate family named Lynch, whose sole social function is to keep on hand a supply of desperately hungry dogs to eat Mr. Knott's leftovers. On occasion, without any impulse to discover anything, the author will simply ring the changes on Mr. Knott's possible peregrinations around his room —"from the window to the door, from the door to the fire; from the fire to the door, from the door to the window; from the fire to the bed, from the bed to the door"—and so on and so forth.

At one stage, Watt undertakes to talk backwards in various ways, reversing the order of words in the sentence, or the order of letters in words, or the order of sentences in the period, or combining all these alternatives in various combinations. Like Murphy, he is a matrix of surds; and, as with Murphy, all his intellectual defeats and impasses seem to flow from a central incapacity to define what (Watt) is mån. In *Watt* we have a first manifestation of that clown-in-waiting around whom *Godot* is built; we have the further pathos of an irrelevant vocation and a mind alienated among its own games. There is the pedantry-*shtik* in the form of a hilarious mock-examination; there are the pratfalls interspersed with metaphysics, the robot-mannerisms interrupted by Pascalian shivers at the silence of infinite space. Yet by and large the book is static, and its disparate parts do not successfully interact with one another. Some people have suggested that the impasse which the book represents derives from its relation to Joyce, its over-dependence on a baroque style. Apart from the absurdity of identifying the baroque style with Joyce, this doesn't seem right in itself. What *Watt* lacked was precisely the kind of inward and unifying passion, the sense of seeing into something and making a felt whole of it, the immediately present example of which was *Finnegans Wake*. Evidently, abandoning English helped Beckett toward a new sort of book by cutting off certain sorts of verbal vaudeville. No doubt the loneliness and the danger of the war years, and the gigantic questions they posed about the nature and the future of man, also pushed him toward the stripped and inward vision. But I do not think the great breakthrough of the immediate post-war years was for Beckett an escape from Joyce so much as a fulfilling of himself through a part of Joyce that he had not previously tapped, at least not very successfully. He could no longer stand outside his characters and watch them perform; he had to get in them and through them. And they were, because of their alien, alienated disposition, and the nothingness immediately beyond them, far harder to get into than any figures in the Joycean *oeuvre*.

By abandoning Norway as a theme, as an idea, as a set of obligations, and plunging into himself, Ibsen rediscovered and in effect re-created Norway. By abandoning Joyce in order to pursue himself, Beckett rediscovered Joyce. He did so not through the use of Joycean techniques—out of the entire panoply of Joycean techniques, Beckett took over only the interior monologue—but in a much less specific way. Locating Joyce in the mature work of Beckett is like locating Christianity in Milton's "Comus": it is nowhere overtly, but everywhere tacitly and by implication. Classical analogues, Viconian cycles, macaronic speech-distortions, mosaic composition, archetypes of all sorts—the great clanking machinery of Joycean fiction drops away. There remains the unbroken murmur of a confession made without a priest, a sifting and straining of the consciousness, a casting aside of everything which is not the quicksilver moment of self-awareness. This is not Joycean, it is Joyce.

The first novel of the trilogy, *Molloy,* is on the whole the most classical and humane, even hopeful, of Beckett's books. It is the story of two interlocked, middle-aged, vaguely Irish males; Molloy is on a pilgrimage to his mother's house, Moran is under a mysterious injunction from Gaber, representing Youdi and his entire apparatus, to seek Molloy.* Though we are not told how, we do know from the beginning that Molloy has in fact somehow reached his mother's house, in however battered and decrepit a condition. His mother is evidently dead, but at least, at last—despite temptations to linger with a siren named Lousse, and many more serious physical impediments —he ends his story in the place where he wanted or thought he wanted to be. Moran, on the other hand, though sent out to discover Molloy, may or may not have crossed paths with him by the end of the book and certainly has not discovered him. He returns to his own house, under orders as he went out; like Molloy, he has radically deteriorated in the course of his quest, but spiritually he has changed, more radically than Molloy and perhaps in consequence of having imagined, if not actually encountered, him.

The two stories, which are largely separate and particularly hazy at the moment when they coincide (if they do), must be joined by the reader through counter-poised judgments of Molloy and Moran. The former is ascetic, unworldly, a physical wreck but somehow marked with the almost visible trait of nobility. With policemen and churches he has nothing whatever in common. Moran, on the other hand, is mean, prudent, spiteful, and legalistic—a rate-payer, a church-goer, a model of minor officialdom; his treatment of his son is a nightmare of petty tyranny. The pair might be variously considered as open and closed, as ethical and acquisitive, as libido and superego, as artist and functionary—Beckett leaves them plastic to all these dualisms, and to many others. But the crucial episode of the book seems to involve the bending of one before the other. Somewhere in a dark forest where he is waiting for his son to return with a bicycle, Moran is accosted

* The novel has an overture, perhaps a schema, describing two outline figures, A and C (A and B in the French), who enact a brief, inconsequential encounter in an abstract landscape. They suggest thereby, though in a tantalizing and not wholly consistent way, certain characteristics of the chief protagonists, and a qualification on the significance of their meeting—if, indeed, it ever took place.

by a gaunt, pale figure whom he does not recognize, but who might be Molloy. The man asks for bread and is given a piece; Moran asks to heft his club, and finds it surprisingly light. That is all. They separate. But the encounter sets Moran's personality or subpersonality to crumbling and shifting. As Beckett describes the process in a sequence of dark and beautiful metaphors,

> I seemed to see myself ageing as swiftly as a day-fly. But the idea of ageing was not exactly the one which offered itself to me. And what I saw was more like a crumbling, a frenzied collapsing of all that had always protected me from all I was always condemned to be. Or it was like a kind of clawing towards a light and countenance I could not name, that I had once known and long denied. But what words can describe this sensation at first all darkness and bulk, with a noise like the grinding of stones, then suddenly as soft as water flowing [Grove Press, p. 148].

What he sees next is a calm, indefinite, underwater face, which he cannot decipher; and this, he supposes, is a mark "of my growing resignation to being dispossessed of self." (The French original is a little different, and softer, here: "et combien il me devenait indifférent de me posséder." Being dispossessed is quite different from not possessing.) But I think the last phrase is to be read dramatically; Moran feels he is being dispossessed of self; in fact, it is a new and different self which is taking him over, as the sequel indicates. For shortly an ugly, thick little man appears, with a "face which I regret to say vaguely resembled my own"; they hold a brief, rough colloquy, in which it appears that the newcomer is looking for an old man with a club. Moran denies having seen him, there is a scuffle, and "a little later, perhaps a long time later, I found him stretched on the ground, his head in a pulp." The invitation is clear to suppose that Moran's new self has killed his old self; and the point is underlined when Moran's stiff leg bends normally, and the victim is said no longer to resemble his murderer.

Having thus liberated himself from a grotesquely rigid person-

ality, Moran is gradually and partially liberated from the compulsion
to pursue his quest. When Gaber appears, to order him home, it
merely confirms an inner decision. Drained and exhausted, but also
exalted by the experience, Moran makes his painful and solitary way
home. His son has faded from view, and his faith in the church of
which he was once a pillar has also evaporated. All the snug amenities
of provincial domesticity have crumbled—his bees are dead, his garden is overgrown, his housekeeper has left, he has no prospect of
further employment in the service of Youdi, and he even denies that
he is going to try anymore to be a man, having apparently found that
state unrewarding. Yet in his condition of ultimate dispossession, in
the last paragraph of the book, he is able to ask if he is not freer now
than he was. It is a question he, as a character, is in no position to answer, but the reader is likely to make his own affirmative. By contrast
with what he used to be, there is no question that Moran is more free
at the end of the book; and even if his immediate task is one of servitude (to write a report on the case of Molloy), the report, in its
deliberate defiance of physical fact, is an act of imaginative liberation.

Molloy is thus a novel which reaches its climax in a desert flower-
ing—a triumph of the liberated imagination, as in 19th-century
novels. It is able to do this because it starts Moran in an almost Dickensian far-back. Molloy, who starts much farther out, does not get so
far—fulfilling thus the paradigm of A and C given us at the beginning of the book. The two pieces of the novel, which are easily
separable, would make a wholly different book if their order were
reversed; thinking of it that way may make us feel that Moran's victory
is only the Pyrrhic one of having fitted himself to advance faster and
with fewer impediments toward the grisly end which stares Molloy
in the face.

Malone Dies, the second novel of the trilogy, has never had a very
good press, for reasons that are fairly clear. Though its basic situation is grimly absorbing—a moribund, semi-paralyzed pauper, bed-
ridden in a hospital for incurables, and calculating the terminal stages
of his existence—the narrative is often distracted and distracting. It

consists of *disjecta membra* which the reader is under no great pressure to assemble, even supposing it were possible to do so. That Malone is sometimes Malone but sometimes Saposcat and sometimes MacMann is not particularly disturbing; but there are also suggestions that he may be a late stage of Molloy, Moran, or both. He remembers, for example, being stunned in a dark forest by a blow on the head; and he himself possesses a bloodstained club. The pretense that he, rather than Samuel Beckett, is telling the story is allowed to wear uncommonly thin: though there's a great deal of business about his pad and pencil, he mentions names like Murphy and Mercier as those of characters whom he has created and destroyed, mentions entire episodes, like the ex-butler's suicide in *Murphy*, as his own accomplishments. Sometimes he speaks of himself in the third person, sometimes in the first; as he assumes the freedom to abolish other characters when they bore him, the reader comes more and more to experience him too as a paper cutout. The stories he tells to while away his long day's dying are inconclusive and sometimes irrelevant. There is a fairly detailed account of a family named Lambert in the English translation though known as Louis in the French original. (An allusion to Balzac's novel is obvious, the point of it less so. At one stage in the translation Beckett neglected, whether deliberately or inadvertently, to transform "Louis" into "Lambert"—the first name stands there as an isolated signpost to nothing in particular, or as a frank anomaly, one can't tell which.) The father butchers pigs, and the family lives in indiscriminate squalor; Saposcat knows them. But the story breaks off at that point and never goes further. There is a brief and carefully disgusting love affair between Malone and his repellent nurse Moll; it ends when the author, frankly weary of his work, tells us he is going to kill Moll off, and does so. The murders with which the book terminates are also unmotivated and unexplained; and we are left with an image of mankind aimlessly adrift on the empty waters, six men in a boat, the imbeciles, the murderer, and the moribund MacMann, all floating off into the void.

The novelty of *Malone Dies* lies, I think, in a systematic derange-

ment of the narrative for which there doesn't seem to be much precedent, in Joyce or elsewhere. Malone, for example, begins his narration
in a hospital bed from which he is scarcely capable of stirring; when
he drops his pencil and notebook, he has to spend several days groping with a stick to recover them. Yet "much later" he comes to again
"in a kind of asylum," and registers the kind of surprise at this development which implies that he hasn't been in asylum all along. Not
only so; he is now much more mobile and energetic than previously,
yet says nothing to explain or indicate that he's aware of the change.
He runs out into the asylum grounds, attempts to escape, conducts a
series of quite active exercises with Moll, is taken on an expedition
by the keeper. These and other absurdities of similar nature are cracks
and incongruities in the physical texture of the story, designed, one
supposes, to discredit the story as a mock-reality. They are not the
product of a hallucinated vision (psychological, that is), nor are they
puzzles planted in the fiction for the reader to decipher like a docile,
clever schoolboy. They are not, in that sense, structural. They are a
product of the history of the English novel, a history which Beckett
was in process of shedding—as inevitable a product as that superb
sentence of Malone's, at the climax of his description of the asylum:
"A stream at long intervals bestrid—but to hell with all this fucking
scenery." All the way through *Malone Dies* one can feel the impatience of an author itching to discard the simulacra of fiction, to be
rid of that code of meaning and artifice of economy by which fictions
are bound to regulate themselves.

The Unnamable takes the full plunge, sweeping aside the whole
gallery of Beckett "characters" and their stories, as mere "mannikins"
and "a ponderous chronicle of moribunds." Not without some disgust, the author must push these away to replace them, as fictional
characters, with himself, who in addition to being Samuel Beckett in
person is noman and everyman, nowhere and everywhere, timeless
and yet submerged in the stream of time. By a brief streak of fantasy
he can also be a head in a jar hung out as a sign before a bistro ("Ali
Baba") in the street where Beckett was living when he wrote the

book. Though he may be unnamable now (we cannot be sure the title applies to him, it may also apply to the process he is trying to define, conventionally and corruptly known as human life), the speaker of the book has had various names, Mahood most recently, perhaps Basil before that, and Worm even before that; he obviously faces a serious prospect of being Worm again very shortly. His meditation is on first and last things in an effort to define what is or should be the quality of his existence as Mahood; the pun on "manhood" is not very remote, and is surely intended to be felt. It is a meditation, remorselessly monotonous and persistent, on a single aspect of the human condition; it proceeds on the unspoken assumption that to define self it is necessary to strip away externals and accidents—repeating, thus, a famous experiment carried out by Peer Gynt with the aid of an onion. Beckett's working out of this paradox has few of the characteristics of fiction. There is no action, no contrast of motives, no manipulation of sympathy, no "rendering" in the Jamesian sense. Though it implies sustained and serious thought, and imitates the processes of thought, the stream of monologue is more like worry than thought, a ceaseless shaking and gnawing and teasing of the question, what is it to be a man?

Like the *Wake, The Unnamable* has to be read slowly and with painful concentration on each sentence; skimmed across, it yields chiefly a sense of endlessly reiterated, musclebound depression. But read slowly and questioningly—preferably with the French original close to hand—it yields an enormous sense of imaginative vitality struggling under crushing pressure.* A comparison that doesn't aim

---

* Because the text has few typographical features (the last 110 pages of the English are printed without paragraphing, the last five pages without a period), the practical way to make comparisons is to mark the French page-numbers in the margin of the English text. The effect of bilingual reading is not only to render the meaning of many passages much more explicit, but also to make one aware of the great freedom Beckett exercised in translating his original, and of the many errors which in one way or another crept into the English version. The contours of the book are much more sharply defined when it is read in this admittedly cumbersome fashion.

to be more than impressionistic would be with Michelangelo's gigantic shackled "Slaves," intended for the tomb of Julius II.

The "voices" which provide the speaker of this monologue with
so much material for speculation may perhaps prove an obstacle for
readers not at home with inner voices, the more so since Beckett *in
propria persona* claims to hear voices and to recite in his books words
spoken by outside agents. Within *The Unnamable* these voices make
some sense as the voices of the past, of history, or of conventional
moralizing. In one very moving series of metaphors they are teachers,
badgering the backward student Mahood to recite a rote definition of
man that he cannot get through his head. Indeed, it wouldn't be hard
to see them as the structure, not only of society but of "systematic"
thought and "formal" language, such as the narrator is struggling to
use against itself, in the forlorn hope of cutting it short. They are the
rags, not only of respectability but of conventional categories, all of
which must be stripped off if we are to see unaccommodated man
(the allusion is trite but inescapable) as the poor bare forked animal
he is.

By contrast with the vaudeville turns of *Murphy* and *Watt,* the
language of *The Unnamable* is taut, stripped, and very limited in
vocabulary. There is an occasional freaky bit of theological pedantry
or anatomical specificity; in his Ali Baba incarnation, the narrator
blurs the proprietress of his bistro by calling her now Marguerite and
now Madeleine; but his uncertainties lie deeper than those of perception, and he focuses on them myopically, monomaniacally, struggling
to the end of the book to say himself, to be said. In these closing passages the counters get fewer and more familiar, the moves are shorter
and bump more abruptly into their own contradictions, the transitions
blur, and the pace quickens, as the prose seems to slide irresistibly
under its own momentum toward the last, utterly simple, impasse. It
is a supreme imaginative achievement.

The trilogy as a whole, and *The Unnamable* in particular, could
probably not have been written without the example of Joyce, and
particularly of the *Wake,* before them; but they draw on only one

area of the Joycean empire, and as in all cases of creative influence, bend it to purposes and interests which are Beckett's own. The given from which Beckett scarcely wavers is the dilemma of post-Cartesian philosophy; if the only evidence of being is thinking, and thinking is largely conditioned, no man can know who he is or that he is, save by a ruthless process of pulling down and putting off. That process Joyce never approached with Beckett's zeal for getting down to the raw bones of the human anatomy; but if he had not dug into the intuitive substructure of life, Beckett might not have been emboldened to dig beyond it to the ontological sub-substructure. Even as it was, the path of approach—indirect, hesitant, and beset with false steps— suggests how hard Beckett found it to reach the center of his subject. In this sense, *The Unnamable* validates the entire previous career; if it is not a supremely difficult achievement superbly accomplished, then the entire discussion of Beckett as a literary artist moves down several pegs. I think that step will not be necessary.

A narrower vision, a different focus, a much more limited and less symphonic art, were first conditions of Beckett's liberation from Joyce. One consequence of these choices that can't be burked is a kind of instability of tone and uncertainty of taste that draws him, from time to time, into two different eccentricities where it's neither easy nor rewarding to follow him. One is self-pity and self-dramatization, the other a kind of mechanical testing of the written language by depriving it progressively, and arbitrarily, of its resources. An example of the first might be Youdi's words to Gaber, which the latter relays to Moran as he lies, cold, lame, and wretched, in the dirt:

> He said to me, said Gaber, Gaber, he said, life is a thing of beauty, Gaber, and a joy forever. He brought his face nearer to mine. A joy forever, he said, a thing of beauty, Moran, and a joy forever. He smiled. I closed my eyes. . . . I said, Do you think he meant human life? [pp. 164-65].

This sort of dialogue seems to me broad to the point of sophomoric cynicism, especially in its milking of a phrase which even the adoles-

cent Keats used with more precision than Beckett allows it. The
French original is less crude than the English translation; life here,
according to Youdi, is "une belle chose, une chose inouïe"; but in
either language, it is a passage of posturing, and stands out as such,
almost as much as Clov's late soliloquy in *Endgame,* the one beginning, "They said to me, That's love, yes, yes, not a doubt, now you
see how . . . how easy it is." Surely these gassy idealisms, invoked
only to earn pity for the protagonist, are unworthy of Beckett; his
bitterness doesn't have to be earned at such an exaggerated price in
naïve idealism. It can be drawn, and in most of Beckett's work is
drawn, from a severe if limited contemplation of the real world and
a conceivable mind within it.

The second fault is illustrated by Beckett's one major fiction since
the trilogy, *How It Is* (1961 French, 1964 English). The problems
which this narrative poses itself, in the form of deliberate deprivations, are so massive that they overwhelm anything that can be
achieved within their limits. Throughout the book the unnamed
speaker grovels and gropes aimlessly, face down in icy mud; he
speaks only in gasps and broken ejaculations, dispensing entirely with
punctuation and often with syntax. In the one episode, he encounters
a similar being, Pim, with whom he communicates exclusively through
sadistic devices (clawing, pounding, gouging with a can-opener), but
to no particular conclusion. Abandoned by Pim, he looks forward
only to encountering a creature named Bom, toward whom he will
play the same role that Pim played toward him. Perhaps the process
will continue indefinitely through countless random combinations
and permutations; there is certainly no thought that it will lead to
any conclusion. Evidently this is how Beckett came to see it; and this
is certainly how he tells it. A monotony of pain has seldom been rendered so monotonously or so painfully. The language of *How It Is,*
like the landscapes inner and outer, is scrupulously drab—literal, flat,
and repetitious, with only a rare indulgence in nuance or rhythmic
subtlety. One can't fail to stand in awe of the artistic integrity that

brought Beckett to this dark, dead pocket of imaginative prose, while still feeling that in the course of assassinating the novel—an avowed aim—he has killed a good deal else.

Hitherto, I have said almost nothing about Beckett's dramatic work, not because it seems unimportant, but because from the special aspect of Joycean influence, it seems to embody a set of themes and devices which Beckett had to isolate from his fiction before he could write what seem to me to be the very finest of his works. The time-killing tragic clowns of *Godot* and *Endgame* have to be seen primarily from the outside, by the physical eye, so that we get only rare and selective glimpses of what goes on within them. It's the irregular in-and-out of this motion, the alternation of anguish with a vacancy which is particularly effective and possible onstage, that gives Beckett's plays their agonizing rhythm. (Vacancy onstage is effective because in the theater-situation we anticipate poise, intention, action, and are in a state of active imbalance when we don't get it; it is possible because characters on a stage can stand still, do nothing, and yet be overwhelmingly present, while on the printed page the flow of words has to continue, and the reader simply loses sight of what is not actively presented.) As a writer for the stage, Beckett not only owes little that is distinctive to Joyce, he is far and away superior, primarily because of his extraordinary gift for interweaving the rhythms of speech and action. A classic example occurs toward the end of *Godot,* where Pozzo and Lucky have tripped over each other, Vladimir has fallen trying to help them, and Estragon, torn between trying to help them all back up and an impulse to go off by himself, is suddenly revolted by a bad smell:

ESTRAGON: (*recoiling*). Who farted?
VLADIMIR: Pozzo.
POZZO: Here! Here! Pity!
ESTRAGON: It's revolting!
VLADIMIR: Quick! Give me your hand!

ESTRAGON: I'm going. (*Pause. Louder.*) I'm going.

VLADIMIR: Well, I suppose in the end I'll get up by myself.
(*He tries, fails.*) In the fullness of time.

ESTRAGON: What's the matter with you?

VLADIMIR: Go to hell.

ESTRAGON: Are you staying there?

VLADIMIR: For the time being.

ESTRAGON: Come on, get up, you'll catch a chill.

VLADIMIR: Don't worry about me.

ESTRAGON: Come on, Didi, don't be pig-headed!
*He stretches out his hand which Vladimir makes haste to
seize.*

VLADIMIR: Pull!
Estragon pulls, stumbles, falls. Long silence.

POZZO: Help!

VLADIMIR: We've arrived.

POZZO: Who are you?

VLADIMIR: We are men.
Silence.

That seems to me to be metaphysical low comedy of a very high
order, purer because more physical and elementary than anything
which lay in Joyce's range. The sequence is perfect as it is; and we
have only to imagine it in the prose of *Watt*, or in any prose fiction
at all for that matter, to sense that in that form it would be a lot less
than perfect. The schism that Beckett underwent when he divided
himself into dramatist and narrator must have been quite as important
to his development as his passage from French to English.

Underlying all these formal considerations is a matter which is not
very easy to talk about, but which any reader of Beckett's *oeuvre* can
hardly avoid sensing—I mean the presence of a quality which, for
lack of a better word, can be called the sacred. Beckett himself does
not try to represent directly this condition. (In *Molloy,* there is a use

or two of "azur," Mallarmé's sacred word; but it disappears in the translation, and is never used, systematically or otherwise, thereafter.) His nasty, disintegrating, foul-mouthed old men do not appear likely candidates for canonization, and in fact they do not so much contain the sacred as stand (or crawl or creep) in its presence. Through their rage, their impatience, their compulsion to make and destroy formulas, we sense something that moves them far beyond the prudent accommodations of the here and now. They are willing to shred the world and themselves into little pieces if only they can understand before they die what it has meant to be a human being. This quality, at which one can only gesture inadequately with words like "sacred," is wholly unrelated to ecclesiasticism or any sense of reverence for the divinity—who, to the Beckett spokesmen, often seems like the cruel perpetrator of a set of inhuman practical jokes. There is no sense of awe or hush in Beckett's approach to the sacred, no strained spiritual effort, no talk of the soul or patter about its dark night, *via negativa,* and so forth and so on. Beckett's saints are do-it-yourselfers. They have a healthy sense of reluctance about the saintly vocation; they spit and snarl, they try to shirk and evade their responsibilities. But by incessantly adding, subtracting, multiplying, and dividing the meager quantum of their thoughts, they bring themselves into the presence of, or at least very close to, the pure, informulable, minimal essence of being—close enough so that its radiance is felt. Admittedly, this is not "the sacred" in the sense of "the other-worldly," but it is quite as remote from the easy quotidian as the old "sacred" used to be; and alongside its pains, palaver like Joyce's youthful talk of "epiphanies," and the Shelleyan ecstasies of Stephen Dedalus, start to sound pretentious and inauthentic. I speak here only of the youthful Joyce. At the height of their achievement both Joyce and Beckett bring us into the presence of a direct vision, beyond the genres of tragedy and comedy, from which most of the screen elements of traditional fiction, such as "action," "characterization," and "rendering," have dropped away. They are replaced by a silent mutual enfolding, a perception of, if not contact with, oneness of being—congruent structures of mind, mood, and cosmos effortlessly flowing into one another. Probably Beckett does not carry this vision further than Joyce; but he pursues its traces more single-mindedly, perhaps because he doubts it more deeply.

Seen as a spiritual activity which reaches through art to some sort of ultimate, however defined, Beckett's writing is inevitably self-destructive—that is, it uses literature, and uses it up, in the service of an imperative which lies beyond words arranged to produce effects. Having found, essentially in the trilogy, the path to his end, Beckett in his later writings has been chiefly concerned with shortening it. One is reminded of chess problems which specify, "White to play and mate in three moves." Or else he is in the position of those prisoners who had been locked up together for so long that they did not need to tell their jokes at full length, but merely referred to them by number—"Twenty-seven!" "Forty-three!" and so forth—each number followed by a roar of laughter. In the case of Beckett, there would also have to be a shriek of despair, intermingled.

All this bespeaks a rather special attitude on Beckett's part toward the absurd; it is a quick unsettling perception, leading elsewhere. One could think of secular Buddhism, if that isn't a tautology; Beckett's vision is the last step this side of Zen, and his absurdity serves the same end as Zen-absurdity, to open cracks in the texture of things for the vision to shine through. Joyce is an artist of transparency, Beckett of these cracks and grotesque disparities. But the fact of vision, hard as that concept is to define or illustrate, is the main element uniting Beckett with Joyce. Beckett is the chief post-Joycean novelist to throw away his predecessor's machinery and concentrate on the attempt at vision. In Nabokov, for example, we will find a novelist who has remained relatively indifferent to vision, but concentrated on verbal machinery. Quietism is Beckett's end, and his vision flowers out of a deep, contemplative quiet.

The concepts of ending and finality fascinate Beckett; his books are all studies of terminal cases under indefinite reprieve; and anyone who cites him as a special instance of Joycean influence has to face the possibility that he represents the last closed doorway in that cul-de-sac down which Joyce is said to have led the English novel. He is, in effect, the promised end. Sweeping as it is, such a diagnosis may some day win general acceptance. In music and art, modern culture of the "advanced" West appears to be *in extremis*—why not in literature as well? If not in Beckett, then sooner or later elsewhere, in some figure or other, the working-out of those principles given us at the Renaissance is bound to come to an end, as the classical world is now seen to have come to an end with Boethius. But only hindsight enables us to draw these historic starting and finishing lines, and even so they are no more than mnemonic conveniences. At least for the moment, therefore, an elegiac mood over Beckett is strictly optional. He works only at the very highest pitch, using minimal materials and aiming at a very narrow range of effects; the sense that he is squeezing the last meager drops from a very dry sponge is the consequence of a deliberate artistic decision, not of The Decline of the West. His endings, long threatened and desperately struggled against, are generally equivocal when they arrive, because to say the last word on man is impossible, however grim his condition. (Zeno's paradox has a special application here: if the last word can be said, somebody must exist to say it, about whom at least one further thing can be said.) As he passionately refuses formulas for himself, so it seems misleading or worse to encapsulate Beckett in a formula. He has kept open the possibilities of humanity by cutting the throat of literature and forcing his readers to confront naked conditions of mere existence— without sham exhilaration or despair, but coldly, very coldly.

CHAPTER FIVE

CARLO EMILIO GADDA

IN THE VERY FIRST ITEM within his collection of short journalistic travelogues titled *Le Meraviglie d'Italia,* Carlo Emilio Gadda discusses, with a preternatural solemnity verging on heavy irony, the Freudian theory that behind every pattern of adult behavior lies a childhood trauma, buried but capable of resurrection. Surely there is good evidence for this hypothesis, he concludes weightily; and moves on to describe a veritable cornucopia of his own fixations with their originating traumas. Because as a child he played in the park surrounding the great Sforza castello in Milan, he has always been a claustrophile, addicted to towers, dungeons, churches, closed forms. His mania for the military (a mania which of course is wholly imaginary) he traces to all the soldiers who marched so splendidly through the streets in those far-off days and tried to make up to girls in the park. But the most important trauma, which needs no explanation, came when, as a little signorino momentarily neglected by his nursemaid, he was playing at being a tiger. He was busy being a real tiger, prowling on all fours through the "jungle"—the shrubbery of the park—when he happened to put one of his forepaws into a "marmellata," that is, a turd.

The episode, like most of Gadda's, is simple but controlling. All his major writings, though they start bravely in some ostensible direction and make preliminary progress toward it, fall sooner or later into a filthy and disgusting mess. They bog down in excessive details and elaborate irrelevancies, spin off into linguistic gyrations, and finally—

as if confessing all delays and subterfuges to be useless in the end—plunge toward a vision of ultimate evil, an intricate and accumulated filth before which the author can only shudder and stop. The author's problem is not to reach that inevitable end, but to delay or avoid it. One has a great sense in reading Gadda, as in reading Beckett, that the story is forcing itself out across obstacles interposed by the reluctant author—that he knows where it's going, and doesn't want it to get there. This is part of a rather distinct though never formally defined Gadda-persona, who is severe, withdrawn, ironic, correct—a literary functionary, of rather narrow and old-fashioned tastes. He is not only erudite, but pedantic, much given to planting allusions and personal recollections in his prose, and then footnoting them at the bottom of the page. He often takes occasion to reassure the reader that this or that detail of his narrative is historically accurate; and this crucial point is often a linguistic one, to the effect that such and such a word was spoken when and where he has used it, and carried the peculiar import he assigns it. Being such a clean-minded man in matters of speech, he is inevitably a man of nasty ideas, with a deep relish for garbled and distorted dialects, among which his own, especially in moments of deep feeling, is particularly colorful. The normal run of his prose is elevated, polysyllabic, periphrastic, poised, and slightly aloof; but lists seem to excite him, whether they are lists of objects for sale in a flea market, or foods that might be eaten at an assembly of gross and uncontrollable gourmands. He plunges into such lists like a man frenziedly scratching an open sore; and in the course of their pouring forth, the language is grotesquely smeared and distorted, with accumulated diminutives and adjectival suffixes and agglutinated verbal complexes which seem pasted together by the heat of the author's raging disgust. He makes much use of contaminated language—Italian smeared over with layers of Spanish, Latin, Greek, and the special distortions of regional dialect—romano, milanese, veneziano. And beyond these quasi-realistic devices, always pressuring the language and forcing it out of shape like a landscape of Vlaminck, is the overpowering feeling of the author's own tastes and attitudes, his presence just around the corner of the word.

In an early novel only recently published (this is another Gaddaesque mess, to which we will have to come), he is describing a disagreeable young man whose family and money and connections—and whose interest in things mechanical—have kept him, hitherto, out of various sorts of trouble.

> Fino a quei giorni del '15 la meccanica lo aveva, così, preso e tenuto, evitandogli insomma tutti i rovi e le spine di cui è piantato il calvario tetro di certe catastrofiche adolescenze.
>
> Tutt'al più qualche signorina un po' romantica e fogazzaroide, facile a sospirar de' tramonti e proclive agli esercizi calligrafici a base di Pascoli e Chiesa di Polenta nell'album rilegato e dorato, o tutt'al più qualche serva superlativa in salute, odorosa di rosmarino e di cipolla, avevano avuto occasione, fra un corridoio e l'altro, d'assaporare qualche suo madrigale un po' perentorio: mentre che dalle sale venivano le voci di tutti, "che in quel momento non ci pensavano"; o in qualche passo di montagna difficile, che per combinazione eran "rimasti indietro," al ritorno da qualche gita in Valsàssina, inghirlandata da ciclamini stanchi e di ricordi manzonioni un poco rientrati [pp. 107-8].

> Until these days of '15, mechanics had thus captured and held him, shielding him in short from all the brambles and thorns that one finds planted along the dark calvary of certain catastrophic adolescences.
>
> At most some little girl, a bit romantic and fogazzaroid, quick to breathe in the evening breezes and likely to perform calligraphic exercises founded on Pascoli and the Church of Polenta in the bound and gilded album—or at the very outside, some servant girl in superlatively robust health, redolent of rosemary and onions, might have had occasion, between one corridor and another, to relish one of his slightly peremptory madrigals: while from the salon came the voices of all those people "who aren't giving a thought to us now"; or else in some difficult mountain pass where by chance they had "lingered behind" on their way back from a hike in Valsàssina, the girl garlanded with tired cyclamens and slightly washed-out recollections of Manzoni [tr. RMA].

The girl might, it seems, have been a little romantic and "fogazzaroid"—that is, soft in the head from reading the novels of Fogazzaro; her calligraphic exercises under the poems of Pascoli and Carducci

("Alla Chiesa di Polenta") further show her susceptibility to heroic-pathetic 19th-century romanticism. The servant girl's abundant health is rendered a little rude by the whiff of onion she gives off, as the young man's madrigal loses a good deal by being peremptory; and the paragraph trails off in a sour smell of "tired cyclamens and slightly washed-out recollections of Manzoni." A special ugly little overtone is provided by the apparently irrelevant "cyclamens"; "ciclamini im-boscati" are draft-evaders (shy wood-flowers, hiding out from the draft), and the whole novel turns on the fact that Paolo Velaschi, whose good bourgeois family has found a way to keep him out of the army, takes advantage of his home-front job to seduce dumb Zoraide, the wife of Luigi, who has had to go. The workmen of the factory lie in wait for Paolo and beat him up; it is, as his family says in in-dignation, an "imboscato," an ambush. But Paolo is also an "im-boscato," a draft-dodger. The "ricordi manzoniani" I can't make more specific than a vague recollection of Renzo and Lucia, chaste *promessi sposi* here invoked ironically as a counterpart to blowsy modern promiscuity.

This paragraph is only in the vaguest sense relevant to the funda-mentally trivial anecdote to which *La meccanica* can, as a narrative, be reduced. (More striking as a deliberate digression is a sizable financial, legal, and social history of the charitable foundation in which Luigi got his slogan-ridden education—a sardonic, satiric fable of sublime good intentions adrift in a squalid, rancid, and louche underworld of Milanese lumpen-proletarians.) Paolo, though a fool-ish and empty young man, is not much of a satiric target, and the author is not really much interested in contrasting him with Luigi, who though trained to a different rhetoric is also a foolish and vacant young man. The paragraph wanders within itself, to be sure, and the syntax is loose and sleazy, as if sliding from afterthought to after-thought, without help from grammar or controlling intention. But as the narrative bogs down in these tag ends of hazy recollection, it branches out literally into a tangle of puns and allusions, generally

denigratory. Everything in the description is "sort of" ("qualche" is
the word most frequently used in the passage) and the blurred presentation, like a loosely woven sieve, seems designed to allow ugly
realities to ooze through the interstices.

The end of the novella is not filled out, but can be sensed. As a result of Paolo's beating, the police have been alerted and are now on
the lookout, so that sooner rather than later both Paolo, the victim of
the attack, and Gildo, Luigi's cousin (ex-barber, ex-motorcycle thief)
who organized it, will have to "go"—"go" in the sense of the word
peculiar to 1915, as Luigi has already gone. And the whole fiction
then reverberates to an earlier passage in which the young men tramp
off to inevitable slaughter—their bravery and vitality and pathetic
good intentions all smashed under a war machine run by incompetent
generals, corrupt bankers, and conniving politicians. The time of the
novel is 1915, but in the telling that war is silently contaminated
with the gallant but futile struggles of 1848, when once before, as so
often in history, Italian boys were thrown against the cold, competent
armies of the north, with predestined results. This is the hopeless
mess toward which everything in the novel is gravitating; and in
sensing it, one senses also the reason for the long delays and wordy
descriptions, the irrelevancies and elaborate details which clog the
action. As Bloom progresses toward the hour of his wife's infidelity
through one irrelevancy and time-killing distraction after another, so
Gadda resists the movement of his story toward its end; yet through
indirections and intimations, he admits it, dallies with it, and lets its
presence work to tantalize the reader.

Another sort of mess that Gadda cultivates—it seems trivial, but
has a certain importance—is bibliographical. His books have generally appeared in disconnected pieces, at a considerable interval after
their composition, and several times over. What seems a light, ironic,
journalistic sketch is sometimes reworked—or not even reworked,
simply incorporated—as part of a new and generally darker whole.
La meccanica, for example, includes several units of what was first

published as *Novelle del ducato in fiamme* (1953), and in more developed form as part of *Accoppiamenti giudiziosi* (1963). *La meccanica* was published in 1970, but is described as the first of Gadda's novels, a youthful work from about 1928 or 1929 except for one unit going back to 1924; antedating both *La cognizione del dolore* (1938-40) (which was itself begun as a travel sketch for inclusion among *Le meraviglie d'Italia*, assembled in 1939) and *Quer pasticciaccio brutto di via Merulana* (1957). What then is the status of the fragments in *Novelle del ducato in fiamme?* Are they first drafts toward *La meccanica* or fragments from an already envisioned novel? There's reason for thinking some of them more primitive, less developed, in their first form, than in the context of the "finished" novel; but this is guesswork, and unless Gadda wants to, and is able to, clear it up, it remains one more mess surrounding the interpretation of his mind and thought.* The fact is, I think it is not a particularly unwelcome mess as far as Gadda is concerned. He gives one the impression of a laminated and labyrinthine personality, whose books are created out of a long personal development, and all of them bear the marks of that development. In this respect, particularly, he resembles Joyce, whose career was one long self-dissection, and who never hesitated to let the specific details of his personal situation shine through the fic-

---

* The kind of box one gets into is illustrated by the opening sentence of "L'armata se ne va," third of the *Novelle del ducato in fiamme.* Sans introduction or explanation, someone in the latter says, "Vedrò di parlare per te, come dici. Ma se non ci riesco . . . non sarà colpa mia, credilo, se dovrai andare anche tu . . . ." In *La meccanica,* Zoraide, concluding her discussion with Gildo, smiles and says, "vedarò de metar 'na parola anca per tì. Se po' i me dirà de nò, mi no ghe n'avarò colpa, se te tocarà 'ndare 'nca ti . . . ." If *La meccanica* was a novel in 1928-29, the speech was probably written in dialect for Zoraide, translated into "correct" Italian for "L'armata se ne va," and then returned to dialect for the final version of the novella. On the other hand, it leads directly in both versions to an essay, not a narrative, an essay on the overtones of the verb "andare" in 1848 and 1915. So it's just as easy to suppose that the essay was overlaid by an increasingly dramatic story as that the story was modified to conform with the essay.

tional constructs that he carefully elaborated around it, like an oyster encrusting a grain of sand with pearl-stuff.

A first impression of *Cognizione del dolore*—the first-written though second-published of Gadda's two major unfinished novels— is that its narrator is hopelessly incompetent. In labyrinthine meanders he wanders away from whatever subject he has undertaken, and entangles himself in irrelevant intricacies from which he seems doomed never to escape. *Nistitúos provinciales de vigilancia para la noche* there certainly were in Madaragàl, and veterans from the ferocious war of 1924 with Parapagàl were encouraged to serve in them. But might not their wounds and disabilities interfere with the service of these patriotic heroes as night watchmen? The question, it appears, had been subject to litigation, but ambivalent and contradictory answers had been given: in Terepàttola yes, in Pastrufazio no—though we are carefully *not* told what the question is to which these are the answers. Meanwhile, we have wandered, by way of a certain scandal at a town called Lukones, into a general geographical account of the area, which breaks off abruptly to explain that the bicycle guard of the Lukones area was *not* named Pedro Mahagones or Manganones, as he had indicated and everyone had thought, but instead Gaetano Palumbo. Only slowly, by means of elaborate circumstantial roundabouts, do we learn—by way of the visiting peddler who told the story, but only in hints and indirections, and by way also of the three old women who spread it—that the watchman was really Palumbo, not Mahagones, and that, though deafened during the war by a grenade, he had miraculously recovered his hearing. And then, without further explanation, with the "scandal" still hanging in mid-air, we are off on an account of the various hideous villas—and villette and villule and villone and casa villerecche—built by the Pastrufazian architects and (presumably) guarded by Gaetano Palumbo. But we still don't know anything of how he lost and then recovered his hearing, or what this has to do with a scandal—though we know a lot of useless elaborate circumstance about Peppa the washerwoman and her seven brothers and sisters, Beppina or Beppa with her odd way of urinating, and Pina—three weird sisters with overlapping names, who had nothing to do with the story that we haven't yet been told, but who repeated it. Meanwhile, we're off on a list of villas and villatial or villaresque horrors.

Yet this shambling and disorganized narrator, perhaps as part of his very inefficiency, is always revealing some disgusting or hideous or barbaric facet of life in Madaragàl. All the patriotic rhetoric of the war with Parapagàl is cut down to the vision of illiterate peons from squalid villages slaughtering and mutilating one another over a piece of meaningless real estate known simply as "quota 131." A flood of rhetoric is devoted to covering the surface of things; but as it winds itself up toward an ecstasy of euphemism, ugly truths seep in laterally, as it were, in spite of the words, which are trying to keep them out:

> Tutti, o almeno quasi tutti, d'altronde, nella zona di Lukones, s'erano messi d'impegno e di buona volontà, visto che pagare avevan pagato, a farsi un'idea di quelle pericolose ronde nel buio: e avevano finito per mandar giú anche l'importanza e la delicatezza dell'incarico che gravava sulle sue spalle, per quanto è lunga e buia la notte, e tutti oramai ci credevano, all'importanza: dacché non sempre la buona fama d'un uomo, nel Sud-America, o la notorietà di un funzionario, dipende dalla inutilità delle sue mansioni [p. 50].

> They had all, or at least almost all of them, in the area of Lukones for that matter, put themselves to task, and gladly, seeing that pay they must and had done, to form an idea of these perilous rounds in the dark: and had finished by gulping down both the importance and the delicacy of the responsibility that rested on his shoulders, seeing how long and dark the night is, and they all now believed in it, the importance, that is: since it isn't always, in South America anyway, that a man's good name or the notoriety of an official depends on the uselessness of his tasks [tr. RMA].

The pedantic, yet nervous self-correction with which the sentence begins is characteristic of our narrator's addiction to false starts; "d'altronde" (on the other hand) distinguishes this assertion uselessly as an alternative to the preceding one, with which in fact it has nothing to do. The contrasting ideas of "messi d'impegno" and "di buona volontà" are further entangled by the confusing phrase "visto che pagare avevan pagato" —in which the original idea of "since pay they mus̲t" is muscled under by the safer statement, "since they had already paid." When they finish their meditation on the importance and delicacy of the tasks for which they pay, they are finally able to "mandar giú" at least the importance—delicacy gets lost in the shuffle; and the verb is carefully chosen. Literally the citizens "send it down," idiomatically they swallow or choke down the notion with some repugnance, and on a latent level they put it down with the rest of the shit. And the whole sentence winds up with the solemn, ironic assurance that in South America it isn't always the case that the good name of a man or the notoriety of an official (distinguished yet equated as the pinnacle of aspiration in the two spheres) depends on the uselessness of his functions. This is not always the case, just in general. The shining exception is evidently to be the sinister and brutal watchman, Gaetano Palumbo, about whose "miracle" we are already darkly (and very justifiably) suspicious.

The sentence is typically Gaddaesque in its intricate scheme of inflection (the grammatical involvements are as devious yet tenacious as those of Proust); it is notable for its many uncoiling subordinate clauses, its high level of euphemism, the slow distillation of its irony. The style works down from initial elevation toward a compressed vision of disgust, picking its way with deliberate and meticulous care from one puddle of moral filth to another. Elaborate syntax, a finicky and precious vocabulary, false starts and pedantic self-corrections, all serve our sense of a reluctant narrator. Yet under the author's pomposities or alongside them, the truth emerges, slipping out sometimes despite his apparent intention. Pastrufazio, the most dynamic city of the country, "spàppola" spatters, its suburbs off to the west and south—a bit sticky, and kind of filthy, if the truth be told—for a hundred kilometers or so. It is eight pages later when the night watchman pushes his bicycle into town, avoiding with his shoes and tires the "fianta verdastra e pillacherosa spappata dalle vaccine" along the little road leading to the center of the town. The verb "spappolare" or "spappare," which stands out as just a trifle precious in the first usage, receives its justification in the second, where the suburbs of Pastrufazio are seen retrospectively as greenish, splashy cow-turds spattered along a path.

Gadda's language is highly textured and many leveled, laced with Spanish, Latin, and pompous scientific erudition both real and fake; it is erratic in syntax, as if out of control, prone to run its sentences into obsessive, interminable lists, but also to break off suddenly and then explode in an exclamatory afterthought. The author is very conscious of textures, of material surfaces, their minglings, and their contrasts: at one point a sweaty peon lumbers across a walk and through a doorway, leaving cakes of compressed dung behind him while a cat slips alongside him, a velvety shadow between the man's feet. On the mat before the Villa Agostini is written "Salve Hospes"; a cock crowing nearby asserts himself, "ecco un cocco, ecco un cocco, ecco un cocco," and the two messages run together in a blur, "cocco hospes, cocco hospes, cocco ospite té!" The nervous animism of nature, the constant agitation of objects, their power to stick in the recurrent mind, even to generate themselves by spawning lists which the narrator is powerless to control—all this leads toward and points up the psychic emptiness and sickness of the central character in the novel, Don Gonzalo. An electrical engineer by trade, working in Pastrufazio, he is evidently a philosopher by temperament, a distant and ironic contemplator of the human scene. Plato and Kant are his professed interests, but in lieu of them both, it's not hard to sense that another name could be substituted as the guiding spirit of his life, and that is Schopenhauer.

With his usual spirit of mystification, Gadda refers several times to an ancient Inca curse, an illness without a name, described in an early book of colonial times; he also invokes the solemn spirit of genealogy, and describes a lengthy lineage from which Don Gonzalo presumably

derived a disposition to his withering psychic disease. But it is a disease which has widened and generalized, under the influence of
thought, from a particular *male* (ailment) to a general *male* (evil)
afflicting human nature. If Palumbo and the gangster movement he
serves constitute an expression of will, capable of striking cash money
from the most unlikely villas, Gonzalo the desolate hidalgo lives in
the sphere of thought, of idea; he sees the world under that aspect,
and loathes it. Three areas where his malady of thought, and its con-
sequent denial of self, manifest themselves most vividly are in the
family, at table, and in a diatribe on syntax.

At the age of forty-four, Don Gonzalo is a confirmed bachelor and
an anguished son: anguished, because he feels excluded from the
shower of loving charity that his mother, with her gift of universal
sympathy, pours on everyone. She pours it on him too, but on him no
more than on Beppa and Pina and the smelly peon who leaves a trail
of dung-cakes on the living-room floor as he comes in to light the fire.
Gonzalo's brother, killed in the war, absorbs an inordinate amount of
the mother's grief and devotion—or so it seems to the jealous eye of
the hidalgo; and the rest of her kindness is diffused in the casual,
undiscriminating charities that make her universally beloved—and
that make the villa ramshackle, the house of Pirobuttiro a model of
shabby gentility. Comparisons with Proust have been made on the
score of the scene in which Don Gonzalo tramples underfoot the portrait of his father, and smashes a watch of some sort—whether gold
or silver or nickel-plated, depending on the malice of the particular
scandal-monger reciting the story. But the comparison is superficial
at best; the specific act may be similar, but the complex of reasons behind it is very different. Gonzalo is enraged with his father (as nearly
as we can discover) for having left the family saddled with a useless
and impractical villa; he smashes the watch because it has been given
to him as a graduation present at a time when he is in need of a new
pair of shoes. His exasperation has more to do with that of Jason
Compson (shackled for life with the task of maintaining a myth of

family gentility without the means to do it) than with the sadistic
tantrums and displays of Mlle. Vinteuil.

Basically Gonzalo is an outcast from the feast of life. His appetite
for affection and reassurance is boundless, inordinate; but that is because his sense of ego, selfhood, is dying within him. The contradiction comes out in the matter of eating. Don Gonzalo is reputed to be
a monstrous, uncontrollable gormandizer. That lobster or crab on
which he nearly choked to death in Babylon is exaggerated, in popular rumor, to a great, glaring monster, almost as fiendish as its glut-
tonous devourer. The terrible bottles of wine that he consumes are
enumerated as if they were evidence of hideous and inordinate lux-
ury. Yet in "reality," so far as we are given to see that, the hidalgo is
an abstemious dyspeptic—so eaten up, himself, by jealousy and frustration as scarcely to be able to swallow a mouthful of soup for the
bile that chokes him.

When he figures this great, gross, pragmatical pig of a world—in
a long silent fantasy toward the end of the novel—he figures it under
the guise of a station restaurant full of stuffed shirts pretending to be
individuals, and glutting themselves on food and complacent observ-
ances by way of sustaining this illusion. There they sit, waited on by
frock-coats as empty as themselves, bloated with the empty dignity of
their situations, flattering one another and themselves with empty
postures of mutual admiration:

> Sí, sí: erano consideratissimi, i fracs. Signori seri, nei "restaurants"
> delle stazioni, e da prender sul serio, ordinavano loro con perfetta
> serietà "un ossobuco con risotto." Ed essi, con cenni premurosi, an-
> nuivano. E ciò nel pieno possesso delle rispettive facoltà mentali. Tutti
> erano presi sul serio: e si avevano in grande considerazione gli uni gli
> altri. Gli attavolati si sentivano sodali nella eletta situazione delle
> poppe, nella usucapzione d'un molleggio adeguato all-importanza del
> loro deretano, nella dignità del comando. Gli uni si compiacevano della
> presenza degli altri, desiderata platea. E a nessuno veniva fatto di
> pensare, sogguardando il vicino, "quanto è fesso!" [p. 198].

> Yes, yes; they were most distinguished, the shirtfronts. Serious gentle-
> men in the restaurants of the stations, gentlemen to be taken seriously,

ordered for themselves with perfect seriousness "an ossobuco with rice."
And the others, with eager gestures, complied. And all this in full possession of their respective mental faculties. All were taken with the
greatest seriousness; and the one group was held in the highest esteem
by the other. Those at the tables felt themselves partakers in the distinguished situation of their poops, in the usufruction of a cushioning ade-
quate to the importance of their rear ends, in the dignity of command.
One group was delighted by the presence of the other, a much-desired
audience. And to none of them did it ever occur to say, glancing at his
neighbor, "What an ass!" [tr. RMA].

Under the surface of things, it goes without saying, the restaurant is
a disaster; the food is a greasy mess, none of the fruit-knives cut, the
waiters curse and kick at each other, and in a final vision slimy spears
of asparagus, dripping with butter, spiral off, followed by water-
spouts of risotti. And yet,

> Tutti, tutti: e piú che mai quei signori attavolati. Tutti erano con-
> sideratissimi! A nessuno, mai, era mai venuto in mente di sospettare
> che potessero anche essere dei bischeri, putacaso, dei bambini di tre
> anni.
>
>   *   *   *
>
> E quella era la vita [p. 199].
>
> All of them, all: and most especially the gentlemen at the tables. All
> were most distinguished! None of them, ever, had ever thought of sus-
> pecting that they themselves might be nincompoops, not to say three-
> year-olds.
>
>   *   *   *
>
> And that was life [tr. RMA].

It is life, of course, as seen not by a rigid and disinterested moralist,
but by a man who is starving to death, physically and for lack of self-
esteem. Don Gonzalo rejects the whorish world of appearances, to be
Lord and Prince in the ruined tower of his own soul. Knowing *dolore*
to the very dregs, he negates himself, leaving nothing to possibility,
frozen in the tragic mask of contempt. Hence, when his mother is
murdered by the bestial agent of the Nistitúo, that black night, the

hidalgo is triply responsible—he refused to subscribe to "protection," he fired the peon who might have helped against the murderer, and he went away himself, at the moment when he was most needed.* The book deepens his world of remorse to the point of the absolutely unbearable, then breaks off, leaving the weight still to fall on him, leaving the question open whether the mother will live or die.

The root of this deep, unredeemable disorder, this near-abdication of the author before the horror of his own vision, is found in his diatribe against syntax, particularly against the pronouns "I" and "you." They constitute the myths of individuality—not formally "believed," so much as enacted by the strutting, pretentious "I" of the Roman daylight or the slinking, animalesque "I" of the Celtic forests—in either case, an unknown, unacknowledged, uncriticized, unexpressed subject of every proposition. The disgust it arouses can be expressed only by comparing it to a plate of food:

> Quando l'essere si parzializza, in un sacco, in una lercia trippa, i di cui confini sono più miserabili e più fessi di questo fesso muro pagatasse . . . che lei me lo scavalca in un salto . . . quando succede questo bel fatto . . . allora . . . è allora che l'io si determina, con la sua brava mònade in coppa, come il càppero sull'acciuga arrotolata sulla fetta di limone sulla costoletta alla viennese . . . [p. 126].

> When being gets parceled out into a sack, into a tub of foul guts, whose limits are more miserable and more stupid than this stupid tax-paying wall, which you could hop over at a bound . . . when this fine event takes place . . . then . . . that's when the I is determined, with its fine monad on the back of the skull, like the caper on the rolled-up anchovy on the lemon slice on the wiener schnitzel . . . [tr. RMA].

* I have oversimplified the ending of *Cognizione* here by assuming that the two chapters published in 1963 but omitted from the first publication of 1938-41 are an essential part of the book. We are given to understand that a final chapter, projected for about ten pages, but never written, is still missing and perhaps always will be. But "missing" is perhaps too strong a word; though the chapter has never been written, its general character is easy to envisage, and it's better intangibly sensed than flatly expressed. A good many final chapters of novels would be better off in the same anomalous condition.

This teetery structure, of the caper-self perched atop the anchovy atop the lemon peel atop the wiener schnitzel, is the hidalgo's ultimate abomination—or at least, so he says. Yet of course he can't get away from himself, even in the act of repudiating his self; his hypochondria is at least 90 percent self-laceration, self-exacerbation, preoccupation with self. The very contempt he feels for this railway-station-restaurant called life, and for the wiener-schnitzel selves infesting it, implies a setting of himself apart; physically, spiritually, intellectually, in every possible way, he maintains himself apart—and that implies not only a definition but an emphasis on self as a definable unit. His mother runs everything together; like a Joycean water-goddess, she is all devotion, self-sacrifice, sympathy, accommodation. She diffuses herself through the people of the countryside, indiscriminately, even as her son hardens himself against them, indiscriminately. His common appellation, "the hidalgo," mocks the stiffness of his remote and aloof posture; the trail of smelly gossip and rumor that follows him around cannot help suggesting that, in spite of himself, he is known as a "character."

In fact, he wants and does not want a self, as he really is a glutton on a self-imposed starvation diet, really is a man of profound tenderness self-condemned to bitterness and celibacy. The very form of the novel suggests anguished indecision, radical and immutable disorder, conflicting unresolvable motives. The book moves, not forward to a resolution or a conclusion, but like an ink-stain on a carpet, spreading out and sinking deeper. Intricate contaminations of language and exasperated, difficult syntax express the contaminated life and exasperated spirit toward which the Gaddan universe is inevitably and hopelessly sliding. *Cognizione del dolore* lives by its rhetoric; it is a complaint, an unbeliever's sermon *de vanitate mundi,* all the more despairing because it demonstrates the vanity of the persona delivering the sermon.

At the heart of Gadda's other great novel, *Quer pasticciaccio brutto di via Merulana,* is exactly the same constellation of forces as in *Cog-*

nizione; only the circumstances are slightly altered. The warm, weak woman (adored but taboo) is murdered at the beginning of the book, not at the end; the mordant intelligence is a policeman, tracking down the perpetrator of the murder, not a philosopher declaring *a priori* a condition. There is, thus, a little more semblance of forward motion to the plot: though Don Ciccio's investigation, following the stain-in-the-carpet pattern, spreads out and sinks into Roman society, at the same time it moves heavily after the specific criminal who murdered Liliana. But in the process of finding him, Don Ciccio finds so much filth, squalor, and hypocrisy—of which the murderer is victim and symptom, far more than cause—that pinning the specific outrage on him comes to seem anticlimactic, if not irrelevant. Seeing "justice" done is particularly irrelevant because the reader has come to understand, through Don Ciccio, how little of his motivation for tracking down the criminal is concern for justice, how much is jealousy. Like the hidalgo of the Serruchon, Don Ciccio of the Roman police force is an outcast from the feast of life. His landlady worships him because—well, for the reasons that landladies worship good tenants; but the men whom women adore, on whom they hang those erotic fantasies that color their entire lives, are of another cast altogether. Doctor Giuliano Valdarena, Liliana's cousin, should by all rights have been her lover and her murderer. But he was not, and the revenge that Don Ciccio burns to take on him remains forever smothered. There are other targets for his jealous resentment, men with the same arrogant, half-brutal assurance. Among the criminal element, Diomede Lanciani the pimp, and Enea Retalli alias Iginio, who may very well be the murderer, have all the fawning, obedient women they want—perhaps too many. Among the bourgeoisie, there are Don Lorenzo Corpi the bull-like priest, even Remo Baldinucci, the unproductive husband of Liliana—yet he has, produced by his obsequious wife, a whole string of extremely attractive "nieces," apart from the casual company of his incessant business trips. Insensitive, complacent, self-important figureheads, they are made as it were in the image of the civilization's presiding genius—the Shit, the Deuce, the Death's-Head, Mussolini in a word. Don Ciccio despises these figures of cruel and sterile Priapic vigor, surrounded as they are by fawning and submissive females. Yet he cannot help defining himself as in competition with them, in competition for the sympathy and attention and concern that they monopolize—and in that competition, he has no hope of winning. What Priapus appeals to is the sheer mindlessness of the rutting female, the impulse, of which she is but the agent, to spawn and submit. What defeats Don Ciccio in the end, producing an impulse which is just about to become repentance when the book breaks off, is the universal human mess of the world, a vision—alas!—of flesh and blood.

The whole movement of the novel is a smear. The criminals are incompetent as well as bloodthirsty; they murder unnecessarily and ferociously, while leaving obvious clues and marks of their identity. The detectives are crude in their bullying, clumsy in their deductions, as blunderheaded in following wrong leads as right ones. Everyone they question lies to them, evasively, confusingly, diffusely, inexhaustibly: "You've got a fine heap of lies, enough to last a month," says Corporal Pestalozzi at one point; and it's true, most of the characters are lavish in irrelevancies. And the author of the novel is just as likely to get entangled in stringy, irrelevant snarls of description or fantasy. A scrawny, one-eyed, semi-featherless chicken who flaps up before the corporal and drops a couple of small, elaborate turds in front of him is like an emblem of the story itself, and is described in devastating detail. Like the chicken, the phantom of justice, as Don Ciccio pursues it, leads from one splotch or puddle of human misery to another. Poverty has its own grotesque and fetid squalor, but the relatively rich also lead mean and miserable lives. The mess on via Merulana shows no signs of ever untangling itself properly; it simply spreads into the other stains on the smeary carpet of Italian society, till it is practically indistinguishable from the other messes. And there the novel, without concluding in any ostensible sense (other than the detective's revulsion and the start of his self-questioning) abruptly stops.

For all his elaborate irony and deep cynicism, Gadda seems to me a more humane writer than Joyce—less cold, less distanced in his point of view—at least that point from which he starts. He owes more to Manzoni than to Dante—that is, he likes to toy, not only with dialect and idiom, but with point of view, after the fashion of that novelist who, in the opening pages of *I promessi sposi,* could let you see life momentarily from the point of view of a couple of chickens being carried by the legs, upside-down, to market. Gadda too likes to get close up to life, though he never forgets to remind us of how bad it smells. To a much greater extent Joyce tends to stand above his characters, looking at the patterns they make or looking through them. I do not get the sense that for Gadda there is much to be seen by looking "through" a character. His personages do not have much depth of character, and there is nothing much beyond them; yet they are not flattened, one does not get the sense of dealing with stencils. The stupid ones contain no hidden wisdom, they are just stupid, and usually dirty and brutal as well. The thoughtful are helpless in the torment of their own thought. Like Joyce, Gadda celebrates in the end a failure of mind—a failure of accommodation to the mess and inexactness of people and history. Both men alternate between seeing this disaster of the mind on the one hand as hilariously comic and on the other hand in the darker tones of self-pity. The grotesque distorting mirror of other minds gives back to them fantastic, shivering images of themselves, with which they love to play elastic games—they are everywhere present in their fictions but nowhere explicitly.

The strongest influence of Joyce on Gadda has evidently been in the matter of prose style, where one must fight hard to avoid the adjective which is Gadda's pet abomination, *baroque.* On the whole, Gadda is less devoted to imitative form than is Joyce; as noted before, there's a strong side-flavoring of Proust (stylistic, I think, more than thematic); and an exercise like "Oxen of the Sun" is well outside

Gadda's range. His is a highly allusive and literary style, however, full of buried and not-so-buried allusions to literary history, literary analogues, and literary predecessors. Like Joyce also, Gadda is likely to get snagged at any moment on some of the author's personal history or hangups, he is ponderous with the weight of his erudition, but frequently punctuated with hoots of laughter or mockery of his own pretensions. Every tiger-hunt ends with a hand in a turd; and the anti-phase of this cynicism is a kind of strained emotional writing, more than a little reminiscent of Joyce's addiction to purple patches, which he is prone to enrich with swoons, languors, and other trappings of glimmering passion. One is intensely conscious of both authors as stylists, of the dynamics, contrivances, and contrasts into which the language flowers under their hands. It goes almost without saying that both move with the extraordinary modern fluidity that Joyce and Dostoevsky created from the realm of fantasy to the realm of "reality" and back again; a set-piece like Corporal Pestalozzi's daydream (in the *Pasticciaccio*) would be wholly unthinkable outside the context of the English novel of the 1920s. Gadda and Joyce both use inter-lingual punning, but to different effects; for Joyce the device often implies a mythic substructure or connection, for Gadda it is more likely to be a curlicue or roundabout executed either for its own sake or toward an ironic juxtaposition—in any case, an opaque rather than a transparent device.

Gadda, I think, has a deeper, more ingrained sense of vulgarity and its opposite than does Joyce; that is to say, lacking Joyce's powerful sense of original sin, in which all men are involved together, he has fewer democratic instincts, and is more conscious of manners. Joyce's social spectrum doesn't rise much above, or sink much below, the sphere of the ignobly decent: Gadda's grammar alone is aristocratic. Joyce had an immensely elaborate sense of structure, and used it primarily to enlarge the definition of the novel beyond what any previous writer of novels had ever dreamed of—he enlarged it, that is, in different and contradictory directions, making it more epic, obscene, mythical, parodic, visionary, and realistic than novels had ever been before. This was a tremendous individual achievement, it goes without saying, but it beat human nature thin to the point of transparency, and pointed the way toward dispensing with it, if not altogether, at least in very good part. The key to Gadda's lesser ambitions is the presence in his background, not of Dante, Blake, or Yeats (passionate schematizers, all), but of that eminently humane and proportional man, Alessandro Manzoni. They are evidence, as is Manzoni's single novel, of an immense and agonized humane consciousness. I'm not sure whether or not Gadda finds his humanity a burden, as in certain moods it is undoubtedly a torment; but it enables him to represent the common condition in a different and perhaps more direct way than Joyce's massive, multi-phase self-dissections.

CHAPTER SIX

DÖBLIN,
BROCH

IN GERMANY, Joyce was known early and favorably. Even where it is most obvious, however, in the work of Alfred Döblin and Hermann Broch, his influence is heavily diluted with other thematic and technical considerations; one sees it quickly, but comes almost as quickly to the end of it. *Alexanderplatz, Berlin* (1929) by Döblin is an urban novel like *Ulysses,* though it deals with a bigger, faster, tougher city, and slices through it at a much lower social level than Joyce ever tried to penetrate. Franz Biberkopf is an earnest, inward ox of a man, determined to be good and doubly determined because, as the novel opens, he has just finished four years in the pen for killing his "fiancée," a girl (like all the girls of Franz's particular milieu) who isn't above eking out a living on the streetcorner. Franz is not only dim of brain but deeply colored by the mores of his lumpentribe; and one of the elegant nuances of Döblin's not-always-nuanced novel is the delicate haze that his hero's brain throws over the professional life of females. Whoring doesn't really interfere with love; it's so normal, it just isn't important, as long as whoring is all it is. Of course if the girl shows a touch of personal interest in one of her johns, that stirs up caldrons of jealous rage in her lover, and is likely to get her kicked and beaten within an inch—either way—of her life. Franz is not a cruel or a bad man; by the standards of his set, he is a good one. But to let a girl feel fond of a customer is about as unthinkable as the notion that she might not be out on the street earning money at all.

The close perspective that this vision implies carries throughout the novel. Unlike the narrative voice, which is consistently sardonic and wise-guy ("I've seen it all before" as from a guttersnipe Koheleth), Franz Biberkopf hardly ever gets or attempts a perspective on events—he takes the rush of them head-on, and they flow over him like a river in flood. The flotsam and jetsam of the big city are here in overwhelming quantities—gaudy storefronts, flaring ads, industrial statistics, weather reports, the sequence of stops on a subway line, fragments of popular song, unrelated episodes and fantasies involving total strangers, the random and the miscellaneous. Stitched through the thick texture of social fact are a variety of leitmotifs and persistent rhythms which convey the mood of our hero.

This is a matter of some importance because Franz Biberkopf is a manic-depressive who, in undertaking to be "good" in a milieu where practically everyone else is "bad," has assumed a superhuman task for himself. His intentions are of the best and his strength is as the strength of ten, but he is not very bright, and he blunders into one trap after another. Each successive frustration is followed by a deeper and darker fit of sulky depression. In these moods, he is prone to see his life under various mythical and legendary aspects, which are presented ambiguously at best, and sometimes in a frankly hostile light. There is a fine and funny discussion of the Furies within Franz Biberkopf that may have led him to kill Ida, as they formerly tormented Orestes for killing Clytemnestra. But the mythology breaks off into an account of the laws of physics, without knowing which we can't possibly understand how the application of a wooden cream-whipper came to fracture the seventh and eighth ribs in line with Ida's left shoulder-blade. And when we've understood these laws of physics, and Franz's application of them to Ida, we clearly don't need to consider the Furies any further. "I'm not a Greek, I'm from Berlin" is one of the leitmotifs of the novel; it implies that when you're hip and sharp, you don't need any classical mythologies, and needn't take them into account.

On the other hand, Franz Biberkopf gets into his third and deepest tangle of trouble because of a purely and obviously mythical action. His most recent and most successful affair is with a gentle and devoted little prostitute whose real name is Sonia, but whom he calls Mieze. Proud of her devotion to him, he invites sinister Reinhold to hide in the bedroom and witness their happiness. The impression is too taking; Reinhold seizes his first occasion to attack Mieze and when she resists to murder her. The entire episode is a re-enactment, of which the narrator at least is very conscious, of Herodotus's story of Gyges. Its consequences all but destroy Franz Biberkopf. As the story develops, they don't quite do so; they lead to a prolonged and terrible struggle in the depths of his catatonic psyche, from which ultimately a new Franz Biberkopf is born. The process is darkly moving. But the very fact that we are concerned on this level with the central character of the novel suggests an affinity with Dostoevsky rather than Joyce. There's little or no transparency to Franz Biberkopf, and even less sense of void; we descend into him and into the roaring traffic of his subconscious (deliberately presented in the same words as the outward traffic of Berlin, forever tearing itself up and rebuilding) as into an ultimate dark pocket. Biberkopf is Biberkopf, not Ajax or Hercules; and the battered peace he finally attains seems to encompass that crucial phrase, "I'm not a Greek, I'm from Berlin." Death, who seems to be from Berlin too (he has the accent), conveys the thought to him in a fantastic colloquy; and so Biberkopf is reborn in humility and caution—good still, as he has always been good, and strong still, but not so confident of his single strength, which has always been the serpent in his garden of Eden. To the critical eye his redemption may seem a little contrived, since it depends on his getting a modest but regular job as assistant doorman in a medium-sized factory, such as he could have had any time in the novel, at least for all we can tell. Still, these are the hazards of the novel of pride, punishment, and personal redemption; and their prominence amply emphasizes the differences of Döblin's action and emphasis from the Joycean model. What produced in the first place the impression of

Joycean influence (which Döblin vigorously repudiated) was chiefly the counterpointed and jazzy rhythm of the background, the mechanism of city life. But the heart of the action was elsewhere.

The influence from Joyce that Döblin vigorously and rightly repudiated, Hermann Broch went out of his way to emphasize, though not so justifiably. He was an articulate man, with strong feelings about the destiny of the European novel and European culture in general; like many middle-Europeans of his age and milieu (1920s Vienna), he felt that with the war something solid and important had fallen out of the center of things, and that the very existence of the artist-poet-*Dichter* had thereby been called into question. Joyce, as the most intricate and resourceful writer of the age, was a crucial figure for Broch, partly as a symptom of a world-condition, partly as evidence of a possible set of responses to that condition. Apart from many private and occasional references to the work of Joyce, Broch on at least one occasion made explicit public profession of his views on Joyce's achievement. It is a complex declaration of abstract principles, compounded with deep admiration not only for *Ulysses* but also for *Finnegans Wake,* and yet tempered with some misgiving. It was published as a somewhat belated tribute on the occasion of Joyce's fiftieth birthday, as *James Joyce und die Gegenwart* (Wien, 1936); and, like everything Broch wrote, it's a curiously suggestive document. The abstract principles center around that by-now-familiar topos, the disintegration of the object (illustrated with examples from modern painting and modern physics); the admiration is primarily for Joycean polyphony and symbolic ingenuity; the misgivings are chiefly over the increasing privacy and incommunicability of the Joycean universe, in which language as a subject in itself has usurped over representation and communication. Joyce turned the polyphonic novel from an ethical course into an aesthetic one; Broch in his own work undertook to return that novel to what he understood as its proper course.

Of these various considerations, those involving specific fictional techniques might be expected to carry over most directly into Broch's own fiction; but on the whole they didn't, at least not in any explicit or obvious way. A reader without previous mental preparation could, I think, very well read straight through the trilogy of *The Sleep-walkers* (1928-31) and that immense lyrical-historical-epical romance, *The Death of Virgil* (1945) without thinking more than momentarily and peripherally of Joyce. But in fact there's very good reason to think of him more than occasionally and more than casually.

The three novels of *The Sleepwalkers* are carefully dated at fifteen-year intervals, 1888, 1903, and 1918; they trace (or, rather, imply) a developing state of moral and physical entropy, in which a general system of categorical and universal values is splintered and disintegrated to the point where even its absence is no longer remarked. Joachim von Pasenow, the central figure of the first novel, is a Prussian officer vaguely and sleepily aware of a moral code and his own relation to it. He is partly and momentarily led away from it, from his duties to the uniform, to his ancestral estates, and to his destined bride; the chief instigators of this restlessness are his dark, sensual, semi-literate Hungarian mistress, and his cynical, sophisticated friend, Eduard von Bertrand. But he is not led very far; as Eduard prophesies, not without a broad streak of disdain, he returns after a fleeting flirtation with the wide world and its disintegrated values to his traditional pre-fabricated role: he manages his estate, serves obediently the military machine of his country, and marries the expected girl, the blonde (not to say pallid) Elisabeth, heiress of a nearby squire. The final unit of the first novel underlines, in the author's person, Bertrand's contempt for these shallow and childish persons. Between docility and timidity, Joachim and Elisabeth go through the form of a chilly marriage, and the author dismisses them with perfunctory contempt:

> Nevertheless after some eighteen months they had their first child. It actually happened. How this came about cannot be told here. Besides, after the material for character construction already provided, the reader can imagine it for himself [p. 158].

So much for Joachim and Elisabeth; and in fact with these words the lady disappears from the trilogy for good, while her husband turns up in the third volume, thirty years later, under a wholly different configuration; if it weren't for his name one would hardly recognize him as the same neutral, negative person that he was in the first novel.

These transparent and unassertive characters, who amount to so little in themselves, nonetheless make up an interwoven counterpoint of voices which is greater than the sum of its parts—and here we start to sense, among these sleepwalkers, the looming presence of a pattern that transcends their conscious intentions and in fact their consciousness as a whole. In a first and wholly negative evidence, the characters as they advance through the trilogy become more and more transparent and ghostlike. Pasenow in the final novel is literally possessed by an idea; Esch, the obsessed bookkeeper who is the central figure of the second novel, is increasingly, throughout it and through the third, the solitary inhabitant of his own fantasy; and though Eduard von Bertrand reportedly commits suicide toward the end of the second novel, he reappears, modified almost unrecognizably, as an itinerant philosopher, lecturer, and seeker of spiritual light, midway through the third. There are intimations that he may be a type of Christ; they are buried intimations, but they are reinforced by the fact that the third novel brings us into the presence of an authentic Lazarus-figure. More positive if less portentous than these intimations of occult import is a persistently skewed and twisted turn to the logic of the characters' represented thoughts. One distorting force is evidently an unsystematic and unobtrusive stream of symbolism that runs just under the surface of the narration. Hats, beards, walking-sticks, uniforms, and hunting are just a few of the trappings with symbolic import; they disturb, perceptibly if only subtly, the flow of thought—without, for all that, constituting a strongly present mythical pattern, such as one finds beneath the surface of *Ulysses*. Finally, Broch's trilogy makes constant use of leitmotifs—recurrent verbal units, used in a variety of circumstances with a variety of different meanings, to strike a resonance between various parts of the book and to suggest musical harmonics heard outside the characters or between them—harmonics for which they are only in the vaguest way intentionally responsible. And these various subsurface devices, working against the increasingly diaphanous surface of Broch's trilogy, give to it a streaming, semi-visionary character loosely akin to that of *Ulysses,* with its fading and increasingly transparent characters, set in an increasingly transparent and timeless cosmos.

Yet though he might have picked up many of these concepts and techniques from a perusal of *Ulysses,* though consideration of them suggests strong affinities with Joyce's work, one can easily overstate the case. Very little of what we might want to call Joyce's contribution to Broch was distinctive to Joyce. Leitmotifs and symbolism, hostility to literal realism, a sense of social chaos and human debility—these a Viennese author did not have to learn from an Irish novelist.* On a much humbler level of reflection, Broch's English left a good deal to be desired, and he must always have known Joyce, as it were, through a veil. And that is the sense of Joyce's presence that one gets from *The Sleepwalkers*—like so many other things in the trilogy, the knifeblade aspect of Joyce's mind, with his Aristotelian fondness for particulars and specifics, is sensed only through a veil and at a middle distance.

The Sleepwalkers provides one exception to the rule of simpleminded characters possessing relatively little inwardness; that is Eduard von Bertrand, who seems to act from deeper layers of reflection, and with greater awareness of philosophic considerations, than any of the other persons. Characteristically mysterious and almost perversely dialectical is his abrupt declaration of eternal passion for

---

* The argument that *The Sleepwalkers* is in effect a fourfold retelling of *The Aeneid* seems to me gratuitously Byzantine, and I've disregarded it. If convincing, it would make Broch more Joycean than Joyce himself; but it's clearly obsessive, and counters the whole tenor of Broch's argument against estheticism.

Joachim's intended Elisabeth—a piece of lovemaking à l'allemand, abrupt, metaphysical, and prefaced by an eternal farewell. Evidently he wishes to imprint on her mind, before she enters on the soggy business of domesticity, intimations of a higher and more spiritual potential. And this is very much the sort of light that in the third volume of the trilogy we find him trying to shine through the murky world of the war years, when he has been metamorphosed somehow into Bertrand Muller, PhD, with a double preoccupation for the Wandering Jew Ahasuerus, and for a Salvation Army girl in Berlin, named Marie. Both these somewhat unlikely figures evidently represent for Bertrand (and, transparently, for Broch himself) a kind of light in the darkness. And the mythic pattern that emerges from the trilogy, visible chiefly in retrospect, is essentially the emergence of this prophetic vision from the ever-darkening greed and vulgarity of an age whose standards are set by cold-blooded sharks like Huguenau. He is essentially an Alsatian Snopes; by the end of the trilogy he has triumphed not only over the weak and decent Joachim von Pasenow but also over a chief actor of the second novel, the intermediate figure August Esch. Esch's moral light is not, to begin with, particularly dazzling; as a commercial bookkeeper he feels, more in irritation than exaltation, that moral as well as business books should balance out. Injustice upsets him as a piece of divine inaccuracy; but as the horizons of the world lower and darken around him, this fretful and anxious morality deepens into an evangelical vision. Because society is so deeply sunk in filth and blind selfishness, only something like a Second Coming can possibly bring about its redemption. But, as seems to be the rule in Broch, the redeeming power works from behind the characters and in some sense against them, rather than through them. Villainous Huguenau manages to gain command over senile Major von Pasenow and to dispose of Esch with a bayonet in the back. The trilogy can then conclude on a reverberant prophetic note from the Book of Revelations: the cycle of history having reached its nadir, the dialectic demands that at this point some transcendent, unifying, regenerative principle is bound to make itself felt—as, duly, it does.

Even so perfunctory and schematic a sketch of *The Sleepwalkers* cannot fail to suggest major areas of sharp difference from the art of Joyce. Broch's work has an overriding moral and didactic dimension that Joyce's work largely lacks, it invokes traditional symbols and creeds in an unequivocal way that Joyce doesn't, and its characters are thinned out close to insubstantiality without acquiring the temporal dimension of archetypes. Disintegration and ironic simultaneity are supposed to be expressed in the final novel by the interweaving of several narrative strains with choral interludes and lay sermons, but the effect of densely intertwined realities, as in "Proteus" and "Penelope," doesn't rise out of Broch's essentially disparate narrative strands. Yet behind the veil of difference, one senses in Broch as in Joyce the emergent figure of the Eternal Return, haunted by that mythical nomad of millennial cycles, the Wandering Jew, and murmuring the intricate, polyphonic music of history.

The appropriate form of the modern novel was Broch's unremitting concern. He worried the question continually, writing and rewriting each of his books till the overlay of first, second, and third intentions, combined with an aspiration for Germanic profundity, sometimes created an opacity verging on muddle. Yet there can be little doubt that his troubles with the form of fiction stemmed very largely from an overflowing of poetic vision, the massive if unusual problem of too much. *The Death of Virgil* is more successful fiction than *The Sleepwalkers* because it gives way more fully to this excess and follows the *Wake* more unreservedly in making language a subject in itself at the expense of usurpation of its expressive functions.

Historically speaking, the death of Virgil was not far removed in time from the death of Ovid, and Broch in planning his book evidently contemplated for a while building it around the author of the *Metamorphoses* and the *Fasti*. Either figure would have served his fictional purpose, for both were poet-mages, makers and reworkers of legend who found themselves at odds with the imperial society for which they wrote. Both lived at the moment of the world's most gigantic transition, when within the accomplished political *pax romana* was being born the new Christian principle of peace. It was a fact of which both poets, though specifically ignorant, showed themselves intuitively, poetically, uneasily aware—or were at least supposed to have done so. Virgil perhaps won out because in the fourth eclogue he was long reputed to have hailed the birth of the savior; because his reputed wish to burn the *Aeneid* implied a wide range of speculative possibilities; and because his death at Brundisium, in the heart of the empire while attending the emperor, lent some dramatic coloring to a novel which, as Broch planned it, was bound to have a minimum of episode.

The external action of *The Death of Virgil*, reduced to its elements, amounts to very little. Virgil returns from Greece to Brundisium deathly ill of a fever; carried on a litter through the squalid port, he is lodged in a room of the imperial palace by the special care of a mysterious boy Lysanias (through whom one is invited to sense the figure of Hermes *psychopompos*). There, in a feverish trance, he reviews and arraigns his career, accusing himself of having betrayed to aestheticism gifts that should have been turned to ethical ends—the civilizing of the Roman urban masses, for instance. This meditation leads to the clear imperative that the *Aeneid* must be burnt, as an act of spiritual betrayal. The third, and in many ways the least successful, section of the book is an argument between the dying poet and the emperor over the burning of the *Aeneid*, an argument all too protracted in the light of the reader's unflagging confidence that it can turn out only one way. The fourth and final unit is an imaginative sea-journey taken by the soul of Virgil backward up the stream of history, pre-history, and the period before human or animal or vegetable life toward the original and ultimate darkness.

By comparison with *The Sleepwalkers*, *The Death of Virgil* is largely uncluttered with characters, social impedimenta, and the dramatic conventions that their presence imposes. This is certainly all to the good. The long, lyrical, inward meditations of Virgil are written in streaming, intricately attenuated, and almost unstructured sentences, rising now and again to hymns of lyric questioning and affirmation which are surely among the most affecting things Broch ever wrote. The four sections of the book are associated respectively with "Water," "Fire," "Earth," and "Air"; in one sense, these designations may appear arbitrary, but in the sense that they make up a complete cosmos, they are not. The speculations of dying Virgil run constantly to the transcendent spiritual unity beyond the cosmic unity beyond the aesthetic unity—to the fullness of inward communion which, for a mind in this life and in the year 19 B.C., is "not quite here but yet at hand."

Toward intimations of this rarefied nature the prophetic mind of the dying poet, by summoning all its energies and sensitivities, can partially and momentarily rise. It does so rise, on the stream of an interior monologue more unbroken and more self-generative than anything even in the *Wake*. The language is extraordinarily insubstantial because it uses so many negative abstract nouns, so many oxymorons, so many adjectives and adjectivals in place of nouns, so many linked, repetitive participles in place of independent verbs—and conversely uses so few concrete nouns and so few active verbs within its enormously drawn-out, strongly rhythmical sentences. Yet, paradoxically, the prose is not only attenuated but opaque, as if designed to delay or impede insight by a series of immediate obstacles to conceptualization, while offering as an incitement to go behind the words only a distant diaphanous shadow of an indefinable phantom. Throughout *The Death of Virgil,* words serve to withhold movement as they do in Beckett, but not in order to sustain and verify individual existence, rather to keep the narrator on dialectical tenterhooks between the perception of everything and of nothing. The end of Virgil's voyage is found in the resonant silence of the Logos itself, which puts an end to all human speech as it stuns the human mind with the enormity of its presence:

—bursting out of the nothing as well as out of the universe, breaking forth as a communication beyond every understanding, breaking forth as a significance above every comprehension, breaking forth as the pure word which it was, exalted above all understanding and significance whatever, consummating and initiating, mighty and commanding, fear-inspiring and protecting, gracious and thundering, the word of discrimination, the word of the pledge, the pure word [p. 481].

The oratorical and prophetic qualities of this diction, to say nothing of its Platonic luminosity, set it altogether apart from any prose of Joyce's devising. But the imaginative process by which Virgil's consciousness advances down a stream of language toward diffusion into a cosmos of light, air, and vacancy is like nothing so much as the processes of the *Wake*. In neither instance do we deal with anything like a deliberate program for the novel; neither author wrote in response to anything but his own deepest intuitions, and as a result neither book is of the common measure. Almost in defiance of his literary programmatics, Broch wrestled like a musclebound Titan with the traditional themes of German romanticism and German philosophy, as Joyce wrought like a blind forger of patterns in the underground caverns of language. There is very little question of influence, but in the hazier fields of affinity one might wander widely for a long time.

CHAPTER SEVEN

VLADIMIR
NABOKOV

IT HAS BEEN WIDELY REMARKED that the terminology of game-playing clings close to the fiction of Vladimir Nabokov. His characters are players of formal or informal games, and the author in his dealings with the reader openly speaks of gambits and devices, not to mention the anagrams, allusions, illusions, puzzles and other obstacles that his odd-ball narrators are constantly placing before the progress of a reader. Sometimes Nabokov in his authorial person mocks the passive or careless reader with his inattention; more often he silently challenges the alert reader by hiding significant clues in insignificant places, covering a real gesture with flashy indirections, hinting through what seem to be accidental correspondences at what seem to be significant significances. The novels click and glitter like sewing machines; they are so active and provoking on their corrugated and baroque surfaces, that one is apt to overlook their retention, at the center, of a touch of romantic sentiment, a shy and well-protected element of human feeling. Beneath even that level, there is occasionally to be found another layer of thought or feeling, perhaps only half-serious but perhaps more than that—persistent enough, in any case, to merit comment—a teasing, tantalizing fascination with the occult and the notion of life after death. In terms of Joyce, the direct influence seems mostly technical: as conscious and self-conscious verbal construct, the Nabokov novel has a good deal in common with the virtuoso passages of *Ulysses,* and the thickness of the verbal texture leads directly to a thinness and an attenuation of the "characters." But its basic themes—as one could only expect of a man with powerful and even eccentric impulses to originality—are Nabokov's own.

Lolita, which first brought to public attention, for largely scandalous reasons, a professor of Russian literature with an avid interest in lepidoptery, has its share of verbal fun and games, its fringe of linguistic fornications around the periphery of another, deeper pool of contamination. Humbert is an instinctive verbal joker, and his counterpart Quilty is another. Behind them, made evident by their very names, is still another joker, the author, who doubled Humbert's name as in one mirror and in the other mirror-imaged (for what reasons?) the Irish town of Quilty in the county Clare. The device of an address to an imaginary jury provides occasion for bravura rhetorical effects of another order; and the long mad pursuit of Q and Lolita through insane multi-lingual puns in motel registries is a triumphant variation on that ancient comic theme (it reaches back through Swift to Rabelais at least) of the scholar crazed by his own learning, for whom the world in its thoughtless stupidity is forever contriving impenetrable conundrums.

Behind these comic and macabre caperings on the surface of the novel lies a comic and macabre collection of feelings in the relationship of Humbert to Lolita and vice versa. Humbert, in the first place, thinks himself a loathsome monster for seducing and corrupting an innocent child. It is his hideous destiny (his disease, his talent) to crave nymphets, and his early story consists chiefly of episodes—absurd, disgusting, silly, touching—in which he tried to satisfy this craving or stifle it. He does not directly blame it for his spells of insanity, but the reader can hardly help doing so; it is responsible for the catastrophe of his first marriage, and for a whole accumulation of humiliations at the hands of pimps, harlots, and nosy psychiatrists too, but also from ostensibly "normal" people. Because of his obsession he is a man wholly alone in the world, unattached to any person or group or belief or task, incapable of communicating the truth about himself to anyone. Yet he also romanticizes his illness, with the story of Annabel Lee and the trauma of his childhood affair on the Riviera beachfront, a story told in mockery to be sure, but with an evident affection and depth of feeling behind the mockery, different even from that which envelops the story of Lolita. If it doesn't fully romanticize his aberration, the childhood story at least explains and in some measure excuses it. In a more immediate sense, events at The Enchanted Hunters further limit Humbert's real guilt. He doesn't seduce Lolita, she seduces him, and she isn't the innocent virgin he (in his innocence) supposed she was. He's not really evil, we are led to think, just dreadfully stupid, in spite of his apparent worldliness and curious history. And afterwards, when, between blackmail and bribery, Lolita settles sullenly but not uncomfortably into the role of Humbert's peripatetic concubine, it seems to be as much her decision as his. He suspects her of constantly trying to run away with other men, it's true, but we discount that as due to his obsession and suspicious nature. But there is a delayed revelation here, carefully withheld for a long time and then released in the middle of things only as a fraction of a sentence, to be covered over almost at once by Humbert's implacable rhetoric: ". . . and her sobs in the night—every night, every night—the moment I feigned sleep."

Everything about the scene is horrifying; his feigning sleep, her sobs, the feelings that brought them on, his indifference to them; the two words "every night" spread through the rest of the book and make of Humbert not only a jailer but a monstrously selfish and sadistic, yet suffocatingly cheery jailer. (This is a figure who began haunting Nabokov as early as *Invitation to a Beheading;* other analogues can be found throughout the canon.) Elsewhere we get images of Lolita putting up with Humbert and his sexual demands, now contemptuously, now for her own sharply bargained advantage. But the sobs in the night are another order of misery, and they gain immense pathos from being mentioned only once, then resolutely stuffed out of sight beneath the narrator's mania. Humbert is ecstatic in the possession of his nymphet; he ignores with brutal deliberation the fact that there's a weeping, miserable person inside that dazzling sexual object.

Humbert, then, is a real monster and no less a monster in 1975 than he was in 1958. His appetite for little girls perhaps looks a little less freaky in the light of the sexual revolution, but it's still freaky, and his readiness to keep a child in sexual servitude is just as revolting as it ever was. Yet at the end of the novel, when Lolita is no longer a nymphet and his chances of ever regaining her are gone forever, Humbert undergoes a kind of transformation. He is said to reach through his sickness, rise out of his selfishness, and recognize in himself nothing less than True Love:

> What I used to pamper among the tangled vines of my heart, *mon grand pêché radieux,* had dwindled to its essence: sterile and selfish vice, all *that* I cancelled and cursed. You may jeer me, and threaten to clear the court, but until I am gagged and half-throttled, I will shout my poor truth. I insist the world know how much I loved my Lolita, *this* Lolita, pale and polluted and big with another's child, but still gray-eyed, still sooty-lashed, still auburn and almond, still Carmencita, still mine . . . [p. 280].

Perhaps the rhetoric carries the reader along; Humbert clearly intends it to, and the fact that she is no longer a radiant child tempts us to think that he has perhaps transcended his hangup, is declaring (as forcibly as the long-debauched idiom of romantic passion will allow) an authentic adoration. Yet the last phrase of the passage all but overtly declares itself a self-deception. "Still mine," indeed!— except as a beast in a cage belongs to its keeper, she had never been "his." To possess a nymphet was a selfish fantasy; perhaps the idea of "possessing" any fellow creature is bound to be a selfish fantasy. Humbert's notion that he ever had "possessed" Lolita is as false as his notion that he can or will possess her again. But I don't think these are the feelings with which we read, or are supposed to read, the passage. (Literary moralists, an extremely offensive subspecies of

an offensive breed, are always tugging us by the elbow and telling us
we shouldn't react as an author has in fact made us react; as a critical
procedure, it simply raises taking-out-of-context to the level of a first
principle.) At least on the wings of his own imagination and his own
undeniable eloquence, Humbert has risen from the state of a loathsome creep to the simulation—at least—of a grand, heroic passion.
And if there is, inevitably, enough egoism in every grand passion to
suggest the possibility of the lover being a loathsome creep, that may
be because grand passions themselves are pretty anachronistic.

Such being the case, we are bound to feel that the very presence
of a grand passion in Nabokov's fiction (however ambiguous, however qualified) is more Proustian than Joycean. Marcel's effort to capture Albertine, Swann's effort to "possess" Odette, are thematically
much closer to *Lolita* than is anything in Joyce—if only because no
Joycean character would be capable of such single-minded self-
assertion, or self-annihilation. Humbert is a descendant of Tristan;
his story is a *Liebestod*. *Lolita* as classic romance is qualified chiefly
by the uncrucial circumstance that the knight is himself half-dragon,
but it culminates, just as securely as any medieval *chanson de geste,*
with the hero standing triumphantly over the decapitated monster.
Joyce doesn't deal much in this sort of finality; for him one conflict
always fades, before it is half-resolved, into another. Before Tristan
ever perishes with his Isolde, they are both likely to have metamorphosed into somebody else.

Nabokov's theme of the pure, sustained, difficult, and ultimately
fatal passion can be traced from the quite early Russian fictions
(*Glory,* for example) through *Ada* at least; though a recurrent
theme, it peeps forth only guardedly and intermittently from under
the carapace of the hard-shelled, trick-playing, exhibitionistic fictions.
One may feel that without this strain many of them would be only
glistening mechanical contraptions; yet it undeniably marks Nabokov
as of an older and more ample generation than our own. He himself
has said something to this effect in *Ada,* by declaring that affairs in

Anti-terra (which I take to be the world of his imagination) lag about fifty years behind those on Terra—the real, that is, the imaginary world common to his readers.

Of all these later novels, *Pale Fire* is surely the most oddly shaped, the most heavily laden with verbal and representational tricks; it has received the most loving attention from those readers who delight in the gamesman side of Nabokov's art. Yet within it too there can be found a kernel of something softer and more inward, the germ of a thwarted and difficult romance triumphing over impossibilities. At first glance, *Pale Fire* seems to be a novel in spite of itself. Divided into four parts, it would consist of a bumbling poem by bumbling John Shade, a predatory, paranoid commentary on the poem by Charles Kinbote, and within that commentary a tale of Ruritanian romance (intrigue, escape, ruthless long-range revenge), plus a wildly comic and very informative index. Telling a pair of converging stories across these several obstacles and through incongruous angles of consciousness is a tour de force in itself. As usual in Nabokov, we must take account of distorted consciousness and several varieties of contrived reticence in order to get anywhere near the heart of the matter. Kinbote is the most obviously disturbed of our narrators. Like the murderer of *Despair,* he is a botched and incompetent artist, vain, self-conscious, self-absorbed, and utterly insensitive to the feelings of others. Apart from his persistent fantasies of humiliation, Nabokov's thought was surely shaped here by an impulse to parody his own parasitic relation, as editor, to Pushkin as poet. The success of his parody is shown by the fact that most readers have been more intrigued by Kinbote and his melodramatic tale of Gradus and Charles-Xavier the Beloved than by the poem of John Shade which provides the pretext for the commentary that provides the pretext for the tale.

Shade's poem is an ungainly and uncouth piece of verse which, from the literary point of view, deserves no better reading than the one it gets from Kinbote. But he is wholly wrong about it in two ways; he thinks it a marvelous piece of writing, and ignores precisely and brutally those passages which do achieve an awkward kind of pathos. (The situation parallels precisely that of Joyce's story, "Ivy Day in the Committee Room," where Mr. Crofton achieves a dictum of precisely calculated stupidity by describing as "a fine piece of writing," Joe Hynes's awkward, stilted, but still moving poem on Parnell.) Shade's poem deals centrally with his daughter—ugly, intuitive, clever, word-twisting, vulnerable, hopelessly unattractive Hazel Shade. Abandoned on a blind date by a brutally callous boy (with whose transparent excuse Kinbote, as by sure instinct, sympathizes), Hazel has committed suicide; and Shade, who has long been subject to queer fits of hallucinated unconsciousness which he takes to be death itself or a foretaste of death, seeks in the course of them to reach her departed spirit—even as she had, while living, tried to reach the spirit in Hentzner's barn, whether that spirit was Aunt Maud or someone else.

The auspices for successful divination cluster closely around Hazel: the hazel bush supplies wood for diviners' rods (dowsing sticks); her mother was named Sybil; her Aunt Maud was a spectacular psychokinetic performer; she sees into words beyond their primary meanings. On the other hand, the book contains a set of fraudulent and ridiculous messages from the great beyond. Countess de Fyler manipulates the ouija board to urge Charles Xavier to marry Fleur, whom he as a committed homosexual finds repulsive and absurd. That message he sees through immediately as a piece of palace intrigue. What Hazel Shade picks up from the spook haunting Hentzner's barn might be equally absurd or even meaningless—as it appears to be on the surface. But Kinbote, who was shrewd enough about the other message, assures us that he cannot make heads or tails of this one; and when Kinbote says something of this sort, it's invariably because he doesn't want to see something, not because he cannot. (In psychic readings he's just as talented as Hazel, to whom in one moment of startling and instantly forgotten insight he compares himself: note

to line 347.) In any case, the message picked up by Hazel in Hentzner's barn from an erratic but playful light is the following:

> pada ata lane pad not ogo old wart alan ther tale feur far rant lant tal
> told [p. 188].

Indeed, it looks unpromising. Cryptographic methods don't yield
much, and the commentators with one accord fall silent. But we are
told, anon, that the barn ghost "expressed himself with the empasted
difficulty of apoplexy or of a half-awakening from a half-dream
slashed by a sword of light on the ceiling, a military disaster with
cosmic consequences that cannot be phrased distinctly by the thick
unwilling tongue." Reading through the murk of the tongue-tied
ghost's indistinct stammerings, one can perceive a sort of meaning
to which Kinbote would naturally be obtuse, for it anticipates the last
scene of the novel:

> Father Atalantis pleads not to go Goldworth where tale from foreign
> land will be told.

Such or something like it might be the prophetic message. Goldworth
is the home of Judge Goldworth, where Kinbote resides and Shade
will die. Atalantis is the Red Admirable or Vanessa (its name from
the Orphic deity Phanes, not Swift's admirer). One of these butter-
flies flits before John Shade as, in the climactic action of the book, he
follows Kinbote to his death. It is a gorgeous but morbid insect,
which makes Kinbote curiously uneasy; in a note to line 238 he
thinks it a flower, but in nearby note to line 270 he knows a good
deal about it, and even informs us that it is known as "the heraldic
one." In the last pages of the novel, I take it to be the spirit of Hazel
Shade, concerned with and distressed by what she can foresee, but
helpless (like many prophetesses) to prevent it. Like the light in the
barn, the butterfly as it dances before Shade is an erratic light, an
enigmatic, incomprehensible herald, leading Shade into deepening
shades. But the words of warning have been spoken, though not
really heard, far less understood.

The parasitic revenant, who has no words of his own, but speaks through the mouth of a host peculiarly receptive to him, and always at cross-purposes, is very much a part of the book. Kinbote the critic is called (by prophetic Sybil) "a monstrous bot-fly," parasitic on his poet; and indeed the procedure of the commentary is to lay a narrative like a maggot in the corpse of a poem. The theme has echoes as well in a more or less contemporary short story of Nabokov's, "The Vane Sisters" (in *Ada* the title will be taken as an ingenious triple pun on Ada and Lucette, the Veen sisters, both in love with Van), where a message from one of the sisters is encoded after her death in an acrostic of a speech murmured by the other sister. Finally, the theme strikes a curious resonance upon a set of historical circum-stances which, though Nabokov denies having known of them, are too curious not to be recorded.

Well before Nabokov's time at Cornell (Wordsmith University, through a conflation of the well-known Wordsworth collection and Goldwin Smith Hall), the Professor of English at Cornell was Hiram Corson, a man of mildly mystic leanings. When his beloved daughter died, the professor sought to be put in touch with her through mediums. Somehow he heard of one in England named Blavatsky (it was HPB herself), corresponded with her, brought her to Ithaca, New York, and put her up in his house. Evenings, she put him and Mrs. Corson in touch with the spirit of their dear departed daughter; during the daytime, he brought her books from the excellent Cornell University library; and under these circumstances, the two volumes of *Isis Unveiled* were composed. The combination of these distinctive elements (a grieving professor of English, his tragic daughter, a Russian outsider with powerful if discordant vibrations, psychic messages among them) is a spectacular if irrelevant coincidence, for there's no overcoming the author's denial. Let it go down, then, among the oddities of literature.* Still, the ungainly devotion

* If memory doesn't wholly fail me, there was even a campus poet at Cornell in the old days, whose versification was much on a level with that of John

and wretched grief of the Shade family are a center of human feeling amid the obsessions, reflections, and self-absorbed word-games of *Pale Fire*.

Setting aside all this moldy business of sources and possible sources (as if a man of such exuberant fancy needed more than a minimum), an important new element in *Pale Fire* is surely the sustained contrast between Shade, the provincial at ease in his own New Wye environment—interpenetrated as it is with intimations and correspondences of another existence (see Alison Lurie's *Imaginary Friends* for confirmation)—and the haunted, haunting outsider Kinbote, who is in so many respects Shade's mirror image, moon to Shade's sun. In another analogy, Shade is very like transparent glass, Kinbote a mirror; the one (like Bloom) is the vehicle of intuitions to which he offers no obstacle and so hardly perceives, the other (like Stephen) carries his own story with him, always and everywhere the same. But both characters, and in this respect they carry forward strikingly a feature of late Joycean technique, are penetrated and infused with messages and images, intimations and intuitions, from outside reality. Some effort has been put into the thesis that Kinbote's Zembla and the entire story woven about it are nothing but a private hallucination. Kinbote in fact is nothing but an inept scholar in a second-rate university, gone slightly loony of course; Gradus is only an accidental madman, Jack Gray from the local asylum. All the rest of that fantasy for which only Kinbote vouches—Zembla, its history and its court, its revolution and its conspiracies—is simply his sick imagination at work. There's very little doubt that if one starts to mistrust Kinbote as a "witness," that part of his story which is "verified," and must be

---

Shade, though his themes were less lofty. He was associated with the Agricultural College, printed little pamphlets containing samples of his verse, and sold them in the Faculty Club; his name was Bob Adams, and in the early days of my residence at Cornell, I used to get mail addressed to him. He predates the sweet singer of later days, Alexis Romanoff, author of the more-than-respectable, encyclopedic treatise on *The Avian Egg*.

true if anything in the whole book is true, can be reduced to about these proportions. On the other hand, we are not dealing here with an essay in ontology. It's precisely the struggle between two different (and rather awful) modes of reality that creates the interest of the fiction; and to make one of them (however Ruritanian) wholly fictitious is to throw oneself into the arms of the other, however drab. Like others of Nabokov's artist-criminals (Humbert of *Lolita,* Hermann of *Despair*), Kinbote winds up in a mountain refuge, writing the story of his crimes and applauding his own insane ingenuity. Precisely because he's so unchecked, so unreliable, we are not supposed to believe or disbelieve whole-heartedly what he says; we must guess, grope, blunder among the probabilities. And so with the novel of which he forms a part. *Pale Fire* no more affirms or denies anything, including the potentiality of its own cosmos, than does the *Wake*—it is simply an achieved book. Its theme is the invasion of a haunted ordinary by an obsessed fantasy, a zombie in bondage to a spellbound ghost. The inevitably inconclusive conclusion of such an encounter throws us back on the tricks of language, synchrony, mirror-imagery, and recondite reference interwoven with fancy, that make up the detailed texture of *Pale Fire.*

Gamesmanship in this book is more ostentatious than in Nabokov's other novels because it consists, not just of little knots in the narrative lines, but of direct and massive opposition between one theme and another. Kinbote of course is determined that Shade's poem shall not be itself, but rather the poem he would have imposed upon (inspired in) Shade; in addition, the basic structure of footnotes and index imposes on the narrative abrupt leaps backward and forward in time, as well as sidelong motions from theme to theme. There are as many false leads along synchronic lines as there are significant ones. For example, it can hardly be coincidence that Jacob Gradus and Charles Kinbote were both born on July 5, 1915; on the other hand, it may well be coincidence that John Shade suffered a heart attack on October 17, 1958, just as Kinbote was reaching America. Whether coinci-

dent dates like these do or don't have tangential significance is up to
the reader to guess; but hardly a fragment of Zemblan is cited that
can't be heard as a variety of deformed English, anagrams and backward spellings are everywhere, and playful fantasies like the garden
containing all the trees mentioned by Shakespeare entice one into
further reflections than they can possibly reward.

Nabokov's fondness for his lost Russia and lost Russian floods
these later novels with a kind of rich Amerussian quite unlike, for
example, Pnin's merely clumsy English, or Humbert Humbert's adventures into merely decorative French. Not only the language but
the landscapes of *Ada* deliberately conflate spheres of existence—and
these are more than the spheres of two very different minds, as in
Pale Fire; they are two entirely different nations and cultures and
even two mirror-images of the cosmos, Terra (our world, which occupies the same ambiguous status as heaven or the afterlife) and the
world of the fiction, Demonia or Anti-terra, which all the characters
accept as the "real" world. (Note, however, that life on Anti-terra is
said to lag "about half a century" (p. 341) behind events on Terra,
so that Van's first book, *Letters from Terra,* has a great vogue on
Anti-terra when events there have caught up with it. Dates, however,
are carefully calculated and always given in Terra years—that is, the
A.D.'s with which we are familiar.) Nabokov distances this imaginary
"real" world not only in time (the entire action of *Ada* takes place
after the Revelation, also known as the L-disaster), but in a cosmos
of incalculable, though peripheral, strangeness. The law of gravity is
now and then suspended through the operation of flying carpets, and
there is a permanent ban on the use, or even the mention (except
covertly) of electricity—which seems to have taken the place of sex
as a taboo topic. People speak a mongrel mixture of Russian, French,
German, English slang, and erudite English from the small-print section at the bottom of the page of Webster's Second International.
Trans-lingual puns abound, along with bastardized place names
(Akapulkovo) and a rich array of verbal off-rhymes and almostings

(Kaluga, Raduga, Ladoga, Luga, Laguna, Lugano, Lumbago, Ladore, Ladorah, Radugalet); the effect is to blur and diffuse one's sense of Anti-terra by dissolving it into a set of unsteady and constantly shifting overlays. In the large sense, Anti-terra is haunted by fitful glimpses and unreliable intimations of life on Terra.

I don't doubt that Nabokov is particularly delighted with some of the proofs invented by modern physics for establishing the existence of life or anti-life on other planets—proofs which levitate giddily on the laws of bare probability and the total absence of factual evidence. Just so the Anti-terrans can neither accept nor dismiss the existence of Terra. Knowledge of the strange otherworld reaches them through dreams, visions, the delusions (illusions, collusions) of shamans, hysterics, and madfolk; and it's very upsetting indeed to the "normal" order of things. But quite apart from these fleeting intimations of another cosmos, life itself on Anti-terra is a blur of fantasies. Czarist Russia, Hollywood, Canadian frontier-life, and international high society blend together in a froth of cinematic collages. Literature spills over into life repeatedly; we find Chateaubriand's oak in botany textbooks, Chateaubriand's mosquito biting bare legs, John Shade's poem being translated by Ada into Russian, Maupassant meandering through the watery labyrinths of Mlle. Lariviere's mind. Van, as ostensible author, intervenes from time to time; Nabokov as real author does the same; Ada interjects, and so (discreetly) does an unidentified Ed.

Set in this layercake of contrasting contexts, the romance of Van and Ada Veen contains too many elements of derring-do and pre-fab fictional claptrap not to be seen, at least in some measure, as parody or self-parody. (There's an awful possibility that parodic intent may *not* underlie Van Veen's vacant meditations on time, which occupy so much of Section 4; but that's an alternative to be avoided for as long as possible.) In the other direction, the romance is qualified by the inhuman egotism of this marvelously self-satisfied couple and a frank recognition, even on their part, of their own hideous brutality toward others—like a gang of birds setting on a weak member of the flock, they have literally pecked Lucette to death. But at root the romance is to be accepted romantically—one sign of which is the sardonic little review that Nabokov has appended to his own fiction. It is, of course, a silly, sentimental, and superficial review—as if Nabokov were trying to ward off, by parodying, a view of his novel that in fact it invites. Amid the phantoms, demons, delusions, and echoes in which his novels delight to play, amid all the skepticisms and sterilities with which he must surround it and ridicule it, Nabokov retains a core of feeling whose intensity we sense for the most part only reflexively, through the *cheval de frise* of verbal fortifications with which he protects it.

Of all Joyce's influences on Nabokov, probably the most important though the least easy to document is in the matter of imitative prose. The influence is hard to document, not for lack of examples, but because a master of prose style will find the special rhythms and images of his subject, regardless of predecessors or authorities. Prose style in fiction is, after all, not a thing in itself, so much as a matter of fluidity and flexibility in intimating both a scene and a set of feelings surrounding it. Like Joyce, Nabokov writes a wonderfully adaptable and various prose which at its best freezes a bundle of widespread particulars into an instant of suddenly stopped unity. Van catches sight of twelve-year-old Ada washing face and arms over an old-fashioned basin on a rococo stand,

> her hair knotted on the top of her head, her nightgown twisted around her waist like a clumsy corolla out of which issued her slim back, rib-shaded on the near side. A fat snake of porcelain curled around the basin, and as both the reptile and he stopped to watch Eve and the soft woggle of her bud-breasts in profile, a big mulberry-colored cake of soap slithered out of her hand, and her black-socked foot hooked the door shut with a bang which was more the echo of the soap's crashing against the marble board than a sign of pudic displeasure [p. 60].

The passage makes a tableau—the figures form up in the first part of the sentence, the snake curling up the basin as Adam moves past the doorway, both stopped involuntarily to watch Eve, and then the door slams in one uninterrupted sidewise movement of her foot, while the sentence moves on to unwind an explanation of her motives. It is a sentence as swift and sinuous as the complex of actions that it embraces. On the other hand, when the narrative disappears into the strange sick minds of Aqua or Lucette, though it maintains a difference between them, the language moves with a quick and frightened vivacity, as if disordered and out of control but drawn irresistibly forward by a power outside itself. In moments of stress, when the mind of some character is darting back and forth, seeking some way out, the prose follows it down its different narrative pockets, shaping out the future into a dozen different forms all more convenient than the present. It is an old trick with Nabokov to move uninterruptedly from straightforward third-person exposition into the fantasy of a character, leading the reader unsuspectingly along until "reality" catches up with him, he blinks, and looks back to find the spot where a private fantasy-trail branched off a public one. There is a classic instance of this in *Ulysses,* where Bloom responds to Zoe's phrase, "Go on. Make a stump speech out of it" (p. 469) by ballooning off into an immense fantasy of his triumph and failure from which he does not return till p. 488, when he finds Zoe saying, "Talk away till you're black in the face." There's a striking example of the device in the last chapter of Nabokov's *The Gift;* but in the later books, it is used less as a trick for its own sake than as a way of weaving into and out of the minds of characters, sometimes only for a fleeting adjective or the intimation of a point of view. And again, there are moments when Nabokov takes great pains to keep out of the minds of his characters; how determined and appropriate is the superficiality and impressionistic allusiveness of the scene in which Ada and Lucette combine briefly to entertain Van in the large bed of a New York apartment. It is a scene painted entirely in colors, lights, darks, dimly perceived shapes, as if the observing eye were high and distant—a wonderfully poised and discreet piece of pornography, as if seen through Seurat's distracting vision.

This mobility of Nabokov's prose distinguishes him, it seems to me, even from such great admirations of his as Proust and Chateaubriand—indeed, from most of the past masters of "fine style." By the same token, it is surely mobility that distinguishes Joyce from *his* avowed master of prose style, Newman. In a twentieth century of insubstantial, phantom persons who nonetheless manage to write wooden and obtuse prose, it is Nabokov's peculiar accomplishment to have inverted the process. His characters may be agitated outlines, but they inhabit a glittering and slippery element of prose that is always capable of, and sometimes achieves, genuine events.

CHAPTER EIGHT

COUNTERPARTS

MOD-ROMANTICS: DURRELL, BURGESS

THE ALEXANDRIA QUARTET of Lawrence Durrell struck a rather sour note at its first hearing, because the last novel of the four was felt to represent a sharp falling-off from at least the first two. The announced order of the novels is *Justine, Balthazar, Mountolive, Clea,* and it's impossible to deny that the folded mysteries of the first volumes and the strong interest of physically exploring Alexandria are more potent fictionally than the explanations and resolutions, which lie flat on the page. Beyond all this, the mystique of sex linking Durrell with Henry Miller and D. H. Lawrence is a soft theme and a limited one, on which, apart from lyrical rhetoric, there's not a great deal to be said in the long run. When Darley settles down with Clea to live happily ever after, the reader is more likely to sigh in disappointment than in satisfaction: we had thought there was more to the novels than that, and indeed there was. The last volumes escape all too successfully from the baffling relativity which was the chief interest of the first two.

A mechanical but genuine source of power in the early books was multiple points of view. Quite apart from tacit transitions from one narrative eye to another, events were watched and recorded by three professional authors—Arnauti, Darley, and Pursewarden—in addition to diarists, letter-writers, and commentators, all of whose work was conveniently made available to the scribe: they included Leila,

Justine, Clea, Balthazar, and Nessim himself. In addition, we saw Darley at a variety of different stages in his career, and information was filtered into the novels from a number of different and competing intelligence agencies. All this made for an ingeniously interwoven fabric of times, places, and points of view, across which the reader's studious eye wandered in search of patterns and ever-deeper patterns. One part of the book called another into question; the various novelists circled around the problems of complex personalities in complex situations, throwing off ideas for novels which might or might not apply to the present one. All this uncertainty was more potent fictional stuff than any conceivable resolutions of it could be: especially since Durrell, though his characters are all erotically obsessed, and he himself proposes eros as an ultimate form of cognition, skimps actual erotic scenes and any definition of the knowledge gained from them as primly as any Victorian novelist in Mudie's Lending Library. The palimpsest-novel is a lot richer in its implications than the novel of erotic exploration and intrigue; it is also much more Joycean.

The basic idea of having the manuscript of the first novel shipped to Balthazar for commentary, expansion, and revision produces in the second novel what Darley, growing in wisdom, calls an interlinear text. Most of the romantic illusions in which the first text abounds are here shattered by a more dispassionate and deeper-sighted observer— above all the romantic egotism with which Darley has experienced his affair with Justine. (In terms of prudential motivation, the question of why Justine, who's already involved in one massive intrigue, should jeopardize it by indulging in two others, with Darley and Pursewarden, never gets answered; but the novel's balance of forces is all the better for being precarious.) Balthazar, as invert, mystagogue, and medicine-man, is admirably suited to bring about these ironic counterpoints. Although this resource is not largely exploited, we sometimes see verbal tags familiar from one context given new resonance by being heard in another. Justine, looking at herself in a mirror, and denouncing herself as a "pretentious, hysterical Jewess," is later seen to be quoting from the book of her first husband, Arnauti. The idea of an interlinear text, which depersonalizes the narration and corrects the errors of egotism, dovetails particularly well with the notion of a *genius loci,* which seemed at first just another rhetorical Darleyism, but takes on serious content though of a grain precisely counter to the personalized ending of the series. The Alexandrians as Darley comes finally to know them are not free persons. At first glance they seem enormously liberated: most of them wealthy, sexually on the loose, intellectually skeptical, culturally cosmopolitan. But they turn out to have little or no control over their own lives. More even than by the cross-currents of international politics, they are controlled by the spirit of the city itself—by its intellectual traditions, its many layers of historical actuality.

With its mixture of Pharaonic, Greek, Jewish, Christian, and Moslem elements, with its special desert-oasis atmosphere and its faded traditions as a cosmopolitan pleasure-resort, Alexandria usurps heavily on the Alexandrians; and Durrell, with a vivid pen for colors, smells, and popular oddities, can render a bazaar, a cheap cabaret, or a hunchbacked barber briefly and brilliantly. With profundities of thought or feeling he's less successful: the Cabala and the doctrines of the Gnostics remain bits of lifeless window-dressing, and the grand passions don't get much beyond the stage of cliché. Of course, that is one of the points of the tetralogy. With its gift for factoring people down to their common irreducible elements, it forms Nessim and Melissa, Darley and Justine into a crystalline quartet of compulsions and frustrations before which the explanations of time and history (whether personal or public) are relatively helpless. Racially and religiously the quartet is as balanced and unstable as the city itself, and its conflicts are quite as insoluble. But then solutions are not really in order; certainly the Joycean vision would not have encouraged Durrell to think that in *Mountolive* he could effectively lay out a political background along with an explanation of Pursewarden (so much better as an enigma than as a case history!) and in *Clea* score up a pseudo-Proustian ending-return. One senses that even though he carried it off, the romantic ending with Clea did not sit well on his artistic conscience, and in the desperate amputation of Clea's hand, he tried to set it off with a bit of strong stuff. But the redemption is very partial; and it's my own impression, having tried it both ways, that the tetralogy reads much more effectively backwards than forwards, which makes it wind up instead of winding down.

Among other things, the success of the first two novels is due to some consciously mosaic prose. Durrell is fond of writing what amount to epiphanies of Alexandria, though he never labels them as such. They are hard, brilliant, descriptive sketches, done with all the senses and nerves alight—really the finest pieces of writing in the sequence. It's an oddity that the man who writes so well can also fall into the weary, loose clichés of the romantic novelist. For example: "Clea was too noble to love otherwise than passionately and yet at the same time quite capable of loving someone to whom she spoke only once a year" (*Balthazar,* p. 44). Unfortunately, as the opportunity narrowed for the first sort of prose (Alexandria having already been presented to us in all its sharp immediacy), the second sort came more and more to predominate. And there are still other veins that the author has tapped, in this eclectic sequence of actions—Scobie, for example, who flows forth like a Pickwickian eccentric given his head, indefatigably and to some extent irrelevantly. One can sympathize with Durrell in feeling that he is too good to waste, yet among the major themes of the novel he hardly fits at all, and apart from his own rich self-display serves no purpose except to demonstrate Clea's charity and the city's polymorphic religiosity—a bit of Boffin's Bower in Alexandria, so to speak.

As all this suggests, there's a lot of uneven work in the *Quartet*—a splash of metaphysical prestidigitation mixed with a swatch of exotic Oriental sex, some menace after the manner of E. Phillips Oppenheim, with homely Malaprop humor at the Sarah Gamp level. The books are written to impress, to dazzle, to titillate, to enthrall; there are sustained passages where they do these various things, but there are also areas where the flats betray crude painting, the machinery creaks, and the characters stand about contriving stage-business to conceal the fact that they really don't know what to do with themselves. Durrell is a superior entertainer, who has found various elements of Joycean composition useful in putting together his kaleidescope. But he's a long way from the cold and distant perspective of Joyce even toward his own creation; one doesn't get any equivalent feel for the architecture of a fiction. Durrell in the Alexandria Quartet was evidently in a delayed Stephen-Dedalus stage of development—his books are built more in the loose form of theme-and-variations than after the strict mode of a quartet.

Another fringe-Joycean is Anthony Burgess, who has written so many novels so fast that one is limited, for sheerly practical reasons, to mentioning only a couple of them. The Joyce-presence in Burgess is mostly linguistic, and perhaps beyond that musical; like Joyce, and like no other novelist in English, Burgess is fond of using language harmonically or impressionistically, and not just in nostalgic moods— he likes to strip words of their representational values and use them for their tonal values. This was apparent almost from the beginning. Without its special dialect, *A Clockwork Orange* would be not only a sparse but a muddled book, with its bare bones in evident disarray. There is a *1984* or *Brave New World* component in the book, a totalitarian society savagely conditioning its subjects into conformity; there is the urban gang-leader as outlaw-hero, a slummy Robin Hood; and there is Alex's particular hangup on classical music, which balances uncertainly in the middle of things—one moment a barbaric incitement to indiscriminate violence (in the rape of the two preadolescent ptitsas), one moment a nobler and more civilized vision, which is contaminated and degraded by being associated with violence. As a matter of fact, the whole conditioning-experiment which is the center of the novel is unconvincing, because it consists of giving Alex a representational overdose of what he obviously enjoys in everyday life, sadistic cruelties. (One is not convinced that—even with the help of drugs—the movies he's forced to see would revolt him; there's just as good a chance that they'd incite him.) In any case, having set up his alternatives—Alex *au naturel,* a bloodthirsty gutter-snipe, versus Alex brainwashed, a whiny, sanctimonious guttersnipe —Burgess clearly was unable to resolve them, and so bundled his novel toward an inconclusive ending.

But the dialect of the novel performs several services for this rather crude fable. Being relatively opaque, it absorbs a lot of attention in its own right; it's a rich mixture of Russian conflated with English, Romany, rhyming slang, and Burgess-coinages, so that initially a lot of the meanings have to be guessed from the contexts. The reader is thus kept well occupied, not to say distracted; a good deal of his attention goes simply to the surface of the novel. Reading the book also involves a lot of back-and-forthing—that is, a word used in one context is given further meaning by its use in another context further on, which reflects back on its first usage. All this to-do on the linguistic surface of things blurs one's attention to the overall shape of the novel, and the scenes of gleeful sadism work to reinforce that desirable superficiality. It's a flat novel written in a thick, impasto style. The theme of music is integral to the novel, defined in this way; it makes for tonal unity on an immediate and impressionistic level, which is just another way of saying that the book is put together more like a movie than like a novel.

It is also a book, like those of Joyce, largely unconcerned with morality in any form. No doubt this was part of the reason for its popular success; it was an authentically cold book, at which a reader was entitled to shiver. Partly this was because of the society that Burgess envisioned, but partly also it derived from a personal artistic option within the book. One can almost feel the pathetic, beseeching figure of Poetic Justic imploring the novelist for admittance to his book and being roughly shouldered away. The writer whose book gives its title to Burgess's, whose house was vandalized and whose wife was raped by Alex and his droogs, is later allowed to play the samaritan to beaten Alex, and to suspect who it is that he's helping, but never to know it. The "brothers" to whom the story is recited are never identified, but we are bound to assume they are a new set of droogs of whom Alex, now a casehardened pro, has become or will become the leader. Droogery is thus unrebuked, even triumphant; if only by contrast with the alternatives, its appeal is allowed.

Music in this novel which slants across all the categories, doesn't work in any logical way on the narration, nor is it an integral part of the plot, yet it's no less functional. In conjunction with the language, which is a major source of the book's vitality, it suggests a sphere of instinctual and uncorrupted response, such as neither *1984* nor *Brave New World* ventures to represent, and which contrasts with the asphalt jungle of the book itself. It's this intimation of the primeval and healthy barbaric, if only as a possibility within the corrupt, sick barbaric of the city slumster, that's distinctively Burgess and at the same time strongly Joycean.

Even more marked is the application of Joycean prose in a pure entertainment like *Tremor of Intent*. Burgess, like Joyce, is delighted by the linguistic patterns that form in the fading shadows of unconsciousness; and in this wholly implausible thriller, the most impressive and inventive passages are those where various characters (Hillier, Roper, Theodorescu, and a Russian KVD-agent) wander off for one reason or another into gaga-land, letting words, their sounds, and their associations take over for the common order of discourse, or imposing on them a whole new order of non-meanings:

> I was not surprised. In a way I was pleased [writes Roper]. My sense
> of betrayal was absolute. I fetched the barnaby out of the cheese-slice,
> fallowed the whereupon with ingrown versicles, then cranked with end
> less hornblows of white, gamboge, wortdrew, harimon, and prayrichard
> the most marvellous and unseen-as-yet fallupons that Old Motion ever
> hatched in all his greenock nights [p. 201].

We couldn't, perhaps, take this wamble-speech in extended and uninterrupted doses, and Burgess doesn't give us a great deal of it. Even the Clockwork Orange dialect runs down perceptibly in the latter part of that novel, and the freakyspeak in *Tremor of Intent* is even more carefully spotted than that. Still, though it's only a dash of Joycean seasoning on books which are of a pretty common order, Burgess unmistakably uses that garnish, and not by any means to contemptible effect. Where Durrell escapes *from* Joycean structure in the course of the Alexandria novels, Burgess at the high point of his fictions escapes *into* Joycean language. The one author is no more interested in palimpsest-effects, narrative discontinuities, and classical analogues, than the other is in twilight states of consciousness; neither has much of a hand for parody, neither is a self-vivisector. Both are entertainers, and in that capacity both are willing to settle for varieties of short-range effect that come close to claptrap—*coups de théâtre* with suave, ice-cold heavies and sultry, fire-lipped temptresses—all suffused with the aroma of musty theatrical trunks, from which they were just dragged. To point out that elements of Joyce served authors of this character is not to add very much to his permanent glory on the Homer-Dante-Flaubert scale, but it humanizes and facilitates him, suggesting the dimensions and directions of his work that were most readily domesticated. In neither case is there any question of pushing Joyce's work further than he himself carried it; on the contrary, Burgess and Durrell use only one aspect apiece of the Joycean enterprise, and handle it very gingerly in their own novels. Yet for the most part, that salt is what gives the rest of the dish its savor.

ARABESQUES: PYNCHON, LEZAMA

Atrophy of narrative, ironing out of paper-thin characters, multi-directional anti-narrative reading habits—such depletion of fiction's traditional energies and inertias seems to lead toward a kind of stasis, best exemplified in that gigantic, endlessly busy, but almost motionless book, *Finnegans Wake:*

> With centric and eccentric scribbled o'er,
> Cycle and epicycle, orb in orb,

the *Wake* is like one of those complex Rube-Goldberg machines whose own operation is its sole, and fascinating, purpose. One is always aware of its rotations, repetitions, and above all its resistance: it is an impedance-machine, intent on getting elaborately nowhere. The novels of Thomas Pynchon, *V* and *Gravity's Rainbow,* offer interesting analogies and extensions of the principle.

On its surface, *V* is an incredibly active novel, with an immense cast of characters as vigorously in motion as a swarm of paramecia in a drop of swamp-water. They penetrate the sewer systems of Manhattan, yo-yo up and down the East Coast, rattle around Egypt, Florence, Malta, and South Africa; they change appearances, change identities, couple like rabbits, group and regroup, diffuse and drop out of sight as fast as motes in a beam of sunlight. The activity isn't completely pointless, since plots and semi-connected actions form and reform, sometimes unbeknownst to the participants, sometimes accidentally; but often all pretense of sequential behavior disintegrates in a whirl of miscellaneous partying, a picturesque but gratuitous act. In the end, the various plots don't cohere, the individual actions are spaced out. Why does Paola Maijstral feel she has to enter a black whorehouse in order to become, or in spite of the fact that she is, the preferred girl of McClintic Sphere? Why after a spell there does she feel inclined to go back to Pappy Hod, with whom life seems distinctly less preferable? These things, and many others, happen, but without apparent motivation, or at least only with such motivation as the reader wants to impute to the character after the event. Uncertainty and actual provocation are built into the structure of the fiction. For example, the heading of Chapter 3 advises us that Stencil, a quick-change artist, plays a role in each of the eight episodes comprising the chapter. Some of his identities are more obvious than others (blue spectacles and a peeling face are perhaps clues), and I won't say that any are completely impossible to guess, especially with the aid of information given much later in the book. But essentially those readers are right who complain that "they can't follow the plot." They can't, and aren't really supposed to. For the plot (in the sense of "what happens to the characters," and even in the sense of "how the characters' inner life develops") is not the vehicle of the book's main interest. Its function, and the function of all that frantic, superficial activity, is to distract and impede, not to express. One can't say that it does or doesn't function in other ways as well; there's an uncertainty principle at work as we read, in that no action is so far-fetched or remote that it can't, perhaps later, tie up on some level with another; and the construction isn't so tight that what looks important can't be simply forgotten or erased by a coincidence.

In any event, all the hurry and scurry in the novel—drunken brawls, promiscuous beddings-down, aimless wanderings, mistaken identities, weird acts of violence, and arbitrary linkages—lead nowhere. For one tale that is tied up in pink ribbon—probably sardonic —like that of Paola and Pappy, there are dozens that the author leaves hanging in mid-air, without bothering to conclude them. Fina disappears after the gang-bang; to have her reappear for an instant at the airport, about to embark for Puerto Rico, gives the book a ragged and inconsequential look that's surely deliberate. And apart from all the characters who simply split off the action and disappear, the action plot itself is meaningless. Profane, the schlemiel-Redeemer, makes the point about all his "experience" at the end of the book, when he says "offhand" (but he means "in deepest seriousness"), "I'd say I haven't learned a goddamn thing."

What is important to the book takes place outside the realm of the characters' actions, and to a large extent outside their comprehension; and it's only indirectly, semi-allegorically connected with Stencil's search for V. That is more in the nature of a private anxiety, since the woman in whom the principle of V was momentarily embodied, insofar as she was an individual at all, was dead well before the action

of the novel starts. She has a name (Victoria Wren), an origin (Lard-
wick-in-the-Fen, Yorkshire), a history crowded with incident (she
is probably the Alice who at ten years old converted Ralph Mac-
Burgess, actor, to Maxwell Rowley-Bugge, bum; she is the chatelaine
who hires hideously disfigured Evan Godolphin; she is the transves-
tite Bad Priest of Malta). But in the last of these capacities she was
evidently crushed to death in an air raid sometime in the early 1940s,
and picked to pieces by various curious children. The search for V is
therefore pointless and obsessive as it's carried on after the war; it
goes beyond the person, beyond even the several perhaps-conspiracies
of which she may have been an intermittent agent, into her existence
as a malignant or at best indifferent principle of nature. Stencil's father, who knew perhaps too much about her, was swallowed up in the
vortex of a waterspout; it is paranoid to think that she was somehow
responsible for this event, but the book intimates it. Her powers of
malignant fascination are shown extending to Stencil, junior, who
had only fleeting and fragmentary hints of her existence, and no notion whether she was even female in more than the metaphorical
sense assigned to ships, hurricanes, and some nations. The fact that a
number of other people can get caught up in a search-program as
flimsy as Stencil's shows by strong implication how loosely they're
attached to the texture of everyday life. Yet the fact is that everyday
life itself includes alien and even hostile elements, as is shown most
gruesomely in the discovery after her death and dismemberment that
the lady largely consisted of inanimate prosthetic materials—a wig,
a glass eye, false teeth, a wooden foot, a star sapphire imbedded in
her navel. Thus, though the search for V as protracted by Stencil is
insane, her reported nature ties her closely to a theme running through
the entire book, the encroachment and usurpation of the inanimate
world on the animate. V as a physical principle needn't be sought
anywhere because she (it) is present everywhere; V as a person can't
be sought, because she is dead. There's a potent unspoken connection
here.

Rachel Owlglass makes love to her MG, beer is dispensed to maniac sailors through rubber breasts, Esther Harvitz gets her nose erotically bobbed and her baby aborted, Lieutenant Godolphin has his face hideously rebuilt, Kilroy is explained as a circuit-diagram, Eigenvalue practices psychic dentistry, Mondaugen tells ghastly stories of dehumanized behavior in Southwest Africa, the wartime bombardment of Malta creates fantasies of stone-like personalities crusted over as a result of life in caves, automata take major roles in a ballet—and on page 270 the author simply transcribes from the world almanac six months' worth of natural disasters, to illustrate the predominance of the inanimate over the animate world. As a sensitive schlemiel, Benny Profane is at hopeless odds with all natural things, a Redeemer limp and helpless against encroaching evil; he sees it but is helpless to do anything about it. This is why—against superficial probability—he is such a magnet for women who want to protect, mother, and be personally intimate with him. Yet hardly any of this vision of a world gradually depersonalizing relates more than hazily to the narrative. Reified people are simply a condition of the world within which the novel takes place, and Stencil's preference for connecting it with lady V (or Vernichtung or Valletta, or Victoria, or vortex, or all of them) is hardly shielded at all from the suspicion that it's a private obsession. Stencil's search and the structure of the world are like two giant vortexes the tips of which meet in the paper-thin plane of the narrative action.

Stencil, junior, has the interesting mannerism of referring to himself only in the third person, as if he were an outline to be filled in; it's a revealing individual mannerism, but the condition it bespeaks is general, striking in him mainly because he has such a phantom-image of what his life must contain. Nobody remarks his transparency because nobody is more opaque than he is; on the contrary, his insane energy contrasts with their random jittering, catches them up and organizes them for a moment, before moving on and out. At the book's end, Stencil is racing off to Stockholm in pursuit of one Viola who may or may not be in possession of V's glass eye—it is as sensible an objective, in his terms, as any other, and not much different, as a principle of world or individual order, from that of Benjy in *The Sound and the Fury* when he's being driven around the square in the accustomed direction.

The V of V's that Pynchon uses as an epigraph to his novel intimates the narrowing of the ordering mind to a point of monomania, the simultaneous reduction of life to a single point of vitality, and so the limiting of kindly intent among or between human beings to an automatic gesture of self-defeat—like a secular saint walking through life under the name "Profane." The great compelling structures of the *Wake* lie within the "characters" and they do cheer if not inebriate, by providing an instant rebirth for every inevitable mortality. Pynchon's characters are thinner and flatter; the arabesques of their activity are strictly limited, and behind them—bad if it's only an obsession, worse if it's something more—is the encroachment of an inanimate, impersonal, inhuman power. It speaks in Pynchon's prose, which is frequently colored gray by scientific and technical terminology; it speaks even more coldly in a constant fascination with abstract and impersonal process. Pynchon's outline-characters caper across an ice-cold universe. Their relation to Joyce's outline-figures (who yet never fail to be full of other outlines) is neither intimate nor immediate. But in the sense of a fragile and fearful existence maintained against the grain of an ostentatiously pointless plot, they are a true Joycean development. Like Joyce's personae, they swim the waters of a sea thick with the plankton of learning both vulgar and encyclopedic; and the fable they unfold has no more to do with morality than with politics or religion. Heroes and villains of the book are its underlying patterns, the real plot is our ability to see them; and in that respect, rather than in other, more immediate characteristics, the book declares its parentage.

"Oneiric chill," a phrase used somewhere in *V* for a specific purpose, characterizes the book as a whole, and carries over with special relevance to *Gravity's Rainbow*—an extraordinary tour de force of paranoid fantasy, cloak-and-dagger romance, and technological poetry. The period of this book is the last days of World War II, when Europe is literally falling apart. The powers of technology (corporations, apparatus, situations, technical processes themselves) have largely taken over for human nature; hence the plans and desires of individuals or even groups are absurdly erratic and unimportant, and everything that happens or seems to happen is or may be a front for something else. As in *V*, there's no following the chain of events; it isn't a chain but a Jackson Pollock of wiggling lines, blobs, blurs, and smears. Many words are spoken, but only rarely by individuals; thoughts and impressions occur, but are rarely localized behind any specific pair of eyeballs. What the novel represents is not what happened over a period of time to a few chosen individuals, but the nightmare of the disintegrating European mind in the final stages of a war that was as much enacted as fought. There's no order or economy or coherence to this story: the survivors who emerge from it would be quite as justified as Profane in declaring afterward: "I'd say I haven't learned a goddamn thing." In its erratic and tangled course, the novel blossoms into extravagantly decadent orgies, narrows down to Keystone-Cop chases, turns to brutally sadistic animal episodes, and always, always weaves developing technologies and corporate mergers, chains of command and task-force terminology into the weft of human intentions.

On one jocose level, the novel veers off to present us with a full-length biography of an electric-light bulb; on another, every conceivable variation is played on the theme of the rocket as male sex organ. Against all probability, a central element of the novel flowers from an ancient obsession of the author's, discernible already in *V*. The Vernichtung-campaign waged by General Von Trotha against the Bondel and Herero tribes of German Southwest Africa was a first and fearful stage in the dehumanization of the world. In *Gravity's Rainbow* it is assumed that some of the tribesmen have survived genocide, have survived their own highly organized suicidal impulses, have come to Germany, moved into abandoned mines, and been incorporated as a military-tribal unit of their own, connected with the rocket program at Nordhausen and Peenemunde. They are known as the Schwarzgerat or Schwarzkommando, their relation to the V-1, V-2, V-x rocket series combines fetishism with technical skill of a high order; and thus they are a matter of great interest to various Russian, American, and English intelligence agencies. In celebrating this marriage of the savage and the technical intelligence, Pynchon is most ingenious; the emblem of the rocket is the very shape of primitive African villages, and the arc that is implicit between that origin and the present terminus—the arc of human civilization—is but one of hundreds of arcs and parabolas worked into the background pattern of the book.

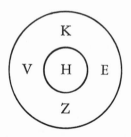

The deciphering of novel by reader parallels the persistent, paranoid effort of the "characters" (but they are transparent cutouts, not true characters) to decipher the twisted and tormented face of Europe; a collective message works its painful way toward consciousness. The world is a palimpsest, but the topmost message is not letters at all, it is a tangle of squirming, semi-animate shapes. Characteristically, one major achievement in deciphering is accomplished by a gang of black rocketmen, careening on high-speed motorcycles through the ruins of a bombed-out North German chemical factory:

There doesn't exactly dawn, no but there *breaks,* as that light you're afraid will break some night at too deep an hour to explain away— there floods on Enzian what seems to him an extraordinary understanding. This serpentine slag-heap he is just about to ride into now, this ex-refinery, Jamf Olfabriken Werke AG, is *not a ruin at all. It is in perfect working order.* Only waiting for the right connections to be set up, to be switched on . . . modified, precisely, *deliberately* by bombing that was never hostile, but part of a plan both sides—*"sides?"*—had always agreed on . . . yes and now what if we—all right, say we *are* supposed to be the Kabbalists out here, say that's our real Destiny, to be the scholar-magicians of the Zone, with somewhere in it a Text, to be picked to pieces, annotated, explicated, and masturbated till it's all squeezed limp of its last drop . . . well we assumed—naturlich!—that this holy Text had to be the Rocket, orururumo orunene the high, rising, dead, the blazing, the great one ("orunene" is already being modified by the Zone-Herero children to "omunene," the eldest brother) . . . our Torah. What else? Its symmetries, its latencies, the *cuteness* of it enchanted and seduced us while the real Text persisted, somewhere else, in its darkness, our darkness . . . even this far from Sudwest we are not to be spared the ancient tragedy of lost messages, a curse that will never leave us. . . .

But, if I'm riding through it, the Real Text, right now, if this is it . . . or if I passed it today somewhere in the devastation of Hamburg, breathing the ash-dust, missing it completely . . . if what the IG built on this site were not at *all* the final shape of it, but only an arrangement of fetishes, come-ons to call down special tools in the form of 8th AF bombers *yes* the "Allied" planes all would have been, ultimately, IG-built, by way of Director Krupp, through his English interlocks—the bombing was the exact industrial process of conversion, each release of energy placed exactly in space and time, each shockwave plotted in advance to bring *precisely tonight's wreck* into being thus decoding the Text, thus coding, recoding, redecoding the holy Text. . . . If it is in working order, what is it meant to do? The engineers who built it as a refinery never knew there were any further steps to be taken. Their design was "finalized," and they could forget it.

It means this War was never political at all, the politics was all theatre, all just to keep people distracted . . . secretly, it was being dictated instead by the needs of technology . . . by a conspiracy between human beings and techniques, by something that needed the energy-burst of war, crying, "Money be damned, the very life of (insert name of Nation) is at stake," but meaning, most likely, *dawn is nearly here, I need my night's blood, my funding, funding, ahh more. . . .* The real crises were crises of allocation and priority, not among firms—

it was only staged to look that way—but among the different Technologies, Plastics, Electronics, Aircraft, and their needs which are understood only by the ruling elite . . . [pp. 520-21].

Pynchon has written, in *Gravity's Rainbow,* an appallingly intelligent, deeply disbelieving, almost unreadable parable of the modern
world; it has the frigidity of a nightmare, along with a nightmare's
lurking suspicion that there's another and worse nightmare lurking
behind this one. You can't even trust your sense of horror. The book
perhaps suffers, like those of Joyce, from too slavish a devotion to the
principle of imitation—chaos is altogether chaotic and void is bleakly
vacant; like Joyce's novels, too, it defies all principles of economy,
and sometimes its black humor is a little jejune. But in the large it's
a deeply moving and very serious book. Slothrop, the free-lance
American agent who masquerades now as Rocketman, now as a giant
Pig-hero, falls into and out of situations, simultaneously ironic and
straight. He is caught up in the functions of apparatus and squirms
free of them with such incorporeal elusiveness, that in the end we're
not surprised to find him fading, almost unremarked, out of human
existence altogether. Like Stencil, he is absorbed into his own obsession, spiraling off (we're clearly given to understand) on a rainbow
that has slipped the pull of gravity entirely. At the same time, and
quite without sentimentality, America moves into the novel, as a fantasy almost of the "normality" Slothrop might have returned to and
didn't.

Though it's deeply rooted in specific locales and a limited period
of time, *Gravity's Rainbow* again reminds us of Joyce in suggesting
behind the immediate scenario a timeless and universal process. People intrude on objects only peripherally and blunderingly, objects advance on people inexorably, and people cooperate with this process
by calmly converting others or themselves into objects. In a book
that's saturated with sex, mostly the kinky varieties to be sure, some
of the most passionate and sensitive writing is devoted to a celebra-

tion of the special molecular affinities of different families of plastics. The book's perspectives are inhumanly long. Pynchon appears to have less than no interest in morals, in politics, in religion, in what used to be called "human nature." He doesn't write an "art novel" properly so called, a realistic novel, a novel of ideas, a horror story, a psychological study, or a science-fiction fable—though traces of all these ingredients are perceptible. Though the phrase doesn't characterize it very closely, *Gravity's Rainbow* could be called a visionary apocalyptic novel, Joycean less in specific techniques than in its scope, penetration, and cold perspective.

José Lezama Lima was well known as a poet, editor, journalist, and functionary in Havana long before he was an achieved novelist, but various chapters toward a novel started to appear, at irregular intervals, in the pages of *Orígines* as early as 1949. A ten-year silence followed the last of them, and then the finished book finally appeared as *Paradiso* in 1966. Lezama is said to be working on a sequel, perhaps to be titled *Inferno;* meanwhile, he must be treated as a one-novel novelist. But that novel is so tremendous that no apologies are required. *Paradiso* is an undoubted instance of Joycean influence, but it is infinitely more as well. Giving some conception of it as a piece of fiction in its own enormous right calls for some poising and balancing.

To begin with, Lezama's *Paradiso* is a chronicle of middle-class family life in the Cuba of the 20th century's first years. Specifically, it is rooted in Havana. Though he doesn't advertise the fact in the text itself, the author makes no effort to disguise a sizable autobiographical element. The head of the Cemí clan in the novel is a colonel of artillery who, like Lezama's actual father, died young of that particularly virulent flu that was making the rounds just after World War I. The first six chapters of the novel, viewing events through a relatively wide-angle lens, lead us in and out among the roots and branches of the Cemí family, dwelling on their brief migration to Florida and back, the marriage of the colonel and Rialta, the special idiosyncrasies of delightful Uncle Alberto, the brief and miserable musical career of Uncle Andresito. Though it's too much to say that the tone of these chapters is nostalgic, it's warm and affectionate—leisurely and ample, too, after the fashion of Proust. The colonel's son, little José Cemí, lends us his eyes from time to time, but is far from dominating the landscape; we follow his development as one more theme in the family chronicle, reminded of Proust once again by the fact that he is an asthmatic invalid, surrounded despite his precocity by rough and often incomprehensible events. After Chapter 7, the book focuses more and more closely on his intellectual development at school and university, and on his association with his prodigious schoolmates Fronesis and Foción, and in the end—but the end is a separate topic to itself.

So baldly outlined and truncated, *Paradiso* sounds a little like a Cuban *Portrait of the Artist* writ large and long; and to a degree this is so. Lezama doesn't cut and chop his scenes as finely as Joyce; he isn't as sparse of episode and detail, and doesn't rely to the same extent on reiterated symbolic particulars. But the relationship to Joyce, however close or distant, makes itself felt chiefly as an afterthought and on the basis of the book's slow-developing structural characteristics. As one enters into it, one is most struck by its stylistic and expressive features, and they appear Joycean only to the degree that baroque prose—complexly allusive, radically metaphorical, and highly elaborate syntactically—may remind us of Joyce but also of other artists in similar vein. Spanish critics often speak of Góngora; a glance at the list of Lezama's critical writings reveals a predominant interest in Mallarmé which might equally well lead to the kind of explosively metaphorical language in which the imagery seems to take on a life of its own, and escape from the humdrum task of recording facts or narrating events.

The combination of allusive learning—Lezama is as much a poet of the library and its *disjecta membra* as Borges—with metaphorical orchids that seem attached to the ground from which they spring only by trailing tentacles of private association reaching down not up, bring the stylist himself center-stage where he tends to stand well above his "characters" and lecture about them. The process is accomplished more persistently and also more violently, though in essentially the same way as by Joyce's continual changes of style from chapter to chapter of *Ulysses*. As a result, Lezama's novel is, to a much greater degree than Joyce's, phantasmagoric. Phrases in a character's mind become reified, they start to enact parts in a drama of some strange sort, being played out on the page before us rather than anywhere within the fictional cosmos. A single, if somewhat strung-out, paragraph makes the point:

> The house, in the middle of the farm, had all its rooms dripping with light. It was deliquescing in the excess of light, imparting to its surroundings the surprise of marine currents. Inside the house was the feverish couple, and the unrecognizable Isolde began to raise her voice to the animistic possibilities of song. There was Señor Michelena, twirling the champagned stem of the glass, while the woman grazed him, barely turning, stretching out her loins and trailing seaweed, uncertain on which square of the board to begin her song. Sometimes, her voice detached from her body, slowly evaporated, she recognized herself among the lamps or in the water's sound on the tiled roof while her body became harder as it freed itself from those lunar subtleties and currents. The door half-opened and she appeared, livid, shrieking as she turned, the woman slowly opening and straightening her mouth as if fighting against the liquid resistance, with small laminations given her by the sweat of caresses. From the farmhouse door at the bottom of the steps, swaying with lanterns and fleshly phantoms, she barely opened her small mouth, slapped in the dream and requiring new muscles for the sticking plaster. Facing this house of druidic lunar suspicions and with tunics left behind by the Stymphalides, sitting in a stone rocking chair of ground mother-of-pearl, the Chinaman of the swift golden crullers, wrapped in apotropaic linen, was moving osseously inside that big stone house, inside his linen billowing in the strong wind. From the weariness inspired in him by a leftover glass egg, he fashioned a very delicate ceremonial baton, sometimes carrying the dream of antelopes and frontal candelabra to the leafy ashtray at his right hand, sometimes lifting the cottons of one leg to the chair, determined to resist the nocturnal projections behind the crisscrossing of the instrumental ossein. His celibate weariness snaked here and there like a hand that could draw out any of the charlatan, inopportune, and intemperate

pieces, and place them on the other side of the river, where it was no longer permitted to look, or even to hum through one's teeth, a guitar whose strings they will no longer be able to charge, a guitar that points and stretches its throat toward the whirlwind of the eastern gate. But disdaining Lully's long baton to mark the entrances and exits, in his ocular inspection of the vegetative growth, he heard within the exception to the law of the whirlwind being devoured by the tides' growth in the pianistic desolation of Monday [pp. 48-49].

Some of the details of this dreamlike picture are explained by previous passages. Señor and Señora Michelena are the employers of Andrés Olaya, momentarily a secretary; the Chinaman of the swift golden crullers is their servant, who out of jealousy swept the food past Andrés so fast that he couldn't take any. Childless and eager for children, the Michelenas pamper Andrés, and he hears from a hotel-clerk about certain less-innocent orgies of which this is evidently a vision—not a representation of things seen, but an imagining. Whether the "woman" is Señora Michelena or a third party isn't definite, but it's probably the latter; she could be an Isolde or a sea-siren, as later she will turn into a manatee, but already she is trailing seaweed and singing, presumably the Liebestod. The Stymphalides are harpies, either the ladies before us or some other harpies; Monday's pianistic desolation may well occur when the whole orgy will have come to a halt, the weekend being over. But within the frame-work supplied by these guessable details, words and images are given pretty much their own way. Before long we shall be into sentences like, "A terrible argument begins between Two Obeisances and Clouds Rushing allied with Quick Slow, about letting themselves get trapped by the Nusimbalta, walking backwards without looking at him and even managing to cross one wing over the other." In the whirl of the imagined orgy, even the routine bonds of syntactical coherence are released, while the allusiveness reaches into privacy beyond any reader's power to follow it more than impressionistically. There is nothing before or after the quoted material to identify Quick Slow or Nusimbalta. Not surprisingly, shortly after this loosening of all the ties, the Michelenas find themselves the proud parents of twins.

The passage represents a striking showpiece within a few pages of the start of the novel, but it doesn't come as a shock. We have already had "French-fried potatoes as carbonized as Cenozoic crystals" and a drop of rum "which, poured on a handkerchief, gave it the quality of the scarf Marius had used to dry his perspiration among the ruins of Carthage." The deliberately explanatory quality of the latter comparison is frequent in Lezama; it combines with the often-exaggerated formality of the dialogue to make the texture of the composition very present to the reader, almost as a screen through which he has to grope. The later lectures of Fronesis, Foción, and Cemí, chiefly on sexology, would be thought stiff and pedantic (with their intricately periodic sentences, their elaborately offhand allusions) if read from a script; as allegedly improvised, they're high fantasy.

And yet the polyphlusboious richness of *Paradiso* is to be sensed on every page; it may be chiefly a verbal phenomenon, but that's far from implying a sense of impoverishment. Like Joyce, Lezama has a gift for mingling the obscene with the erudite, for phantasmagorizing gobbets of realistic detail, for deep-plowing the subconscious. The various miscellaneous ingredients of the fiction are never held under such strict control that one can't envision them exploding or spiraling off into separate nebulae. From the beginning, it's an anxious, a high-tension performance; and after the disappearance from the book of Fronesis and Foción (abrupt and inconclusive, hardly mitigated at all), the orbits widen still further, the narrative chunks whirl through vaster and more evident distances of empty space. Characters become detached from their surroundings, their names, the laws of nature, even from a consistent set of pronominal references (*he* and *we* are particularly apt to get interchanged), and the prose becomes even more remotely metaphorical, more fragmented syntactically, than before. The book does close a sort of narrative circle by bringing José Cemí back into timely intimacy with the dying Oppiano Licario, who had been present long ago at Colonel Cemí's deathbed. But these last units are not seen through the eyes of José Cemí, so far as can be told; and if he is the achieved artist who wrote them—he, whose development we have primarily followed through the body of the book—that has to be our own surmise. Actually, the final pages come close to being disembodied writing—image generating image, as in a poem by Yeats, without explicit reference to a hypothetical speaker or even an ostensible subject.

In this liberation of language to its own inner energies, Lezama surely represents the fulfillment of a major Joycean potential, one that we're more likely to associate with the *Wake* than with the *Portrait;* one, too, that transcends all questions of influence and even inspiration, but can only be intimated under the loose formula of affinity. One doesn't pass very confident judgment on a novel such large parts of which are, and are likely to remain permanently, indigestible; but there's enough fascination in *Paradiso,* even for a relatively uninformed reader, to give it a major place among the books that have fulfilled and extended lines that Joyce first began to trace.

MOTLEY: BARTH, O'BRIEN— AND THEN BORGES

Inevitably with time, Joyce has become domesticated, miniaturized, and fractionated. It's hard to say this without implying that the followers are like Penelope's eager, impotent suitors, striving to bend the bow of Odysseus but incapable of doing so. In fact there's no need to do again what Joyce already did so well, and a good many of his techniques, perfectly valid in the first part of the century, are no longer really operational. For example, the entire mystical-erotic-artistic side of Stephen Dedalus would be an embarrassment to a contemporary author, appropriate to a period-piece perhaps, but irritating to a reader with 1976 values in mind. John Barth's *Lost in the*

Funhouse provides a sort of loose parallel, though the sketches are far more discontinuous than those in Joyce's Bildungsroman, and in the last part of *Funhouse* the artist is present chiefly by self-mocking implication. The sequence in the collection leads us from the meditations of a sperm through the boyhood adventures of Ambrose to the mythical life history of an anonymous Homeric bard marooned on a desert island and forced to create a life-work out of his own life. From infancy through childhood, and then to the province of the mythical, Barth seems intent on writing large that wonderful sentence of Joyce's, "God becomes man becomes fish becomes barnacle goose becomes featherbed mountain." One thing is largely omitted, to be sure; that is the development of the individual sensibility. We leave Ambrose before he has become much more than a very embryonic artist; and what takes his place in the latter part of the book is simply the narrative process itself.

In playing the games of self-consciousness, Barth is in his own sportive element; he delights in sound-box, mirror, and echo effects, which turn every story into a wry questioning of its own processes. He raids an imaginary textbook on fiction for comments on the fiction that's being told, takes over the mind of a writer complaining about the process of writing, or enters into a story bewailing the mode of its own existence. His mythological fables are contaminated by an awareness that they are already mythological, but they are also cast, not just linguistically but motivationally, in the mode of the present. Most of Barth's mythological figures are in fact self-conscious writers, mocked by their own clichés and trapped by their own narrative reflexes. Character thus diminishes into the jokes and paradoxes of a quick-trick dialectic that's always pretty much the same, whatever the name attached to it. It's a spry and elegant kind of funny; but it's often very private too, and there's a lot of protesting—half dramatic, half quite personal as I hear it—against the narrow twists and turns of thought compressed by its own means of expression.

In fact Barth makes use of mythology, when he does so—in

Chimera as well as *Lost in the Funhouse*—for more limited and defined purposes than Joyce does in *Ulysses*. He feels the classical
world, or that of the Arabian Nights, as decisively distant and different from the casual, colloquial American dialect in which his retell-
ings are cast. He sometimes puts so much new wine in his old bottles
that they bulge alarmingly, and comically, far out of their original
shape. Joyce, to be sure, does something of the sort; but he implies a
kind of interpenetration between the classical model and the modern
instance, a reinforcement of either by the other, a sense of depth.
Barth is a joker who gets most of his jokes from cross-cultural incongruities. In the process not only the original fable but the identity
of the reteller is remarkably attenuated. There's little that's positive
about Barth's artist-in-the-making. He is programmed to run through
the funhouse of his own personality, as through the museum of the
world's cultures, more in terror and anxiety than in delight. He is
also afflicted with a terrible sense of *déjà vu*. The funhouse has been
here a long time, we have visited it before, and it's a closed experience
in any case, because it always bends the story-teller back into the cor-
ridors of his own story.

Where Stephen Dedalus draws his learning around him like a
magician's cloak, Barth's artist slaps it down between a nudge and a
nervous giggle. He acts as if we all knew it all the time, and in fact
seems to prefer mythological skeletons that we have known very well
on the formal pages of Bulfinch, so he can set them to jigging by
means of his own nervous syncopations. Indeed, the big pastiche- and
burlesque-novels—*The Sot-Weed Factor* and *Giles Goat-Boy*—are
more spacious and outward, but over the long run they fall into another trap, when the capering narrator outwears his welcome. It's an
old complaint, that a narrator who walks in front of his puppets splits
the reader's interest, and risks making his story or himself seem intrusive. In the shorter fiction, there is really no center of interest apart
from the story and its teller, who are one. But in the big fictions, the
novelist is perceptibly present behind his capering creations, yet he
isn't present enough to be felt as a deepening of the story.

Barth is a serious comic novelist, with more interest in language than in character, a performer and even a bit of a clown; all these qualities make him as legitimate an heir of Joyce as is Updike. And even more than Updike or Burgess, he gives evidence of a careful reading of Joyce. His prose, in its rhythms and concentrated impressionism, reminds one of Joyce again and again: its rendering of experience, by slipping from object into mind and back again, is exactly similar. And yet there's one great difference, as a result of which one leaves Barth, as one leaves Updike, with a sense of thinness and insubstantiality. His books seem written to be read at a rapid canter, catch as catch can, take it or leave it. Even Barthian puzzles aren't heavily elaborated like Joycean labyrinths; reading them the second or third time over is like reading them the first. It's not to be expected, of course, that a man will write in palimpsest who doesn't see the world in palimpsest; Barth isn't worse as a writer because he's less weighty—only different. My own sense is that miniatures constitute his best work so far—and that, in its own terms, is praise. But the intimidating quality of a man like Joyce is that his simple presence constricts the terms in which you praise other writers. His comedy is gut but it also makes you think; his writing is intricate, but it is also gigantic. He stretches the critical vocabulary to the point where it looks condescending when hung on another man. But that I guess is the price you pay.

Flann O'Brien's crazy, wonderful novel, *At Swim-Two-Birds,* was published in Joyce's lifetime (1939), though just barely, and won the master's generous approval. It is a phantasmagoria which takes place essentially in the mind of the author, a classically quiescent university student who spends his days in bed and his nights cadging cigarettes and drinks. The bed is a place of repose, much to the disgust of the author's mean-spirited uncle, in whose house he lives; but it is also a place of contemplation and reverie, and of childbirth as well, since it produces the novel we know, with its chinese-puzzle of stories within stories. Indeed, there's such a swirl of mostly fantastic activity inside the novel that the external torpor of the nameless novelist is more than justified. But of course none of this is visible to the uncle, any more than the various marks by which the book's characters are distinguished are apparent to readers for whom the author hasn't bothered to describe them. O'Brien seems to have put some effort into the ancient wheeze that language was given to man in order to conceal his thoughts.

Much as he resembles Beckett's figure of Murphy, who was born just the year before, O'Brien's somnolent author is not yet psychotic, he is simply distracted. The Greek motto at the head of the book declares that "All things naturally draw apart," and under the analytic gaze of the author (who helpfully provides many sections of his book with solemn descriptions of their rhetorical modes), that's exactly what they do. A gang of wild-west cowpokes begotten by Mr. William Tracy, a recognized expert in that genre, gallop with six-guns blazing through rural Dublin; Giant Finn MacCool and Mad Sweeny the bard assert themselves under the impulse of ancient Irish legend. An unctuous but vicious Pooka and a nasty but ineffectual Good Fairy carry on a private war out of the realm of folklore; and there are large beery sections of Irish pub-conversation—maundering, moronic, and accurate to the last curl of a cliché. The hero of the book is not the story, as with Barth, partly because O'Brien sets so many stories going, and the characters involved in them start so many counter-stories, that none of them really gets told. Here language itself is the hero or villain, language which is able not only to transform and then reflect itself, but to give events and ideas and objects instantaneous new characters—often in a surprisingly literal sense. Language itself is the first mover, under whose impulse "all things naturally draw apart."

It is therefore fitting that the characters created by Dermot Trellis (an imaginary character created by the nameless imaginary author) should conspire against him, making use of his imaginary bastard son Orlick (cf. Dickens's *Great Expectations*) to concoct a counter-story. In this narrative-within-a-narrative-within-a-narrative the characters created by Dermot Trellis gleefully and hideously torture their creator, and finally put him on trial for his life before a panel of phantom judges and a phantom-jury of his own creation, making use of the evidence supplied by characters out of his own book. Like Bloom before the bar of his own unconscious, the badly battered Trellis is struggling hopelessly against the foregone conclusion when the scene breaks off.

On an episodic level, the novel ends with a kind of mechanical happiness. Even as he is fighting for his life, a stupid maid burns the last few pages of Dermot Trellis's latest manuscript, thus destroying the various hateful characters who have been tormenting him so malignantly. He returns from his nightmare, somewhat the worse for wear, into the world of the everyday, the comforts of which are suggested by the swinging haunches of the maid as she climbs the stairs before Trellis. And, after being relentlessly sour and begrudging, the uncle of author number one proves himself unexpectedly generous and considerate when the young man has passed his examinations. As the innermost story collapses, the outer ones are resolved: sweetness and light seem to prevail. But the *Conclusion of the book, ultimate,* which the author appends, is a curious and very beautiful prose poem after the manner of Robert Burton, on the fragility of the human mind, its frightful susceptibility to its own *idées fixes.* Two images predominate: Mad Sweeny, a prophetic bag of bones hung in a tree between heaven and earth like a starved bird or a sibyl, listens to the barking of dogs, a creaturely noise that only deepens his sense of the infinite immensity of space: and a man run mad on the number three goes home and cuts his throat three times, scrawling with his blood on the mirror a last note to his wife, "good bye, good bye, good bye." As an ending to a comic novel, it is as grim a passage as the ending of *The Sound and the Fury,* which is also a novel about the mind's inability to keep things from falling apart.

At Swim-Two-Birds is a Joycean novel, but it's Irish as well, and fantastic in addition; there's no way of saying very clearly where one element leaves off and the other begins. The trial scene, the burlesques of epic tradition, and the derisive report of a learned conversation between three villainous pub-crawlers (they are as full of solemn, disjointed, useless miscellaneous information as the "Ithaca" section of *Ulysses*) are among the passages that stand out as directly derivative. Then there's an area where without the Joycean precedent O'Brien perhaps wouldn't have written just as he did, but where the resemblance is too general to justify talk about "influence." The knack of rendering colloquial speech is only to be picked up by listening to colloquial speech, but with *Ulysses* beside him, O'Brien evidently found certain rhythms and certain hard, funny vulgarisms within easy range of his discourse, as earlier practitioners of vulgar Irish English had not. The contemptuous hash made of narrative, the drying out of description, the intrusion of the author as stylistic manipulator—all these conventions, with some others, mark O'Brien as a *post*-Joyce if not wholly *propter*-Joyce writer. The elements of fun and play are purer in him than in Joyce, the labyrinth of the author's language is less intricate and perhaps less oppressive: for all its illusionistic entanglements, the story comes closer to being a story than anything in Joyce. But the evidence of influence is too strong to need further emphasis.

As prestidigitators, illusionists, and artists in trompe-l'oeil, Barth and O'Brien point us toward a calculating contriver of verbal mini-labyrinths like Jorge Luis Borges, with whom this provisional account of post-Joycean fiction-writers can fittingly come to an end. Borges, when we look at him closely, is no more a real descendant of Joyce than he is a proper writer of fiction. His literary ancestry, however far back it reaches, is bound to start with that unlikely couple, Franz Kafka and H. G. Wells; his art does not lead toward an act of luminous vision, but via equivocation and uncertainty to a sense of the duplicity of things. Borges appears before us with the modest but cheerful demeanor of a stage-magician performing small acts of legerdemain with rapid confidence. Linguistically his surfaces are plain, not to say ordinary; his mode is eminently common-sensical, or at most owlish and scholarly. Far from being the mad scholar beloved of fiction-writers since Rabelais, he is reluctant and skeptical. But the train of his investigation leads as abruptly as may be to a logical crux, impasse, or surprise, involving more often than not a second order of nature, a cunning imitation of nature, or an esoteric order in nature.

Apart from Borges himself, there are few characters in his stories who amount to more than stick-figures. Like Erik Lonnrot the detective in "Death and the Compass," they tend to be wholly without background or features; or else they are unidimensional, like Vincent Moon in "The Shape of the Sword"; or they are purely mythological, like the metempsychosing hero of "The Immortals." Very often Borges dispenses with characters altogether, and quite as often with the merest pretext of a story; his essays are fantastic speculations, his stories speculative fantasies—it would be a bold man who tried to draw a straight line between the categories. The fact is that Borges is a gymnast of rationalism. He does not seem to have any deep feeling for the irrational, as it takes the form of deep feeling or private association or mental disease. Even his irrationals are alternative rationalisms. His favorite game is with public systems of counter-logic. The archetypical story in this context is "Tlon, Uqbar, Orbis Tertius," in which one small anomaly in one copy of one volume of a well-known encyclopedia gradually expands into a whole new and intrusive cosmos. The Kabbalah, the Zahir, the Lottery in Babylon are other instances of an occult system of relationships that intrude on "real life" in such a way as to supplant a long-accepted structure. They are often barbaric or mysterious, but that is because the normal occupants of the established system, including our pedantic friend the narrator, don't have a proper key to the new system; when they start seeing the new system from the inside out, resistance fades.

The mental traveler who is Borges's unvarying hero has many traditional roots. The first paragraph of the first chapter of the first book of *Gulliver's Travels* devotes itself assiduously to rooting Gulliver in the most normal, unimaginative petty-bourgeois English milieu that

Swift can fantasize; the time-travelers and scientific discoverers of
H. G. Wells are the most plain and practical fellows treading the face
of the earth. Such a witness, full of homely details and often pedantic
accuracies, is the character More assumed for himself in relation to
the *Utopia,* and it's ideally suited to insinuate the unsuspecting reader
into a world of fantasy before he has a chance to realize how he got
there. But of course this is just a decoy-figure, behind whom we recognize an author intent on mystification; and it's another, less mechanical dimension of Borges's fictions that he often brings this
mystifying author directly onstage to demonstrate that he not only
mystifies us, but is himself a victim of his own questioning, mystery-
spinning mind. An intriguing parallel here is with the remote figure
of Sir Thomas Browne, who like Borges is ostensibly concerned with
pseudo-learning—the more copious, intricate and esoteric, the better.
Both in this sense are structuralists, in that they are fascinated by ar-
rangements and patterns of belief, symbolic systems which have an
inherent delight far beyond the matter of their truth or falsity. And
thus both, under the guise of scholarship and science, are really engaged in an exploration of their own temperaments, their own
equivocal positions in the world.

The model for self-consciousness is an infinite recession of self-
reflecting mirrors, and Borges as the central figure of his own magic-
show reserves the mystification-vocabulary and mystification-syntax
(rhetorical questions are highly favored) very largely for the question
of his own identity. He is not only elusive here but illusionistic, his
figure of Borges resists definition by multiplying definitions. Hardly
anyone who asks, in the course of a fiction, who he really is, really
wants to be told. In Borges's case, the question gives depth and resonance to the labyrinths that surround it, as no specific answer to it
could possibly do, for it suggests a receding sequence of labyrinths,
the last of which are a mystery even to the labyrinth-maker himself.
Actually, the word "labyrinth" though it constitutes the title under
which Borges's writings have become known in English, is of Joycean

provenance. It is not the title of any Spanish collection, though it's a
recurrent concept.

In all these matters, while there's a kinship with Joyce, I think
it's a left-handed, third-cousin kinship, defined as much by antithesis
as by sympathy. Certain relationships lie on the surface. The very
concept of a labyrinth implies an antagonistic relationship between
the artist as mage or adept, and his disciples; they will be such only
as long as he stays ahead of them, so that his position in the fictional
relation rises as theirs is depressed. This alone is enough to set Borges
apart from Chesterton or Wells. As does Joyce, Borges often gives us
nuts to crack that are more shell than kernel; and of course the
atrophy of narrative is apparent in both. But the whole visionary-
symbolic side of Joyce, which leads us to sink under the surface of his
language, and exposes us to painful and wracking violence wrought
on our most intimate phonemes, is absent from Borges. Joyce har-
rows, Borges at his best hypnotizes, so that even his self-division and
self-questioning are felt to take place at a distance and on a stage.
Even if we feel ourselves moving from labyrinth to deeper labyrinth,
it's deeper within Borges, not within ourselves, nor in any sense on
an outward spiral.

CHAPTER NINE

THE
JOYCE ERA?

WHATEVER THE POINT from which you start, if you draw enough lines out from it, the finished diagram will look like a sun. A powerful book has been written to persuade us that the age of modernism, after passing for many years as the age of Eliot, should in fact be retitled "the Pound era" because Ezra Pound is at the center of so many important developments of style and thought. The point is made by suppressing a lot of Pound's eccentricities and emphasizing as his originalities some elements that should probably be sent elsewhere, or divided between Pound and others according to a still-problematic formula. All the same, if that particular bipolar choice were the only one available, I should not be very reluctant to side with Mr. Kenner in thinking Pound's position more pivotal than Eliot's, though even here hindsight gives us no unquestionable privileges. But the options are more than two. Prose fiction has its claims—by which I don't by any means wish to say that the early- and mid-20th century should be titled "the Joyce era," because there are large sections of it that will make better sense if we call them "the Kafka era." In turning from one facet of the past to another, we are so far limited by literary assumptions; but a sensible outsider might well supplant us all by proposing to rebaptize the age with Picasso's name and image. And beyond that I see an argument that needs making (so I can only imagine what it will amount to) that much of the art, music, literature, architecture, and philosophy of the early century was stirred by the revaluation of classical antiquity which began around the turn of the century. As symbolism has been described as a second wave of romanticism, so modernism might perhaps be described as a second wave of neo-classicism under the stimulus of the Cambridge anthropologists. No doubt it's too obvious to need saying, but all these alternatives aren't mutually exclusive; in fact they require mutual supplementation. It's only in "Outlines of History" and the like that historical eras are equated with proper names, and only by simple minds that these useful mnemonic devices are thought to bear even a rough resemblance to reality.

We of the early 20th century have been as fortunate in the variety and multiplicity of our literary artists as was 15th-century Italy in the variety of its plastic artists. No one rubric will satisfactorily define a time-stratum that included figures as powerful and distinct as Lawrence, Mann, and Rilke, Kafka, Proust, and Valéry. Affinity-groups are going to be a long time sorting themselves out; and very likely they will shape up in response to the needs of the future historian and his age, quite as much as in response to the facts of the case. Modern critics don't hesitate to link together as the "metaphysical school" of 17th-century poets individuals who never knew or cared to know one another—men whose very styles were as different as those of Marvell and Cleveland, Herbert and Cowley. What sense posterity will be able to make of our crowded and confused era is in a very real sense posterity's business; nothing precludes their seeing us as a broad current flowing in one general direction, with numerous eddies, counter-currents, and backwashes associated with particular figures and groups. But they will define these different elements for themselves, from a point of view at which we here and now can do no more than guess.

In this general climate there can be little doubt that one of the major systems of literary weather will turn out to focus on Joyce; looked at over all, it will turn out to involve writers of importance in many different tongues over many years, who responded in highly individual ways to different varieties of Joycean stimulus. If one were able to show that wherever it reached, the influence of Joyce produced row upon row of plaster-cast miniaturized Joyces, the argument for his pre-eminence would be overwhelming, no doubt; but the "influence" thus demonstrated might better be called a blight. In fact, the record shows the exact contrary: where the influence of Joyce struck strongly on strong indigenous materials, it met with no passive reception, but provoked an active and individual response. Beckett, who of all men was closest to Joyce and was inspired by him most, "imitated" him least. In their different ways, Faulkner and Virginia Woolf fought to free themselves from Joyce, and found their own voices in the process of doing so, yet not without taking on a tincture of the force with which they had had to cope.

Pope has a rather funny passage on Virgil's perplexities over whether he should copy Homer or copy Nature:

> But when t'examine every part he came,
> Nature and Homer were, he found, the same.
> Convinced, amazed, he checks the bold design,
> And rules as strict his labored work confine
> As if the Stagirite o'erlooked each line.

Well, I don't think it was much like that for most of those who followed Joyce. He helped to show many of them that previously sacrosanct representational conventions needn't be followed rigidly; he enriched many artistic palettes; he cut off some lines of development by fulfilling them with paralyzing completeness; he provided an array of techniques of which smaller talents could copy a few; he hardened those who found repellent the whole development of which he was the culmination, and made it imperative for them to seek alternatives to him. Mythological parallels and stream-of-consciousness narration, neither original with Joyce, were among the first and most striking elements to be identified with his style; but neither technique was ever much used as he used it, on his scale or in his kind of context.

Those who adopted some elements of his labyrinthine, mosaic style of construction hardly ever worked to his scale; those who worked to his scale generally relied more than he did on the impetus of narrative. *Finnegans Wake* led to thickets of comparative mythology and linguistic contortion where very few writers indeed have felt impelled to follow. Yet even here an influence has been felt in a frequent sense of an immanent mythical past at work within the active present, in a deliberate contamination of languages with one another and with their own roots. O'Neill's trilogy *Mourning Becomes Electra* stands in the same knight's-gambit relation to *Ulysses* as Tolkien's *Lord of the Rings* sequence does to the *Wake*. The comparison of Nabokov with Conrad—as stylists who came to English relatively late in life from another primary tongue—is trite by now; but the enormous difference is the amount of the original language that each carried over. Zembla and all its fantastic verbal games are out of Conrad's range altogether, and so is the special talk of Burgess's droogs. Direct connections with Joyce are untraceable, but the widening of fictional prose over the last fifty years to accommodate varieties of hybrid and synthetic usage—not quaint dialects, but compound individual languages—is practically tangible; and in that widening Joyce surely played a major role. It is not too much to say that he enrolled prose style and inter-lingual gymnastics for almost the first time in a major way among the *dramatis personae* of fiction.

In one large respect Pound and Joyce exercised a complementary influence: they stood almost uniquely outside and against the commercial tradition in English letters, as prophets antagonistic to the structure and values of the marketplace. Able men of an earlier age, like Meredith, Gissing, and Henry James, had expected and been disappointed in popular success and popular rewards; they had in varying degrees gone out of their way to seek such rewards, and so paid tribute to Mammon even though they despised him. Even Eliot, though by difficult and gradual means, finally carved out a social, cultural, and financial position for himself—indeed, such an imposing one that we are only now starting to separate the façade from the solid masonry. Pound and Joyce stood apart, as pariah-priests of the imagination. This type in itself is common enough to be tiresome: any Bohemia you want to look into contains hundreds of plaintive martyrs to the liberated fantasy. What was unusual about Joyce and Pound was that, in the tradition of Blake and Baudelaire, they were both prophets against the culture that produced them, and supreme flowers of that culture. In a word, they were good, very good; they also saw behind the value-system that conferred that distinction on them, and refused to exploit the consequences of it. All modernism harbored this ambivalence; they not only pushed it *à l'outrance* but lived it. Their independence of popular values and vulgar standards made up an act of defiance in which only a few have tried to emulate them, but which has signaled a vital renewal.

Though the point can't possibly be proved in any formal way, it has to be said that Joyce was one of the renewers of our language. He cleansed it of stale clichés and tired verbal gestures, washing them sometimes in the acid bath of his sarcasm; he excised loose rhetoric, and made language work, sinewy and nervous, as hardly any English writer had done for two centuries. Whatever the ideals of an age may be, the stylist who carries them to their uttermost limit is bound to be an influential man. He moves the standards, and up and down the line all the benchmarks move. But in its nature this is a hard influence to document; Joyce's achievement in prose is almost purely his own, and if Beckett sometimes seems to rival him in strength and purity of expression, their combined examples have not prevented an awful lot of dreary writing by the epigones.

Mimetic solidity, stylistic transparency, consecutive narration, psychological insight, and moral authority within a middle-class framework—such, in a nutshell, are the central values of the traditional English novel. Books are still being written exemplifying substantially these values; and, contrariwise, a fair number of novels were written during the dominance of the tradition, which didn't aim to satisfy its conditions. (Maturin is no realist, Meredith far from a translucent stylist, Peacock has no interest in psychology, and serious morality does not bulk large in Sterne.) Ballad-novels like *Wuthering Heights,* epic-romances like *Moby Dick,* moral disquisitions hung on a slight narrative frame like *Rasselas* existed alongside the main tradition of the novel, and without penalty: a literary tradition is far from a legislative edict. Still, there's little doubt that with the advent of modernism a balance shifted: a central majority mode in the writing of novels dwindled within a few years to a definite minority.

What replaced the great tradition can best be described as a sheaf of alternatives—no one standard format, but wide variations on a common theme. One could spread a number of them out as quickly as a deck of cards—the camp novel (James Purdy's *Malcolm*), the rhetorical novel (Kenneth Burke's *Toward a Better Life*), the allegorical novel (Kafka, *The Trial*), the mosaic or checkerboard novel (Huxley's *Point Counter Point*), the archetypal novel (Queneau, *St. Glinglin*), the obstacle-novel (Nabokov's *Pale Fire*), the dream-novel (Beckett's *Molloy*), the design-novel (Pynchon's *V*), the burlesque or parodic novel (Barth, *The Sot-Weed Factor*), many different variations on the detective story, all involving the completion of an incomplete pattern, the mythological novel (Updike, *The Centaur*), the depersonalized novel (Robbe-Grillet, *Jalousie*), the palimpsest novel (Durrell), the game novel (Calvino, *Il Castello dei destini incrociati*), the erotic-discovery novel (Lawrence), the argot- and dialect-novel (Gadda)—and so forth and so on. Most of these novels disregard all the criteria listed above as the values of the traditional novel, and all of them disregard most.

The turnabout is all but complete, and the resultant diversity so great that the very concept of direct influence from a single central figure is absurd. The decisive gesture was not one of pushing people toward this alternative or that, but of blocking, stopping, cutting off the mold toward which fiction had for a couple of hundred years allowed itself to be persuaded. Even this metaphor is too strong. The mold was never a constraint, just a convention; such authority as it possessed had been diminishing of its own accord during the late 19th century. In Huysmans and Dostoevsky it is already broken, under pressure of very different impulses. In James and Hardy, in Butler, George Moore, and Conrad, one feels it being stretched and distorted out of its old shape, though not yet discarded. The direct and massive challenge to the old tradition came in *Ulysses*. It was especially forceful because *Ulysses* dealt centrally with a number of themes familiar from novels of the old school. It portrayed a young man, an outsider, coming to terms with society; a marriage challenged by the wife's infidelity; the busy and various life of a modern city. Yet it was wholly out of the tradition, wholly uninterested in the classic fictional values. Though it imitated minutely the surface of everyday life, as if to prove that it could, *Ulysses* constantly invited the reader to look under or behind that surface. Its style was often opaque, and by changing so often, called attention to itself. The novel denied psychological insight by its emphasis on pre-determined patterning, and was absolutely uninterested in morality, middle-class or otherwise. Joyce's novel did not destroy the tradition, but simply made it look like what it was to be henceforth—one alternative among many, and the least adventurous.

Though the arts do not know what it is to "progress," change is the law of their being. What has been done once changes the whole definition of what can be done again or must be done next. A series of pot-shapes, arranged in the order they inevitably demand, outline the parabola of a civilization. The change is not dictated by function, in the sense that we can trace successive adaptations of the bones that transform a paw to a hand, a fin to a wing. You cannot do anything with the last pot of such a series that you could not equally well have done with the first; indeed, there's a good chance that thinness of wall and delicacy of form may combine with increasing richness of decoration to render the last pot *less* practical in terms of household chores than the first thick, ugly vessel with which the series started.

No matter, man does not live by household chores alone. As a life-forwarding device, *Pamela* is far superior to *A Rebours,* not to speak of *The Way It Was.* But art-forms are not strictly tied to promoting the biological incentives of their creators. They have a life of their own and they must fulfill it. Apart from time passing, nothing whatever has happened lately to make one think modernism has worked through its cycle, and a *novus ordo saeculorum* is clamoring to be recognized. If anything, the current phrase "post-modern" signifies plainly that we are still forced to define ourselves in relation to the old modernist impulse, even though we know it's no longer ours, and haven't the faintest idea of what has succeeded it, or will do so. When the new age comes along, if it's really going to be new, it will no doubt announce itself as decisively as *The Waste Land* and *Ulysses* announced the advent of that cycle whose brass and iron ages we are, as it seems to me, now experiencing.